ISLAMISM
AND
SECULARISM
IN NORTH AFRICA

ISLAMISM
AND
SECULARISM
IN NORTH AFRICA

⛎   ⛎

Edited by

John Ruedy

**Center for Contemporary
Arab Studies**
Georgetown University
Washington, DC

**St. Martin's Press
New York**

First published in the United States of America 1994

Printed in the United States of America

Library of Congress Cataloging-in-Publication Data

Islam and secularism in North Africa / edited by John Ruedy.
    p. cm.
  Includes bibliographical references.
  ISBN 0-312-12198-9
    1. Africa, North—Politics and government. 2. Islam and politics—
Africa, North. I. Ruedy, John (John Douglas), 1927– .
DT204.I85 1994
961'.0097671—dc20   94-15944
                                                CIP

Interior book design by Digital Type & Design

Contents

II. The Islamist Challenge

III. Reform or Repression: State Responses to the Islamic Revival

Acknowledgments

The editor acknowledges with gratitude the assistance of
Professors Barbara Stowasser, Mary-Jane Deeb, Ibrahim Ibrahim,
and Ibrahim Oweiss as well as that of Dr. Michael Simpson,
Anne-Marie Chaaraoui, Justin Crowne, Bryce Giddens,
and Ellen Fleischmann.

Notes on Contributors

KHALIFA CHATER is a Professor of History at the Faculté des Sciences Humaines et Sociales de Tunis, where he has taught since 1972. He received his Doctorat d'État from the Sorbonne. Dr. Chater is the author of two books, *Dépendence et mutations précoloniales: La Régence de Tunis de 1815 à 1857* and *Insurrection et répression dans la Tunisie: La Mehalla de Zarrouk au Sahel*, which analyzes the history of political and social change in nineteenth-century Tunisia.

MARY-JANE DEEB is the Academic Director of the Omani Program of the School of International Service at The American University. She received her Ph.D. in International Relations from the School of Advanced International Studies at Johns Hopkins University. Dr. Deeb is the author of *Libya's Foreign Policy in North Africa* and coauthor of *Libya Since the Revolution: Aspects of Social and Political Development*.

MARIUS K. DEEB is author of the forthcoming book *Lebanon: State, Civil Society, and External Intervention in Historical Perspective*, and of four other books on Lebanon and Egypt. Dr. Deeb obtained his D. Phil. in Politics from Oxford University. Dr. Deeb is a Professorial Lecturer at George Washington University. He was formerly Senior Fellow at the Center for International Development and Conflict Management at the University of Maryland from 1985 to 1992.

MICHAEL COLLINS DUNN is Senior Analyst of the International Estimate, Inc., a Washington consulting firm, and editor of its biweekly newsletter, *The Estimate*. From 1980 to 1988 he served as group editor of the *Defense and Foreign Affairs* group of publications. Since 1982 he has served as Adjunct Professorial Lecturer at Georgetown University. Dr. Dunn has published numerous monographs, including *Renaissance or Radicalism?: Political Islam: The Case of Tunisia's al-Nahda, Tunisia's New Leadership*, and *Sudan Since the Coup*.

DALE F. EICKELMAN is the Ralph and Richard Lazarus Professor of Anthropology and Human Relations at Dartmouth College. In 1991, he served as President of the Middle East Studies Association of North America. His publications include the books *Moroccan Islam*, which has been translated into Arabic, *Muslim Travellers: Pilgrimage, Migration and the Religious Imagination* (coedited with James Piscatori), and the forthcoming *Muslim Politics and Societies: Russian, Central Asian, and U.S. Perspectives.*

JOHN P. ENTELIS is Professor of Political Science and Codirector of the Middle East Studies Program at Fordham University. He received his Ph.D. in Political Science from New York University. The books published by Dr. Entelis include *Algeria: The Revolution Institutionalized, State and Society in Algeria* (editor), *Comparative Politics of North Africa,* and *Pluralism and Party Transformation in Lebanon.*

ABDELBAKI HERMASSI is Tunisian Ambassador to UNESCO. He is the author of seven books, including *Le Maghreb face aux mutations internationales, Société et État dans le Maghreb arabe, L'Islam protestataire, Third World Reassessed,* and *Leadership and National Development in North Africa.* After obtaining a Ph.D. in Sociology from the University of California at Berkeley, Dr. Hermassi served there as Assistant and later Associate Professor from 1971 to 1980.

DONALD C. HOLSINGER is Professor of History at Seattle Pacific University, and Adjunct Associate Professor of History at the University of Washington. After obtaining a Ph.D. in African and Middle Eastern History from Northwestern University, Dr. Holsinger taught at George Mason University from 1979 to 1989. He has contributed to such scholarly journals as *The Journal of African History, Social Studies Review, The Middle East Journal,* and *The American Historical Review.*

SÉVERINE LABAT is a doctoral candidate at L'Institut d'Études Politiques de Paris. She is the author or coauthor of a number of articles in French dealing with the issues of Muslim religious freedom in France, Islam and secularism in France, the Islamic movement in Algeria, and a comparison between Islamism in Egypt and Islamism in Algeria. She has also taught political economy at the École Française d'Attachés de Presse.

MOHAMED EL MANSOUR is Professor of History at Mohammed V University, Rabat, where he served as Chairman of the Department of History from 1988 to 1992. He received his Ph.D. from the School of Oriental and African Studies, London University. He is the author of the book *Morocco in the Reign of Mawlay Sulayman (1792-1822),* and coeditor of the book *The Atlantic Connection: 200 Years of Moroccan-American Relations, 1786-1986.*

KENNETH J. PERKINS is Professor of History at the University of South Carolina. He obtained his doctorate degree in Near Eastern Studies from Princeton University. He is the author of five books on North Africa, including the *Historical Dictionary of Tunisia,* and the forthcoming *Port Sudan: The Evolution of a Colonial City.* Dr. Perkins has also contributed numerous articles and book reviews to journals and is the author of many entries in reference books.

HUGH ROBERTS is an Associate at the Geopolitics and Internationl Boundaries Research Center at London University's School of Oriental and African Studies. He received his D. Phil. from Oxford. He is the author of three books dealing with Algerian politics: *Algerian Socialism and the Kabyle Question, Northern Ireland and the Algerian Analogy: A Suitable Case for Gaullism?*, and the forthcoming *Revolution and Resistance: Algerian Politics and the Kabyle Question.*

JOHN RUEDY is Professor of History at Georgetown University, where he is also a member of the Executive Committee of the University's Center for Contemporary Arab Studies. He received his Ph.D. from the University of California, Los Angeles. His publications include the books *Land Policy in Colonial Algeria* and *Modern Algeria: The Origins and Development of a Nation.* Dr. Ruedy is the author of many published articles on North African history, as well as a number of contributions to encyclopedias and almanacs.

EMAD ELDIN SHAHIN is an Associate Researcher at the International Institute of Islamic Thought (Herndon, Virginia). He obtained his Ph.D. from the School of Advanced International Studies at Johns Hopkins University. He is the author of two forthcoming books: *Through Muslim Eyes: Muhammad Rashid Rida and the West* and *Surat al-Gharb 'ind Muhammad Rashid Rida.* He has written a number of articles and has contributed to the *Encyclopedia of the Modern Islamic World.*

I. WILLIAM ZARTMAN is Director of African Studies at the School for Advanced International Studies of the Johns Hopkins University, where he is the Jacob Blaustein Professor of International Organization and Conflict Resolution. Dr. Zartman, who received his Ph.D. from Yale

University, is the author of a number of works on North Africa, including *Government and Politics in North Africa,* and on African politics and negotiation analysis. Dr. Zartman was founding Executive Secretary-Treasurer of the Middle East Studies Association from 1966 to 1977 and served as its President in 1981-82.

Introduction

John Ruedy

This volume deals with the interaction of the secular and religious in the Maghribi countries of Libya, Tunisia, Algeria, and Morocco. The product of efforts by fifteen scholars from North Africa, Europe, and the United States, it seeks to explore that interaction from the perspectives of anthropology, sociology, economics, and political science, while at the same time placing the phenomena within historical perspective.

Until the late 1970s, the consensus of scholarly opinion in the West held that, while Islam retained great historical interest, it had little if any role to play in the contemporary politics of the Middle East and North Africa. This consensus—entered into by many scholars and political elites of the region—tended to view Islam as a residual category whose influence in the important realms of political and economic development was on a trajectory of irreversible decline. If its study retained relevance in the twentieth century, it was as a theology or an ethical system, as a framework for cultural analysis, or, more negatively, as the main force of reaction pulling at societies desperately trying to modernize. While the Islamic modernism of Muhammad 'Abduh, Muhammad Rashid Rida, 'Abd al-'Aziz al-Thaalbi, 'Abd al-Hamid Ben Badis, and their followers was of interest at an intellectual level, and the populist protest of 'Izz al-Din al-Qassam in Palestine, of Hasan al-Banna in Egypt, or 'Umar al-Mukhtar in Cyrenaica, elicited concern, these movements were more or less anachronistic manifestations of an era that was ending and did not presage the future. The future belonged to secular modernists. This was true in Tunisia and Algeria, whose heads of state were explicitly secular, and also in Libya and Morocco, which were headed by monarchies with traditional roots. In both cases, development and administrative strategies, coercive functions, information flow, and educational systems were firmly in the grasp of men whose training and outlook were overwhelmingly secular. Many were more familiar with the legacies of the French and Bolshevik revolutions, the works of Voltaire and Rousseau, Marx and Engels than with the Qur'an, the treatises of the great *fuqaha'*, or the works of Nizam al-Mulk and Ibn Taymiyya. A few were more familiar with the life and rhythms of

Paris and London than with village and provincial life in their own countries.

This is not to say that secular elites were never challenged by men still attached to Islamic visions. They were regularly challenged; but neither the elites in place nor Western-educated scholars and policy analysts took much notice of such challenges. It was the 1979 Islamist triumph over the wealthy and apparently invincible Pahlavi monarchy in Iran that abruptly and dramatically readjusted scholarly and analytical focus. With that compelling model constantly in the background, the Islamist challenges to the secular status quo moved from the periphery to the center, not only in the political discourse in many Muslim lands, but also in scholarly discourse.

Both *secularism* and *Islamism*, the principal terms contained in the title of this book, resist precise definition. Secular is a term used to distinguish the temporal or worldly from the spiritual, while secularism has come to denote a philosophy that privileges the domain of the temporal and diminishes that of the spiritual. The former grows to cover civil affairs and education, while the latter is increasingly restricted to the areas of private belief, worship, and conduct. While secularism as a philosophy is central to the Western experience, it should be borne in mind that the concept has evolved historically and that it is still doing so. What was considered the proper province of human rational decision was different in the fifteenth century than in the nineteenth century and is even more different in the late twentieth. Secondly, it should be stressed that the struggle over the frontier between the secular and the religious is one characterized by continuous tension and that, up to now, the exact line of the frontier between the two has never been agreed upon. One must also recognize that in the West there has seldom been agreement among secularists as a group, nor among the religious as a group, as to where exactly that frontier should be.

More important, it should be realized that even though the terms are dissimilar and the discourse is not as explicit, the struggle to define the proper domains of the temporal and the spiritual exists in Islam. That struggle began in the reign of the early Umayyad caliphs during the seventh century and has continued virtually without interruption into the twentieth century. Islam in its early centuries never produced an Augustine of Hippo to distinguish the City of God from the City of Man. It was unable, therefore, to present acceptable theological justification for a distinction between the secular and the religious in the way that

Christians had. Yet, the separation of the political and much of the civil from the religious has been actual in most regions and during most periods in Islamic history. As will be clear at several points in this book, especially in the chapters contributed by Khalifa Chater and Abdelbaki Hermassi, there were many 'ulama in the nineteenth and twentieth centuries who accepted the distinction in various forms. But, the fact that such separation has not been upheld over time and space by the consensus of the majority of respected 'ulama has produced a yawning gap between the actual and the normative that confers upon the struggle between the domains even greater drama than it has assumed in the West.

The term *Islamism,* as used in this book, is relatively new. In the years since the Islamic revolution in Iran, Western readers have become familiar with the term *fundamentalism.* From our point of view, this term has always presented problems, however, since its application to believers of any faith—Christian, Jewish, or Muslim—connotes a return to the basics or fundamentals of that faith, but does not necessarily connote political activism. It is precisely political activism, the movement of the religious into what many had considered the temporal sphere, that is the focus of most studies of the issue. The authors of this book, following the lead of European colleagues, have therefore chosen the term *Islamism* to which they have somewhat arbitrarily assigned the meaning of "political Islam." For our purposes, ideal Islamism is a philosophy or point of view that holds that the realm of Islam should encompass all human action and that is willing to act upon this belief in order to erase the boundaries between the temporal and the religious. With this said, it must be observed that some Islamists in North Africa have expressed willingness to work within constitutional frameworks that admit a diversity of political programs. This being the case, it is clear that there exists within Islamism a range of viewpoints as to whether a secular sphere should continue to exist and, if it does, what its boundaries should be. It would, therefore, seem unwise to insist upon total convergence among Islamists any more than one would insist upon the same among secularists.

The chapters assembled in this volume emphatically demonstrate that the ongoing conflict between Islamism and secularism in North Africa cannot be subsumed within any single paradigm or ascribed to a single cause or set of causes. The conflict is one of extraordinary complexity intellectually, sociologically, economically, and politically.

At one level, secularism is associated with colonialism, neocolonialism, and the Western worldview, while Islamism is associated with the indigenous reaction to the same. In a variety of ways, this fact is attested to by every chapter in this book. But de facto separation of the religious and the secular did not begin with European colonialism. It is clearly associated both with precolonial political systems and with the native religious establishments, the official 'ulama. Whether within the context of the 'ulama's acquiescence to political realities of the precolonial and colonial worlds, within the context of islah, the Islamic modernism of the early twentieth century, or through contemporary secular regimes' co-optation of the religious establishments and the official 'ulama's explicit support of such regimes and their policies, secularism clearly possesses native Islamic roots.

Essentially, secular nationalism was also the dominant ideology of the North African independence movements. It is not surprising, therefore, that, beginning with independence, a range of secular ideologies and programs was propounded by Westernized elites who were the principal beneficiaries of the struggle for independence. But the political systems these elites created were designed to perpetuate their own power and to preclude meaningful challenge from competing individuals, factions, or ideologies. Islamist movements, emanating from unofficial religious institutions and groupings largely outside of state control, have provided the most important vehicles for oppositional mobilization since independence. North African Islamism is primarily a political movement that struggles for power in the name of Islamic authenticity. But, because politics and social action are its priorities, and because the roots of the movement, with a few exceptions, lie outside the mainstream of Islamic theology and jurisprudence, North African Islamism has produced little coherent ideology and few solid academic treatises.[1] Public statements as well as published materials of North African Islamists present a surprising diversity of theological and philosophical positions, social and political priorities, and tactics and strategy. Such diverse, even contradictory evidence has complicated the task of reaching any broad consensus about the essential nature of Maghribi Islamism. A part of the value of this collection is that where consensus is possible, it usually leaps out, and that where it is elusive, that fact is clearly evident. Readers are presented, however, with a significant body of valuable research permitting them to begin working out their own conclusions.

In social and economic terms, several chapters in this book present compelling evidence that the fundamental base of North African Islamism lies in the pauperization of large segments of society and in the demographic crisis that, in recent decades, has brought the impoverished flocking to the cities. Here their deprivation contrasts with the affluence of secularized elites; here, too, they are far more mobilizable for political action than in the countryside. At another level, evidence indicates that the alienated—in Algeria, at least—also include sizable middle-class elements from the merchant and landowning strata, angry at their exclusion by a socialist regime and wishing to open the system to their own profit-oriented activities. The goals of this class are not always compatible with those of the first group, but few have noticed.

One also should take into account the alienation of many scientists and technocrats, many of whom attained high but relatively narrow levels of education. This class was angered by the superior power wielded by the political classes and appalled by their patterns of corruption and mismanagement. Some of this group were apparently estranged by the behavior and attitudes of elites who identified with Western values and systems that they themselves were not exposed to in their own more narrow educations. At a lower level of educational preparation are many who come not from the poorest strata, but from the ranks of upwardly mobile young men who, after spending years within the educational system, found their educations inadequate for the job market, or the job market itself too narrow to accommodate them. Some of the most militant and violent Islamist activists belong to this category.

Several contributors make the point that, at the political level, one of the historic functions of Islam in North Africa was to resist the attempts of central governments to extend control and taxation into the hinterlands. The resistance of populist, tribally based Islam to centralization is a nearly permanent feature of Maghribi history since the late Middle Ages. While there was considerable ambiguity about the religious legality of such confrontations during the precolonial era because of the offsetting claims to Islamic legitimacy of Ottoman and Sharifian governments, such ambiguities disappeared after the government became European. While colonial authorities, like their predecessors, succeeded in co-opting the official 'ulama in Tunisia and Algeria, one could always find during the colonial period Muslim spokesmen urging various forms of resistance against the state. In the wake of the liberation struggles, independent Maghribi states enjoyed three advantages that precolonial governments did not. One advantage was that they were at least nominally Islamic. Another one lay in the popularity and legitimacy that success in the national struggles conferred upon them. The third was the control over national territory and population achieved by the colonial order and now bequeathed to the independent states. In many ways the rise of Islamism is an indicator of the degree to which largely secular contemporary governments managed to squander the benefits they began with. In no case has an independent regime delivered—particularly at the material level—the benefits it repeatedly promised. In every case regimes that routinely resort to populist rhetoric are perceived as having conferred benefits upon very narrow segments of society closely identified with the systems. The most effective response in opposition has been political Islam or Islamism. The magnitude of Islamist movements, their ideologies, composition, organization, and degree of success vary from country to country however. The study of these movements in a range of aspects is the main focus of several of the chapters in this book. Other contributors emphasize more the responses of government and secular parties to the Islamist challenge.

Part I of this book begins with a carefully documented case study of the Islamic response to imperial penetration. It begins with Donald C. Holsinger's analysis of the reaction of the Mizab Oasis in the Northern Sahara to the French imperialism of the nineteenth century. Khalifa Chater examines a large collection of *fatwas* from the nineteenth and early twentieth centuries, to determine how the *'ulama* of Algeria, Tunisia, and Morocco responded to the challenges of a period of unprecedented trial for the region. Kenneth J. Perkins, covering some of the same ground, analyzes the responses of Tunisian political elites to nineteenth- and early twentieth-century challenges and the range of positions taken by the Tunisian *'ulama* to the same, keeping in view the central role played throughout the period by Istanbul in the imaginings of anxious Tunisians. Perkins ends with the contribution of *'ulama* to the Young Tunisian movement and to the old Dustur. Mohamed El Mansour analyzes in Morocco the less-than-successful attempts of 'Allal al-Fasi and other *salafis* to shape the Istiqlal Party along the lines of Islamic modernism.

In an attempt to connect past with present in Algeria, the editor, in his chapter, advances the hypothesis of a Mediterranean, politically dominant Algiers, constantly imposing itself upon a more culturally authentic hinterland. In turn, that hinterland, from Ottoman times to the present, resists that imposition in Islamist terms. The bridge between past and present is continued by Abdelbaki Hermassi, who sees the secularization of Maghribi societies as a process that has been underway for generations with the progressive acquiescence of most of the official religious establishment. The process became more abrupt with independence however. He sees Islamism as the response of classes marginalized or alienated by this accelerating change but he views Islamist doctrine as an "ideologized" version of Islam having little relationship to traditional Islamic thought.

Part II deals with contemporary Islamist challenges per se. The chapter by Séverine Labat presents an in-depth analysis of the origins and evolution of the various components of Algeria's Front Islamique du Salut (FIS). She concludes that the FIS is not a cohesive movement and that, notably, it is distinguished by a wide chasm between those who insist upon a totally Islamic polity and those willing to work within a more pluralistic system. Hugh Roberts, in his chapter on "Doctrinaire Economics and Political Opportunism," highlights the absence of a coherent economic vision on the part of the FIS and its willingness to ally with the reformist policies of the Benjedid government for the sake of sharing in power. Michael Collins Dunn, in the chapter dedicated to the Tunisian Al-Nahda, argues that Al-Nahda and its predecessor, the Mouvement de la Tendance Islamique, represent the case of an Islamist movement prepared to work within the existing system being driven by government and, perhaps, internal forces to more extremist positions.

The Islamist movement is less well-developed in Morocco than in Tunisia or Algeria. Its most visible movement is the 'Adl wal-Ihsan, headed by 'Abd al-Salam Yassin. In a careful analysis of Yassin's rather sophisticated writing, Emad Eldin Shahin qualifies his thinking as that of an Islamic modernist who rejects ethnic and secular nationalism, but who espouses a gradual approach to implementation of Islamically oriented social and economic change. Concluding this section, Marius K. Deeb explores the relationship of the Qadhafi regime with Islam within the framework of broader Libyan history. While Qadhafi claimed that the "Third Universal Theory" invoked by his Green Book was founded in Islam, his unwillingness to share power meant that by the late 1970s and the 1980s he was marginalizing the Islamic establishment and openly promoting the right of individual interpretation in religious matters.

In Part III, devoted to state responses to the Islamist challenge, I. William Zartman analyzes the problems faced by Maghribi political systems in trying to mobilize democratic alternatives to authoritarian systems. John P. Entelis focuses on the 1992 military coup in Algeria, which overthrew the Benjedid government and annulled the results of the first round of legislative elections won by the FIS in December 1992. He argues that the FIS had inaugurated a political discourse consistent with Algeria's culture, history, and experience, but that discourse represented a challenge that was unacceptable to the military, which had always been the mainstay of Algeria's authoritarian system. In his chapter on the 1992–93 elections in Morocco, Dale Eickelman details the Moroccan monarchy's efforts at coping with changing society and threats to its rule. One of the major strategies consists of "reinventing" both religion and the monarchy, in order to cope with Islamist and other challenges. In the final chapter, Mary-Jane Deeb proposes a dialectal model to explain the successes and failures of Islamist movements in the Maghrib. The thesis she develops is that the more pluralistic the state, the less developed the Islamic challenge will be and that the more the modernizing state succeeds in incorporating Islamic traditions and institutions into its programs, the more successful it will be. Thus Islamism is the most successful in Algeria, the most authoritarian state and one that is explicitly secular, and the least so in Morocco, which has long permitted limited expression of dissent and which has always projected itself as an Islamic state.

Notes

1. Works of 'Abd al-Latif Soltani of Algeria and 'Abd al-Salam Yassin of Morocco, and some others, might well be considered exceptions to this generality.

Glossary

'alim (pl. *'ulama*)......religious leader
'allaliyin ....followers of 'Allal al-Fasi
'asabiyya ....tribal solidarity; esprit de corps
'azzaba ....learned leaders of the mosque in the Wadi Mizab
bashkatib ....minister
bay'a ....pledge of fealty to a Muslim ruler
bid'a.........................innovation
colons (Fr.)................European colonists
diwan ....council
fatwa ....judicial opinion
fiqh...........................Islamic law
firman ....edict
fuqaha' ....jurists
habous......................same as *waqf*
hadith ....usually a saying of the Prophet Muhammed; also a pro-
                                  phetic deed, or the words or deeds of a close compan-
                                  ion of the Prophet
hijra..........................migration; the flight of Muhammed and his followers
                                  from Mecca to Medina
Ibadi...........................a branch of Kharijite Islam found in North Africa, pri-
                                  marily in the Mizab and on the island of Djerba
ijtihad ....interpretation (of scripture, tradition, or law)
ikhwan ....brethren; Muslim Brotherhood
imam...........................leader of an Islamic community; prayer leader of a
                                  mosque; descendent of Ali held by the Shi'a to be the
                                  infallible successor of Muhammed
islah ....reform; the Islamic reform or modernizing movement
jahiliyya
   (adj. *jahili*) ....the pre-Islamic era
jawad ....tribal elites
jihad...........................striving on behalf of Islam; sometimes holy war
kafir (pl. *kuffar*)........unbeliever
khalifa ....caliph, or supreme leader of Islam
Kharijism...................one of the three historic branches of Islam (along with
                                  Sunnism and Shi'ism) which appeared in North Africa in
                                  the 8th century A.D. and of which the Ibadis are a part
khutba
   (pl. *khutab*) ....Muslim Friday sermon
mahdi ....personage sent by God to announce the Millennium,
                                  the end of history

majlis al-shura ....consultative council
makhzan
    (adj. *makhzani*) ....Maghribi term for government; occasionally refers to
                   government troops or tribes allied with the government
marabout ....leader of a local religious sect; holy man; saint
mawna ....war tax
mujahid
    (pl. *mujahidin*) .....one who strives on behalf of Islam; sometimes a warrior
                   or holy warrior
mukhabarat ....secret police
nizam
    (adj. *nizami*) ....shortened Maghribi form of the Ottoman Nizam-i-Jadid
                   or New Order, referring to administrative and military
                   reform on Western models
qadi ....judge
qawmiyya ....nationalism or ethnic solidarity
salafiyya
    (adj. *salafi*) ....An Arab/Islamic philosophy of renewal that calls for re-
                   turn to the precedents of the founders of the Muslim state
shahada ....Islamic profession of faith
shari'a ....Islamic religious law
Shi'ism ....a group of Islamic sects holding in special reverence the
                   lineal descendants of the Prophet Muhammad
shura ....consultation; a council
suff ....tribal subdivision
Sufism ....mystical movement in Islam characterized by hundreds
                   of different paths (*tariqas*) to the divine
Sunna ....the tradition of the Prophet Muhammad and his closest
                   companions
Sunnism ....the majority branch of Islam to which virtually all
                   North Africans belong
ta'ifa ....faction; party
takfir ....accusation of unbelief
tariqa (pl. *turuq*) ......Sufi religious order
umma ....the community of all Muslims
waqf (pl. *awqaf*) ....Islamic religious endowment
zahir ....decree
zakat ....Muslim religious tax; obligatory alms
zawiya
    (pl. *zawaya*) ....religious order; religious shrine, building, or school

I.

Secular-Islamic Encounters in Historical Perspective

Islam and State Expansion in Algeria: Nineteenth-Century Saharan Frontiers

Donald C. Holsinger

Tracing historically the interrelated themes of Islam, the state, and community—three central strands in North African history—is a formidable intellectual challenge. The researcher is confronted with an ever-elusive kaleidoscope of Islamic dimensions (faith, values, ritual, practice, law, brotherhood, mysticism), and of state dimensions (boundaries, institutions, resources, norms, identities). These overlapping and shifting images defy attempts to identify and to analyze structural and historical patterns.

Part of the conceptual difficulty in making sense of North African history lies in the confusion between normative Islam, which prescribes how human society should operate ("There is no separation of church and state in Islam"; "All believers are equal in Islam"), and the everyday world of ambiguity, materialism, inequality, power, and compromise. This tension between the timeless ideal of the what should be and the perplexing evidence of the real applies as well to settings that might be called "Christian" or "Western" or any other cultural setting defined as other than Islamic. However, the fact that an "Islamic" political philosophy and system of law evolved in Islamdom has tempted students of Muslim peoples to impose an idealized and comprehensive "Islamic" explanation on the historical development of these societies.

A comparative historical approach offers one way to gain new perspectives on the historical experience of North African societies.

Placing the sequence of North African history within a context that includes non-Muslim peoples may help to identify ways in which "Islamic" dimensions of Maghribi life have shaped the course of events over the past two centuries. The breadth of vision provided by such a macro-lens approach can be deepened by utilizing a micro-lens approach to study a specific community as it acted upon and reacted to its evolving environment, thereby offering a case study against which to compare the experiences of other communities through time.

This chapter applies such an approach to North African history by first identifying the second quarter of the nineteenth century as a transition era in which structures and institutions of long-term global significance were taking shape, and then summarizing ways in which three comparable societies in widely separated regions were taking form simultaneously. It then focuses on one Saharan community—the Mizab (or Mzab)—as it adapted to the new challenges brought on by the French occupation and expansion in Algeria. It explores ways in which a self-consciously "Islamic" community coped with the challenges of state encroachment during the nineteenth century.

FORMATION OF GLOBAL STRUCTURES, FORMATION OF WESTERN MYTHS

The first half of the nineteenth century witnessed similar events of lasting impact in widely scattered regions of the globe.

Paul Johnson's book, *The Birth of the Modern,* is a recent version of the classical "modernization" interpretation, emphasizing the spiraling out from Europe of beneficial ideas and institutions destined to make the world modern.[1] The competing "world-system" interpretation and its variations offer alternative explanations of global change by stressing the exploitative and destructive relationship between the industrializing core and the deindustrialized periphery of the modern "world-system."[2]

A comparative study of social formations, cultural struggles, and frontier expansion in Algeria, southern Africa, and Argentina during the first half of the nineteenth century highlights similar patterns of political, economic, and cultural change occurring simultaneously in what Alfred Crosby has called the "Neo-Europes" of the world.[3] All three regions, for example, were drawn into a European-dominated global market in which Britain and France functioned increasingly as importers of raw materials and as exporters of manufactured products.

All three regions experienced increased levels of political turbulence as groups, finding themselves situated on advancing state frontiers, and sought to maintain political autonomy. All three regions, sharing similarities of climate and physical geography, became the focus of a substantial influx of European settlers who used the technological advantages of the industrial revolution to overcome overt resistance. They also used local sources of labor and the wealth of stored energy in soils to transform these societies, at least initially, into agrarian export economies. All three witnessed the formation of cultural and political institutions with long-lasting legacies.

The "tools of empire" placed in the hands of the expansionist European states by the industrial revolution transformed previous power relations.[4] The spectacular imperial "scramble" at the end of the nineteenth century has tended to overshadow the unprecedented levels of European expansion that had occurred a half century earlier. Between 1800 and 1878, for example, it is estimated that the average rate of European imperial expansion worldwide was 216,000 square miles per year.[5] Few observers at the time were able to grasp the significance of the historic events of the 1830s and 1840s. Alexis de Tocqueville, reflecting on the meaning of the British-Chinese Opium War, wrote in 1840: "Something more vast, more extraordinary than the establishment of the Roman Empire is growing out of our times, without anyone noticing it; it is the enslavement of four parts of the world by the fifth."[6]

This metaphor of a world enslaved came to be buried under more comfortable self-images in the West; Europeans, after all, were leading the crusade against institutionalized slavery in the 1830s and 1840s. A belief in both the inevitability of Western expansion and its ever-spreading benefits gained widespread acceptance in the West during the nineteenth century. MacGregor Laird, whose family played a key role in the development of steamboat technology, articulated an early version of the "modernization" interpretation of global change: "We have the power in our hands, moral, physical, and mechanical; the first, based on the Bible; the second, upon the wonderful adaptation of the Anglo-Saxon race to all climates, situations, and circumstances . . . the third . . . hundreds of steam-vessels, carrying the glad tidings of 'peace and good will toward men' into the dark places of the earth which are now filled with cruelty."[7]

Laird's racial, cultural, and technological arrogance may appear quaint from a late twentieth-century vantage point, but the widely shared myths that he articulated had deadly serious consequences for peoples scattered over the globe. Laird was partly correct. The "mechanical" advantages bestowed on European powers by the industrial revolution did profoundly reshape global power relations. The steamboat was the decisive force in the outcome of the British-Chinese Opium War; it, along with quinine, new weapons, the railroad, the telegraph, and canals did effect a global revolution.[8] Several of these "tools of empire" were critically important in reshaping the cultural, economic, and political landscapes of North Africa, especially Algeria.

Beginning in 1830, Algeria witnessed the French conquest of the capital, the gradual extension of military control over the coastal region, and the growth and eventual defeat of a variety of resistance movements of which 'Abd al-Qadir's Western Algerian state was the most formidable. State-sponsored immigration of European settlers beginning in the 1840s led eventually to the formation of a sharply divided caste society. Alexis de Tocqueville visited Algeria twice during the 1840s, making some prescient observations about the probable outcome of this new society. Embodying the paradox of liberal imperialism, Tocqueville on the one hand applauded the "civilizing" efforts of the French in Algeria, while admitting "We did not bring to Africa our liberal institutions; instead we dispossessed it of the only ones which resembled them."[9]

In a recent history of colonial Bône (now Annaba), David Prochaska illuminates the dynamics of nineteenth-century social change in eastern Algeria as both the foundations of the colonial order and the seeds of its demise were put in place.[10] Economic geography helps to explain the sequence of decisions that formed the colonial system. Bolstered by the ideology of Saint-Simonian socialism, the new rulers of Algeria expropriated first the urban buildings, then the surrounding agrarian hinterlands, followed by the forests and the mines. Prochaska's detailed study underscores the importance of seemingly minor technological breakthroughs in lowering the cost of state expansionism, foreign immigration, and colonial exploitation. Quinine, the antimalarial substance that French researchers isolated from cinchona bark around 1820, lowered the disease barrier to European settlement at a critical juncture in the 1830s. Road-building schemes during the following decades established the infrastructure of the colonial system by facilitating the exportation of raw materials, allowing for the importation of manufactured products, and easing the movement of French troops to protect encroaching settlers who found themselves in chronic conflict with local populations whose land and labor they coveted. Prochaska's study also illuminates the important long-term ecological costs of Algerian colonial development/exploitation.[11]

Nearly five thousand miles south of Algiers in a climate remarkably similar to that of the North African littoral, another settler society was taking form in the second quarter of the nineteenth century. The turbulent frontier between Europeans and Africans to the east and north of the southern African Cape resembled that of Algeria—for here the forces of land hunger and the need for labor, the logic of the "iron fist" in suppressing overt resistance to the European state, new state-building attempts by African leaders, the formulation of myths to justify expansion, and the critically important advantages in military, communication, and transportation technologies were enjoyed by advancing Europeans in their encounters with resident populations.

In southern Africa, as in Algeria, the second quarter of the nineteenth century witnessed a cyclone of forces that buffeted peoples along shifting frontiers. The arrival of British settlers in the eastern Cape during the 1820s failed to provide the pacifying buffer between Africans and Boers that the British government had intended. Beyond the European-African frontier, African political borders were themselves shifting dramatically as Shaka and his successors led an explosive movement of state restructuring (the *mfecane*) which in turn contributed to massive population dislocation and defensive state-building, most notably by Moshoeshoe among the Sotho people. In the aftermath of the *mfecane,* thousands of Boer farmers, exasperated with British attempts to raise the legal status of their slaves and servants (slavery being abolished beginning in 1834), moved beyond the British political frontier in an attempt to establish their own communities free from British interference. Weapons from the Cape played a crucial role in determining the outcome of conflicts with the inhabitants of the interior, and by the early 1850s, two independent Boer republics were taking shape northeast of the Cape. African state-builder Moshoeshoe, unlike Algeria's 'Abd al-Qadir who was defeated and sent into exile, managed to preserve the integrity of his truncated state in the face of European encroachment.

Following the latitudinal parallel westward from Cape Town, we arrive at Buenos Aires where similar changes were occurring in the second quarter of the nineteenth century. Independent Argentina under caudillo Juan Manuel de Rosas, who ruled the Platine federation from 1829 to 1852, may appear at first glance to be a society entirely different from French Algeria or the British-ruled Cape. A closer look reveals similar patterns in the formation of this "Neo-Europe," as the complex interplay among a powerful rancher elite, nomadic gauchos, and the Indians of the interior was shaping Argentine state and society. Increasing European demand for hides in the 1820s broke the balance that had prevailed among these groups over the preceding decades. Under the leadership of Rosas, who established the pattern of caudillo rule, the authorities conducted campaigns to destroy Indian autonomy, incorporating many as laborers into the pastoral export economy. Rosas gained fame during his command of the "desert campaign" against the Indians in 1833, thereby opening up vast territories for cattle and later sheep farming to meet the export demands from Europe. Although Rosas' period of rule from 1829 to 1852 left a long-lasting legacy in Argentina, his attempts to maintain a weak federation failed to prevent the unification of a centralized state in the decade following his exile to Europe.

The preceding summary of historical transformations in Algeria, South Africa, and Argentina aims to underscore basic similarities in the challenges faced by peoples caught in the path of a systemic process of political, economic, cultural, and demographic expansion. It also raises questions about crucial cultural factors—Islam in particular—in shaping the proactive and reactive decisions made by Algerians as they faced new challenges following 1830.

Frontier Interaction in Algeria

A study of the political dynamics in Algeria following 1830, among Saharan as well as coastal communities, reveals a bewildering range and complexity of actions. Given the diversity of responses to French encroachment, ranging from cooperation to tenacious armed resistance, Islam per se is an insufficient explanation for a particular course of action. The realities and perceptions of economic interests, both short-time and long-term, the variety of "faces" presented by the Europeans (economic, cultural, political, military, and technological), and the uncertainty about the meaning of this new factor in Maghribi society, offered persuasive rationales for a wide range of positions vis-à-vis the European presence.

To grasp the meaning of historical events during the crucial decades following 1830, we need to place ourselves within the torturous dilemmas faced by individuals coping with new challenges and opportunities in an environment where small miscalculations often ran the risk of major disasters. Who could be sure of the intentions of the new regime in Algiers? With hindsight, it appears that imperial expansion was an irreversible process culminating in the partition of almost the entire continent by the end of the century. But in the 1840s, this was not in the least obvious. Spain, after all, had given up its foothold in Western Algeria only a few decades earlier, after several centuries of occupation.

In a situation of extreme ambiguity and turbulence, Islamic ideals, symbols, and institutions offered powerful instruments of inspiration and mobilization for those who perceived the French presence in North Africa as a threat. Dozens of charismatic leaders, drawing on ethnic, brotherhood, or regional allegiances, led movements of reform, resistance, or revolution, calling on their followers to free the homeland from the grip of "nonbelievers."[12]

However, groups that appear socially or culturally similar responded in radically different ways to what appear to be common challenges; moreover, policies of the same group toward an ongoing threat also varied over time. For example, 'Abd al-Qadir alternatively negotiated with and fought with the French regime based in Algiers. In order to make sense of seemingly chaotic and inconsistent positions, we should recall that resistance of local communities to state centralization was a theme of enduring importance in North African history. Whether the encroaching power was the Turkish bey, the French governor-general, or a neighboring rival, local decisionmakers tended to view serious conflicts as struggles between "us" and "them," "believers" and "nonbelievers." Shifting perceptions of interests led to rapidly shifting alliances. Residents of the Sahara, dependent on an acutely unforgiving environment, often faced constricted options, as expressed by a common Saharan proverb, "We can afford to be neither Muslims, Jews nor Christians; we are necessarily the allies of our stomachs."[13]

The turbulent nature of interaction along state frontiers contributed to the impulses and momentum for expansion. Whether the perimeter of the state extended a few miles, as it did in 1830, or thousands of miles through northwest Africa, as it did by the end of the century, all along that state frontier were leaders seeking to protect the short-term and long-term interests of themselves and of their dependents in an environment that was oftentimes ecologically fragile. The difficulty of gathering reliable information, the circulation of rumors, the divide-and-rule tactics of one's rival, all contributed to the insecurity and ambiguity of the situation. In such a fluid setting, the appearance of many competing solutions, including millenarian voices and move-ments awaiting an apocalyptic moment, becomes understandable.[14]

Placing ourselves in the position of state administrators making decisions in Algiers or Paris enables us to grasp the self-perpetuating dynamic of imperialism. As colonial officials looked outward from Algiers, they saw an occupied zone (small in 1830, enormous in 1900) that looked relatively peaceful. Beyond the region of imposed "law and order," they saw an arc of turbulence and conflict. Unable to see that arc as a frontier perimeter whose turbulence was in large measure the political by-product of the colonial order, colonial administrators, metropole populations, and historical interpreters assumed that con-flict was simply the normal and natural conduct of "uncivilized" peo-ples awaiting the arrival of "civilization."[15]

A letter sent to the French authorities at Algiers by seventeen Algerian leaders shortly after the 1830 conquest, describes vividly the nature and impact of the colonial state's expanding frontiers:

[After the initial disruption] commercial relations were re-estab-lished and maintained for a while. Then the Bedouins rebelled, inter-cepted the routes, and fought amongst themselves, some desiring to trade with the French and others in opposition. The latter are the more numerous. We managed to reopen communications only with great difficulty. Then they rebelled once again, accusing the French of depriving them of the means of subsistence and of ruining the country. The result of all these troubles has been the utter destruc-tion of means of livelihood and of industry. The Mitidja plain is no longer cultivated. All the industries are languishing. The inhabitants are enduring terrible suffering; the prices of goods have become excessive. If this situation continues for two or three more months, the battles, the misery, the interruption of communications will end in a massive loss of life. And that will not bring peace. We have been told that justice and equity reign in France. It is only too true that they do not reign at Algiers. From the above we conclude that the province of Algiers will never be tranquil and that only through immense sacrifices in men and money will the French be able to pos-sess it. It would be necessary even to depopulate the country of its original inhabitants and to repopulate it with other men, an impos-sible option.[16]

The authors of this letter incisively identified the political and eco-nomic factors that contributed to their dilemma. From a distance of more than a century and a half, their assumption that a settler trans-formation of Algeria was impossible appears naive. But that is the point. What "rational" person in 1831 would have anticipated the revolutionary transformations that were in store for Algeria? It is instructive to compare the letter of these Muslim leaders to another thoughtful attempt to analyze the situation at about the same time, this also by an Algerian, but one who had been a member of the administrative elite in Algiers prior to the French conquest. In the words of Hamdane Ben Othmane Khoja,

> In short, I ask myself why my country should be shaken to its foundations and all the roots of its vitality attacked? Moreover, in examining the situation of other states around us, none seem condemned to suffer consequences quite like those fated for us. I see Greece aided and then firmly established as a state after tearing itself away from the Ottoman Empire. I see the Belgian people separated from Holland because of their different political and religious principles. I see free people everywhere showing concern over the Poles and the reestablishment of their nationality, and I even see the English government make its glory immortal by the emancipation of Negroes, while the British Parliament spends a half-million pounds to promote that emancipation, but when I think again of the country of Algiers, I see its unfortunate inhabitants placed in the yoke of arbitrary government, of extermination, and of all the plagues of war. And all these horrors are committed in the name of a free France.[17]

Several features of this document are striking—the author's sharp awareness of world affairs and the larger global trends that they represent, his recognition of the central contradiction of "liberal imperialism," and finally, his sense of Algerian national identity. Hamdane also points out the irony of historical events in the 1830s; as one form of slavery was being abolished (referring to the British Parliamentary Act of 1833), another form of subjugation was taking form.

Hamdane's eloquent plea became submerged as an alternative interpretation came to dominate Western public discourse. The following newspaper editorial from southern France, commenting on the 1830 assault on Algiers, articulates a point of view that came to be widely shared in the West: "Who knows what changes we are destined to bring about in these famous, but desolate regions, debased for centuries by the tyranny of Muhammad's followers? Who knows if, in a few years, under the protection of our kings, arts and sciences and commerce will not flourish where today barbarity and ignorance rule and where the banner of the false prophet will soon undoubtedly bow before the flag of France and the revered symbol of Christianity."[18]

Similar editorials, but without the Islamic symbolism, were found all along the expanding Western frontiers during the nineteenth century. What is remarkable in the interpretation of the 1830 invasion is the mixture of symbols linking economic, political, and cultural changes together into a vaguely defined but powerful Western self-confidence and arrogance. The assumption of moral superiority is obviously flawed, but the subsequent military successes on the battlefields, on the plains, in the mountains, and in the deserts of North Africa led to an uncritical acceptance of the accuracy of such myths on one side of the advancing frontier. Once again this highlights the central importance of technological advantage in shaping the outcome of conflicts and giving credence to the myths that followed in their wake.

A Saharan Community: The Mizab

By focusing on small-scale communities as they met new challenges, the historian may be able to illuminate the complex relationship between Islam and the state, raising questions for comparative analysis in other settings and in other times. Even in Algeria, the locus of a particularly disruptive form of colonial expansion due, above all, to the demographic transplantation that occurred, Muslim communities managed to draw selectively on traditional institutions and beliefs in order to adapt to the rapidly changing environment.

A study of the Mizab, a community of five cities in the northern Algerian Sahara, reveals the importance of ecological constraints as community leaders calculated the short-term and long-term interests of their dependents. The expansionist colonial state following 1830 was one more variable in an extremely complex matrix of cross-cutting interests and bet-hedging. The increased uncertainty brought about by the French occupation, the cost in dignity when political autonomy was taken away, and the turbulence of frontier interaction all increased the odds for those who carried the burden of leadership. As the stakes rose in ecologically precarious settings where small miscalculations made the difference between life and death, individuals understandably disagreed on the nature of the problems as well as on the solutions. Who, after all, could claim certainty of knowledge, other than someone convinced that he had received a special message from Allah?

The history of the Mizab is instructive in that its distant geographical location combined with its institutional cohesion contributed to its communal survival. Throughout their eight centuries of existence, the inhabitants of the Mizab had drawn on Ibadi Muslim traditions of cultural solidarity, consensus building, and collective problem-solving to cope with new challenges. But successful adaptations were always costly, a truth underscored again during the nineteenth century as the Mizabis faced the threat of an expanding colonial state. Located 350 miles south of Algiers in a Saharan region (the Shebka) infamous for its desolation, the five small cities of the Mizab, along with the two more distant satellite towns, had been contending with formidable environmental odds for centuries by the time of the French conquest of Algiers in 1830. The fifteen to twenty thousand permanent residents of the Wadi Mizab belonged to the Ibadi Islamic sect, whose origins can be traced back to the first century of the Islamic calendar (seventh century *C.E.*). The first settlements in the Wadi Mizab date probably from the early eleventh century, when Ibadi refugees sought a haven in which to practice their faith unencumbered. Over the centuries, the Ibadis of the Mizab developed an elaborate set of written theological and legal traditions whose preservation, interpretation, and implementation were overseen by the *'azzaba,* the learned leaders of the mosque. These men were expected to forgo clan or town allegiances so as to represent the Ibadi community as a whole. Having committed their lives to study and service, they assumed a crucial function in the community, resolving conflict, overseeing behavior, redistributing wealth, and educating the young.

The Mizabi economic system is a striking example of human ingenuity in adapting to the extremes of a desert environment. Maximizing available soil, water, and labor, the Mizabis had constructed an intricate system of water control through an elaborate network of dams, reservoirs, and conduits that not only protected against the occasional large floods that swept through the Wadi Mizab, but regularly captured and replenished the aquifer and irrigated the palm groves during the irregular but essential rains that made the river rise. Most agricultural effort centered on the production of dates. Women in the community worked on household looms to produce woven garments and tapestries for export.[19]

Mizabi residents cooperated with surrounding nomadic pastoral populations in a mutually beneficial exchange of services and products. In the centuries leading up to the French invasion, the Mizab, and Ghardaia in particular, functioned as an important northern Saharan market for caravans from all directions. Long before the French conquest of Algiers, Mizabi men were active in a commercial dispersion to cities of the northern Tell where they had gained firm footholds in a variety of urban occupations.[20] By the late eighteenth century, Mizabi merchants possessed government-sanctioned control of several trades and services. The merchant migrations between Sahara and the coast often corresponded with seasonal nomadic movements, helping to reinforce bonds of cooperation between Mizabi entrepreneurs and pastoral transporters. The regular migrations also strengthened economic interdependence between the Mizabi desert confederation and the coastal Algerian state. The leaders of the Mizab cultivated friendly relations with the rulers of the Tell while preserving the autonomy of the community from coastal interference.[21]

The basic ecological constraints of a delicate and intricate economic network changed little with the occupation of Algiers in 1830. The remoteness of the Mizab from Algiers, combined with the fact that many hundreds of Mizabi merchants were stationed in the capital of the new regime, gave the Mizabis a certain advantage in assessing their options, for unlike most Algerian groups, they were able to observe continually events from both sides of the advancing imperial frontier. Disagreements among merchant factions over the proper degree of cooperation with the new regime did create deep rifts at times among the emigrants, but despite the turmoil, Mizabi corporations managed to retain their prominence in traditional professions.[22]

In the 1840s, as French military forays extended southward into the Sahara from Algiers, Mizabi political leaders showed little sign of concern about the possibility of losing their traditionally recognized autonomy from coastal authority. Why should the new regime regard the distant desert confederation any differently than the previous Turkish regime had regarded it? True, there had been disruption of supply lines and trade routes linking the oasis communities with the northern agrarian regions, but few Mizabi observers could have anticipated that the traditional independence of the desert community was about to be gravely challenged.

The appointment of Jacques Louis Randon as governor-general in 1851 launched a phase of more aggressive expansionism into the Sahara. Randon foresaw the possibility of extending French commercial sway across the Sahara and viewed the submission of the Mizab confederation as an important step in reaching this goal. He was well aware of the levers of influence that he enjoyed—specifically, the Mizabi emigrant corporations in northern Algerian towns and cities and the supply lines linking the Saharan oases and the rainfed northern coastal plains and markets.

The first major test of resolve on both sides came in 1852 when Muhammad Ibn Abdallah, known commonly as the "Sharif," used Laghouat, 120 miles north of the Mizab, as a base of operations in his attempt to organize a mass uprising designed to expel the French from northern Africa. Randon responded to the uprising by sending two military columns into the Sahara, converging on Laghouat, the reported supply base for Muhammad Ibn Abdallah. Sedentary communities and nomadic pastoralists faced a dilemma. Although the Mizabis were capable of defending their cities behind fortified walls, they risked having their palm groves ravaged or caravans raided by openly defying the Sharif. Were they to throw in their lot with him, they risked losing hundreds of commercial establishments in coastal cities under French control as well as having the supply of grain shipments between the Sahara and the Tell disrupted.

Randon, well aware of the advantages that he possessed over Saharan oasis-dwellers like the Mizabis, demanded that the confederation close its markets to rebellious forces. Reports from the time indicate that severe factionalism was breaking out in the Mizab over the proper course of action.[23] In December of 1852, the two military columns reached Laghouat and stormed the desert town. A French participant recorded the scene: "The carnage was frightful. The streets were strewn with bodies. A meticulous count based on the best information ascertained that 2,300 men, women and children had been killed. The number of injured was insignificant, which is understandable since the soldiers, furious at being sniped at . . . would rush inside and stab anyone who was there. You can understand that in the chaos, often in dim surroundings, they did not stop to distinguish according to age and sex."[24]

The attack, demonstrating the military firepower and political will of the French regime, reverberated throughout the northern Sahara. The French regional commander quickly exploited his new political advantage by writing to the Mizabi confederation, promising a new relationship between the desert community and Algiers.[25] In response, a delegation from the Mizabi towns, instructed by the senior member of the 'azzaba, set out for Laghouat to negotiate with the military commander.

Surviving evidence shows that the Mizabi leadership had no intention of surrendering the community's traditional independence from the coastal state.[26] Randon envisioned a different scenario. He recruited three Mizabi merchants from Algiers to travel to Laghouat to pressure the delegation to continue their journey to Algiers, planning to use the occasion to demand their political submission. When confronted with Randon's request, the delegates hesitated, perhaps suspicious of his intentions, but they finally agreed to undertake the arduous trip to the capital. Randon's plan was to utilize Mizabi political submission to achieve his larger goals of closing off Saharan markets to resistance movements and extending French commercial networks across the Sahara.[27]

Arriving at Algiers in late January 1853, the Mizabi delegates were suddenly confronted with a fundamental alteration in their relationship with the coastal state. Randon handed them an ultimatum demanding formal submission, a political posture that would require recognition of French sovereignty, a payment of an annual tribute, and the closing of their markets to forces hostile to the French. When the delegates countered that they had not been authorized to accept such humiliating conditions, Randon sent them back south with an April 1st deadline for accepting his terms and a threat to cut off supply lines to the Tell if the Mizab did not comply.[28]

The delegates retraced their steps, arriving back in the oasis community several weeks later with the disturbing news. The Mizab now found itself in a classic frontier dilemma. To give up its traditional political autonomy was unthinkable. But to incur a strangling commercial blockade would threaten its survival, not to mention the possibility of Mizabi merchants in the north being held hostage. A meeting of representatives of the seven Mizabi towns revealed bitter disagreements. Cherished traditions and values were at stake—political autonomy, attacks by forces loyal to the Sharif, a devastating commercial blockade, and Muslims submitting to Christians.

As a self-consciously Muslim community, the Mizab faced one of the most difficult decisions in its long history of adaptation to adversity. More than a millennium of Ibadi experience had provided a variety of historical precedents and theological justifications for whichever course of action was decided upon, but never before had the community faced this particular dilemma.[29]

Surviving French and Arabic documents reveal that Mizabi decision makers agonized over the appropriate position to take. Although it is risky to claim that any one response represents *the* Muslim point of view, a letter from the 'azzaba council to the French commander at Laghouat received just prior to the April 1st deadline illuminates the thinking of the most influential leaders of the community at a crucial turning point in its long history:

We beseech you in the name of Muhammad Ibn Abdallah and Jesus son of Mary (the spirit of God) to keep calamities from befalling the Banu Mizab as did those who governed before you. The powerful have never concerned themselves with our community because of its small size, its isolation, its difficult trails, the aridity of its red mountains, and its lack of herbs and plants. From the earliest times the aim of the powerful has always been to seek after that which is grand and to ignore a nullity like the Banu Mizab. The second reason that the powerful have ignored the Banu Mizab is that we follow the maxim of Jesus son of Mary (the spirit of God): do not interfere in the affairs of the powerful and they will not interfere in yours.

The third factor which has drawn the protection of the powerful over the Banu Mizab is that we take charge of our own instruction and commerce, and we gain our livelihood by the sweat of our brows. There are neither thefts nor frauds among us, nothing which could harm trade.

Do not impose on us what we cannot bear, for we adore God from our mountaintops, as did the great Christian priests in their towers and we trouble neither you nor your subjects in any way. We commend to you what Noah said and which was also the inspiration of Abraham, Moses and Jesus: be religious and believe. Those who are closest to your religion are those who have said, "We are Christians," because they are intelligent, have good hearts, are not covetous and spend their time in study.[30]

This letter illuminates themes and encounters that are central to understanding the formation of the modern world. In this instance, Muslim leaders were attempting to hold back the process of state centralization that has engulfed the world in the past two centuries. Their plea was partly moral, as they sought to preserve community autonomy by appealing to a shared set of Judaic-Christian-Islamic symbols and values that would, they hoped, influence the behavior of the masters of the "Christian" state. They were asking the French commander to act out a central tenet of that tradition—treating others as he would want to be treated. From a different angle, they were requesting from the agents of "Western" expansion recognition of a value that is sometimes seen as uniquely Western—political self-determination. Their plea was also pragmatic, as they argued that the economic interests of the state would be best served by preserving the autonomy of the community.

Whatever hopes may have been riding on the Mizabi letter soon evaporated. The appeal for a common cultural understanding was not reciprocated. Although the cultural struggle between Islam and the West would remain an open question for well over a century to come, the Mizabi attempt to preserve political autonomy was no match for the determined power of the colonial state in 1853. Randon was in a strong position, backed by superior military technology, reliable information networks, and centralized administrative structures. As April 1st approached, he increased the pressures on the Mizab by halting grain shipments to the community and by sending a military column south from Laghouat. These actions seemed to tip the balance in the Mizab in favor of submission, for in early April the commander of the French force reported that the towns had sent the *qada,* the gift of a horse formally accepting political submission. Randon, now in the mood for reconciliation, immediately ordered that the Mizab's first tribute payment be utilized for the purchase of wheat for the confederation.[31]

The Mizab's 1853 political submission was a milestone in the community's history. But if the residents of the confederation thought that submission would bring an end to strife in the community and the region, events soon proved otherwise. For one thing, not everyone had agreed on the act of submission; recriminations now split the community.[32] More important, the political status of the Mizab was now left intentionally ambiguous. Randon had insisted on Mizabi submission and cooperation, but he had no intention of setting up a French garrison in the Mizab, urging instead that the Mizabis govern themselves as they had in the past. That, however, was impossible, for the political context of the northern Sahara had been fundamentally altered.

The state had only partly extended its control into the Sahara. The Mizab still found itself on a turbulent frontier, a situation that continued until 1882 when the colonial state formally annexed the region. For several decades, the community found itself caught in a vise— pressured by movements of rebellion appealing for support against the French on the one hand, and the French military outpost at Laghouat, which sent periodic columns south to ensure Mizabi compliance with the terms of submission, on the other. Contributing to the turmoil was the ever-present uncertainty about French intentions. Who could be sure that the regime would not withdraw north from Laghouat (as had happened after the 1844 expedition), or even from North Africa altogether? Who could know whether or not Muhammad Ibn Abdallah, or other resistance leaders who came after, might establish a Saharan state that would take revenge against those who had submitted to French authority?

When examined within the context of frontier interaction, the litany of brawls, assassinations, and civil strife that tormented the Mizab from 1853 to 1882 appears to be less the mysterious endemic characteristics of traditional cultures (the famous *suffs* that so intrigued outside observers) and more the understandable by-products of an ambiguous colonial frontier.

In the decades following Mizabi submission, French administrators assumed that the *'azzaba* were responsible for any anti-French activity or violence that rocked the community. The fact that the clerics, as symbols and protectors of cultural identity and cohesion, were so perceived is a common global theme in the history of colonialism. Colonial authorities sought to undermine the authority of the mosque leaders by rewarding their own protégés. As the role of the *'azzaba* became less overt, raw force and the blood feud gained at the expense of Ibadi legal procedures for settling disputes.[33] The political fabric of the community, always delicate and dependent on the moral prestige of the *'azzaba*, continued to unravel. As expressed by a group of Mizabi leaders in 1855, "We are well aware of what it would take to halt our self-destruction . . . but who among us will take the initiative? We no longer possess the moral authority for that; the first among us to make a move to restrain another would simply give the signal for the exchange of blows."[34]

The long-sanctioned tradition of rule by representative councils and consensus became a liability in the face of anarchy. Whereas outsiders concluded that political turmoil was simply an endemic feature of traditional Mizabi political life, many Mizabis, by contrast, concluded that the turbulent quandary in which they found themselves between 1853 and 1882 was by state design so as to keep them weak and divided. As expressed by one notable in response to a question about the chronic factionalism in the Mizab, "Where is this going to lead us? It will lead to the destruction of one faction or the other after which the Christian will take the rest."[35]

The speaker's outlook may have been overly pessimistic. The Mizab, despite some predictions to the contrary, did not disintegrate. The *'azzaba*, although less publicly visible, continued to exert an important influence in maintaining cultural cohesion. They continued to play key roles in reinterpreting Ibadi Muslim doctrines in order to adapt to the challenges of new technologies, new ideas, new institutions, and new crises. The task of reforming and renewing traditional Muslim beliefs and practices was led by Sheikh Muhammad Ibn Yusuf Atfiyyash, whose life spanned nearly the entire nineteenth century. A reputed scholar and prolific writer, Sheikh Atfiyyash trained several generations of Muslim scholars and leaders who carried on his vision of renewal, contributing to the Algerian Muslim renaissance of the twentieth century.[36]

In conclusion, the experience of the Mizab during the nineteenth century illuminates the nature and significance of imperialism and state expansionism for Muslim Algerians. In this case, an oasis community was severely shaken by the turbulence of shifting state frontiers. Despite the upheavals, the community survived, tattered but intact. Not all Algerian groups were as fortunate. Many experienced permanent disintegration under the impact of defeat in battle, confiscation of land, heavy taxation, and other mechanisms of colonial development and state centralization.

NOTES

1. Paul Johnson, *The Birth of the Modern: World Society, 1815–1830* (New York: Harper Collins, 1991).
2. See, for example, Immanuel Wallerstein, *The Modern World-System III: The Second Era of Great Expansion of the Capitalist World-Economy, 1730–1840s* (San Diego, Calif.: Academic Press, 1989).
3. Alfred W. Crosby, *Ecological Imperialism: The Biological Expansion of Europe, 900–1900* (New York: Cambridge University Press, 1986), pp. 2–7.
4. From the title of Daniel R. Headrace's influential book, *The Tools of Empire: Technology and European Imperialism in the Nineteenth Century* (New York: Oxford University Press, 1981). See also Headrace's *The Tentacles of Progress: Technology Transfer in the Age of Imperialism, 1850–1940* (New York: Oxford University Press, 1988).
5. D. K. Fieldhouse, *Economics and Empire, 1830–1914* (Ithaca, N.Y.: Cornell University Press, 1973), p. 3.
6. *Alexis de Tocqueville: Selected Letters on Politics and Society,* Roger Boesche, ed. (Berkeley, Calif.: University of California Press, 1985), pp. 141–142.
7. Quoted in Daniel R. Headrick, *The Tools of Empire, 17.*
8. Ibid.
9. Alexis de Tocqueville, *Écrits et discours politiques* (Paris: Gallimard, 1962), p. 207.
10. David Prochaska, *Making Algeria French: Colonialism in Bône, 1870–1920* (New York: Cambridge University Press, 1990).
11. Ibid., 73–77.
12. See, for example, Julia Clancy-Smith, "The Saharan Rahmaniya: Popular Protest and Desert Society in southeastern Algeria and the Tunisian Jarid, c. 1750–1881," Ph.D. diss., UCLA, 1988.
13. Quoted in E. Daumas, *Le Sahara algérien* (Paris: Langlois and Leclerc, 1845), p. 10.
14. Julia Clancy-Smith, op. cit.
15. Scholarly works are still being published that present this view. See, for example, Thomas Pakenham, *The Scramble for Africa* (New York: Random House, 1991).

16. Archives du Ministère de la Guerre (Vincennes, France), H 6, French translation of petition dated February 1831 signed by seventeen Algerian leaders.

17. Hamdan Ben Othmane Khoja, *Aperçu historique et statistique sur la Régence d'Alger intitulé en Arabe Le Miroir* (Paris: Goetschy, 1833), pp. i–ii. Published in Lucette Valensi, *On the Eve of Colonialism: North Africa Before the French Conquest,* Kenneth Perkins, trans. (New York: Africana, 1977), pp. 106–107.

18. April 17, 1830, editorial from *L'Echo Provençal.* Published in Valensi, op. cit., 108.

19. See Donald C. Holsinger, "Migration, Commerce and Community: The Mizabis in Nineteenth-Century Algeria," Ph.D. diss., Northwestern University, 1979, for a detailed study of the economy of the Mizab.

20. See Donald C. Holsinger, "Migration, Commerce and Community: The Mizabis in Eighteenth- and Ninteenth-Century Algeria," *Journal of African History,* vol. 21, no. 1 (1980): 61–71.

21. Venture de Paradis, *Grammaire et dictionnaire abrégés de la langue berbère* (Paris: Société de Géographie, 1844), p. xxi.

22. See Holsinger diss., op. cit., Chapter 5.

23. Archives du Gouvernement Général de l'Algérie (Archives d'Outre-Mer, Aix-en-Provence), hereafter refered to as *AGGA,* 1 1 104, correspondence dated August 23, 1854, to the Algiers division commander.

24. T. Pein, *Lettres familières sur l'Algérie* (Paris: Tanera, 1871), p. 371.

25. *AGGA,* 1 1 18, correspondence dated December 14, 1852, from General Pélissier addressed to the Mizab confederation.

26. *AGGA,* 1 X 32, Berbrugger correspondence dated January 30, 1853.

27. *AGGA,* 1 H 10, letter dated January 20, 1853, from Randon to the French minister of war.

28. *AGGA,* 1 H 10, correspondence dated late January 1853, from Randon to the French minister of war.

29. Four principal political dispositions were theologically justified, based on more than a millennium of Ibadi history. These included the state of glory (*zuhur*), the state of defense (*difa'*), the state of quietism (*qu'ud*), and the state of concealment (*kitman*). See T. Lewicki, "Al-Ibadiyya," in *Encyclopedia of Islam,* vol. III (Leiden: E.J. Brill and London: Luzac, 1971), pp. 650, 658.

30. *AGGA,* 22 H 12 and 1 1 104. The letter was received at Laghouat around March 23, 1853.

31. *AGGA,* 22 H 12, correspondence dated April 27 and May 6, 1853, from Randon to the division commanders.

32. *AGGA,* 22 H 13, correspondence dated July 23, 1853, from the Algiers division commander to Randon.

33. See Holsinger diss., op. cit., 356–359.

34. *AGGA,* 22 H 13, report dated April 21, 1855, by Laghouat commander.

35. *AGGA,* 79 1 3, report dated March 31, 1855, by Laghouat commander.

36. For Sheikh Atfiyyash's life and works, see Pierre Cuperly, "Aperçus sur l'histoire de l'Ibadisme au Mzab," *Mémoire de maîtrise* (Sorbonne, Paris: 1971) and Muhammad Ali Dabbuz, *Nahdat al-jaza'ir al-haditha wa thawratuha al-mubaraka* (Algiers: Imprimerie Cooperative, [1385]1965).

◉ ❷ ◉

"The Masses Look Ardently to Istanbul": Tunisia, Islam, and the Ottoman Empire, 1837–1931

Kenneth J. Perkins

The great nineteenth-century Tunisian ruler Ahmad Bey (r. 1837–55) maintained an ambivalent attitude toward the Ottoman sultan, his nominal sovereign. On the one hand, as a practicing Muslim, Ahmad had no wish to compound the problems of his already beleaguered coreligionist by too openly challenging Istanbul's authority; on the other, as a practicing politician, he had no desire to surrender the power he had accumulated, at least in part with an eye toward preventing outsiders, including the Ottomans, from seizing control of Tunisia. Throughout his reign, Ahmad took pains to show the appropriate respect for the sultan as the most potent authority in the Muslim *umma* while simultaneously endeavoring to hold him at arm's length politically.[1] Ahmad's successor, Muhammad Bey (r. 1855–59), attempted to give formal substance to this arrangement by offering his explicit recognition of the sultan's spiritual authority in exchange for official Ottoman acquiescence to Muhammad's administration of Tunisia and the management of its international affairs, as well as his certification of the Husaynid family as the province's hereditary rulers. But a bargain so advantageous to Tunisia had little appeal to the Ottomans, who rejected the overture.[2]

Most of the less cosmopolitan or sophisticated subjects of the beys did not draw so fine a distinction between the Ottoman sovereign's spiritual and political authority. Thoroughly steeped in twelve centuries of Islamic tradition and considerably less well attuned to contemporary international political currents, their allegiance to the sultan was not circumscribed by the reservations of their beys. Indeed, it became clear soon after Muhammad's demise that what reservations many Tunisians outside the ruling elite and the urban bourgeoisie with which it was closely linked did have with the political process actually centered on the policies of the Husaynid rulers themselves.

Ahmad Bey, Muhammad Bey, and Muhammad al-Sadiq Bey (r. 1859–82) all introduced an array of political and administrative innovations that especially aroused the ire of the peasantry and the tribes. For example, Ahmad's programs of military modernization enabled the beylical government to project its power more effectively than ever before into areas remote from the capital; guarantees of Muslim and non-Muslim equality and of the right of foreigners to acquire property, which were among the provisions of Muhammad Bey's 1857 Ahd al-Aman (Fundamental Pact), enhanced the already considerable economic influence of European merchants throughout the country, generally to the detriment of the poorer classes of Tunisian society. In addition, the introduction by Muhammad al-Sadiq of a modern legal system conformed with the provisions of his 1861 constitution but, by virtue of its grounding in Western jurisprudential concepts, alienated many of the Tunisians who needed its services.[3]

To many of the beys' subjects, these, and other newly formulated approaches to government, were *bid'a* (innovation) and thus merited opposition on Islamic grounds. In an atmosphere that had grown steadily more tense, the government made two decisions in 1863 concerning the poll tax (*majba*)—itself a non-Qur'anic levy—that were bound to provoke resentment. In an effort to raise additional revenues desperately needed to meet payments due on international loans contracted to finance the ambitious sociopolitical restructuring envisioned by the rulers, the *majba* was applied universally rather than, as had traditionally been the case, selectively; for the same reason, its rate was doubled. By the spring of 1864, a rebellion of major proportions had erupted among the tribes of southern Tunisia and had spread to the urban centers of the Sahel.

Accompanying the insurrection, and rising to a crescendo in step with the fear of European intervention, were widespread denunciations of the bey for having fallen totally under the sway of foreign, non-Muslim interests and public affirmations of support and preference for

2

the Ottoman sultan as a Muslim leader more cognizant of the needs of his people. What the rebels did not know, however, was that Ottoman diplomacy was steering a carefully "correct" course in Tunisia. Haydar Effendi, the sultan's envoy to the bey, repeatedly stressed that his only objective was to render assistance to the Tunisian ruler. The Ottomans did so by providing the bey with the money he needed to pay his own troops to press the offensive against the recalcitrant tribes and to bribe their leaders to abandon the resistance.[4] Despite this unimpressive Ottoman response, the mere presence of a Turkish official convinced many of the dissidents of the sultan's sympathy for their cause, even if international circumstances prevented him from acting on it (the presence of several European naval squadrons in Tunisian waters during the 1864 crisis virtually guaranteed that no outside force could overtly intervene without risking a major international confrontation). Thus, an inclination to identify the Ottoman Empire as the exemplar of the true Islamic political order continued to recur among Tunisians (and not only those in the ranks of the unsophisticated) until the Empire's collapse following World War I.

One example of this line of political thought was the 1867 political essay *Aqwam al-masalik* (The Surest Path), written by the statesman and reformer Khair al-Din al-Tunisi, in which he advocated strengthening Tunisian links with the Ottoman state, praised the contributions to the *umma* of several particularly dynamic Ottoman rulers, and stressed the importance of a concept that lay at the very heart of the Ottomans' political philosophy—that the ruling class incurred the obligation to safeguard the welfare of its charges in much the same way that the shepherd took responsibility for his flock. Although *Aqwam al-masalik* was a plea for Muslim leaders to blend the best of their own traditions with the political institutions of Europe, Khair al-Din nevertheless endorsed the Ottomans' cautious approach to the introduction of a parliament, citing the heterogeneous nature of the empire's subjects and the questionable loyalty of many of them.

During his tenure as Muhammad al-Sadiq's prime minister from 1873 to 1877, he implemented reforms correcting many of the abuses that had debilitated the country since the 1850s and that were, in his view, unworthy of a Muslim ruler. In doing so, he made powerful enemies among the old-guard politicians who had benefited from the injustices he sought to rectify, as well as among Europeans who were not anxious to see the emergence of a Tunisian government that might eventually limit the prerogatives they had grown accustomed to enjoying in the country. After he was forced from office by his adversaries' intrigues, Khair al-Din resided in Istanbul until his death in 1889. His esteem for the Ottoman political system, and Sultan Abdul-Hamid's appreciation of his views, were evident in his appointment to the post of grand vizier for a brief period in 1878 and 1879.[5]

If Muhammad al-Sadiq's predecessors had sought to keep the Ottoman Empire at arm's length so as to prevent any erosion of their own power, the Franco-Tunisian crisis in the spring of 1881 prompted the bey to strike a dramatically different chord. With France apparently preparing to launch a military expedition against Tunisia, Muhammad al-Sadiq solicited the intervention of the Ottoman government, implicitly acknowledging its rights in Tunisia. But, with none of the European powers prepared to countenance Ottoman interference in an arrangement they had sanctioned three years earlier at the Congress of Berlin, Ottoman leverage was virtually nil.

After its army invaded Tunisia in late April, France chose to ignore the initial Ottoman protests, but evidence that Istanbul was preparing to send a war fleet to Tunisian waters in early May provoked a stern warning that France would take whatever measures might prove necessary to forestall an Ottoman attempt to obstruct its campaign in Tunisia. Already militarily weakened by losses sustained in the Russo-Turkish War (1878) and by the financial woes that had pushed the empire to the brink of insolvency, the Ottomans had little choice but to back down. Abdul-Hamid redirected his forces to Tripolitania in the hope that their presence would constitute a barrier to French expansion into that province of his shrinking empire.

At the same time, he sent a contingent of sheikhs to rouse Islamic sentiments in the region along the Tunisian-Tripolitanian frontier. He also arranged for the extensive distribution in Tripolitania of *Al-Jawa'ib,* a pan-Islamic Arabic newspaper published in Istanbul, certain in the knowledge that many copies would find their way into the hands of Tunisian tribesmen. As French troops swept through northern Tunisia, the sultan even weighed a scheme to endorse Khair al-Din as a replacement for the politically disabled Muhammad al-Sadiq, or at least to send the former Tunisian minister to Tripoli, but both options had to be abandoned when French officials in Tunisia learned of them.[6] In the meantime, the bey had signed the Treaty of the Bardo on May 12, instituting a French protectorate over his country in all but name. Although the international situation had prevented the bey from playing his Ottoman card (or the sultan from playing his Tunisian one) to good effect, the Ottoman Empire nevertheless remained an inspiration for the resistance of Tunisians outside the beylical entourage.

As the French army advanced into southern and central Tunisia, it encountered the first serious obstacles to the imposition of the protectorate in the form of an insurrection among the tribes and stiff resistance to the occupation of the cities of Sfax and Gabès. Although the tribal composition of this rebellion differed somewhat from the 1864 uprising—some tribes that had remained loyal to the bey in 1864 joined the rebels in 1881, while others that had opposed the government in 1864 took a less active role against the French, perhaps remembering the high price they had paid in the brutal repression that had ended the earlier uprising—other features of the two movements were remarkably similar. Once again the insurgents reviled the bey, this time demanding his deposition for "selling" the country to foreign interests and couching their resistance in terms of a jihad to protect Muslim lands and culture from non-Muslim control. Once again, as well, they expressed their loyalty to the Ottoman sultan, whose warships they hoped to see looming on the horizon before the full weight of the French military was brought to bear on them. In this, however, they were destined to be disappointed.[7]

As the French systematically broke the back of the resistance in the summer and fall of 1881, as many as 140,000 rebels and their families sought refuge in Ottoman Tripolitania rather than submit to French rule.[8] The active support that they expected to receive from the neighboring Ottoman authorities did not, however, materialize. By taking in the refugees, Sultan Abdul-Hamid saw an opportunity to demonstrate his commitment to the *mujahidin* and, by extension, to underscore his claim to the caliphate and, with it, the spiritual, as well as political, leadership of the *umma*. At the same time, he well knew that if he condoned the Tunisians' use of Tripolitania as a sanctuary from which to harass the French army in southern Tunisia, an occupation of Tripolitania, mirroring the 1881 French campaign in Tunisia itself, might well ensue. The mutual desirability of "managing" the refugees produced a Franco-Ottoman agreement in May 1882 to establish a buffer zone along the frontier.[9]

In the same month, a representative of the Tunisian rebel leader Ali Ben Khalifa traveled to Istanbul in an attempt to clarify the prospects for meaningful Ottoman support. When he returned convinced that there was no realistic hope of staging a counterattack from Tripolitania, the rebels began to negotiate terms of pardon with the French that would allow for their return. By early 1883, more than 80,000 had done so, and by 1885 virtually none remained in Tripolitania. In the French view, it was better to re-admit these tribesmen to Tunisia, where they could be supervised by the military administration that was emerging in rural areas, than to have their discontent fester just across an extraordinarily porous frontier.[10]

International political realities dictated an Ottoman accession to the French takeover of Tunisia and it was clear in Istanbul that the refugees' presence could only create problems with France that would almost assuredly be resolved to the empire's disadvantage. Although Sultan Abdul-Hamid did make one further attempt to assert Ottoman rights in the country at the time of Muhammad al-Sadiq's death in 1882 by sending the customary *firman* of investiture to his successor Ali Bey (r. 1882–1902), French officials in Tunis so pointedly ignored it as to leave no doubt whatsoever concerning to whom the new bey would answer. Thus, in a manner of speaking, the Ottoman Empire "let down" Tunisian Muslims who had turned to it for support in both 1864 and 1881, albeit more egregiously on the second occasion than on the first. Even so, the symbolic importance of the Ottoman Empire as the last independent Muslim state and the significance of its leader's claim to both the sultanate and the caliphate were hardly compromised and continued to carry great weight among traditionally oriented Tunisians who did not cease to look to the empire's leadership for guidance and succor.

With only a few exceptions, the 'ulama contributed neither to the leadership nor the rank and file of the 1864 and 1881 revolts.[11] Most nineteenth-century Tunisian 'ulama felt a strong emotional bond with the Ottoman Empire as an Islamic state, although many of them, like their colleagues in the empire itself, also had strong reservations about the wisdom of the innovations their political leaders were introducing. (These were precisely the persons that Khair al-Din was targeting in his *Aqwam al-masalik* in the hope of persuading them of the importance of pursuing the progressive path he had outlined.) Such attitudes might have drawn the 'ulama into opposition movements, particularly those with undercurrents of Ottoman support in the defense of Islamic values, had it not been for their even more deeply entrenched tradition of responding to a governmental show of force by reacting, at least publicly, with meek resignation. Thus, after 1881, the 'ulama hunkered down to survive as well as possible in circumstances which, in the minds of most of them, ran the gamut from distasteful to abhorrent.

Arnold Green has written extensively on the Tunisian *'ulama* both before and after the protectorate.[12] His findings help to establish a context for understanding a new set of linkages, although still of Islamic inspiration, that developed between Tunisians and the Ottoman Empire in the early years of French rule in Tunisia. In general, the *'ulama* did not resign from their posts with the advent of the protectorate, made no effort to emigrate, and issued no call for jihad. Instead, they engaged in low-intensity obstructionism to slow down, if they could not block, French attempts to secularize the legal system, Gallicize education (including at the Zitouna mosque-university where many of them taught and where most of them had been trained), and impose various statutes which the *'ulama* regarded as inimicable to Islam or their own socioeconomic interests, or both. The *'ulama* class was not, however, monolithic and from the beginning of the protectorate era, some of its members allowed themselves to be co-opted by the authorities.

Others, especially those who were protégés of Khair al-Din or of members of his entourage, came under the influence of the Islamic reform ideas of Muhammad 'Abduh (who visited Tunisia briefly at the end of 1884 and again in 1903).[13] Regarding the maintenance of states governed by Islamic principles as a concern of the highest order, many of these men were also vigorous proponents of pan-Islamism. These *'ulama* readily developed a working relationship in the late 1880s and the 1890s with members of the Young Tunisian movement who, with the encouragement of the French, were promoting themselves as interpreters of Western culture to Tunisia's Muslims and of Tunisia's Islamic heritage to the French. But the persistent French refusal to liberalize the sociopolitical environment in Tunisia soured relations between the Young Tunisians and their would-be mentors in the French administration in the first decade of the twentieth century. The latter retaliated by shifting their position and beginning to cultivate the country's traditional elites, who had resented and feared the implications of the Young Tunisian movement from the outset. By 1910, an alliance between the protectorate authorities and Tunisian bastions of conservatism, including the mainstream *'ulama,* was firmly in place, as was the intent and the will to curb the Young Tunisians.

Historian Arnold Green argues that Young Tunisian leaders had accepted the reformist notions and the pan-Islamism of the progressive *'ulama* less out of true conviction than from their pleasure in discovering "a readymade ideology with which they could twit the nose of a . . . French Resident General in Tunisia."[14] Nonetheless, most of the Young Tunisian activities that eventually precipitated the institution of martial law and the arrest or flight of many of the movement's militants in 1912 were Islamo-centric: support for Tripolitanian Muslims' jihad against the Italian occupation; efforts to prevent the desecration of the Jellaz Cemetery; and demands for the reform of the Zitouna mosque-university curriculum. The Young Tunisians may have been opportunistically exploiting Islamic sentiments that few of them fully shared—although many of them sought refuge in the Ottoman Empire—in order to thicken their ranks, but their assessment of the importance of Islam to most Tunisians was entirely accurate.[15] Of crucial importance was the fact that Islam constituted an inextricable component of Tunisian culture in the view of the secular Young Tunisians as well as in the views of both the conservative and progressive 'ulama. Each group might employ that component in a different manner and toward a different end, but none failed to recognize its existence and its centrality.

Indeed, by the turn of the century, even protectorate administrators had concluded that the Ottoman sultan-caliph enjoyed such genuine and intense support in Tunisia that they should abandon the practice, followed almost instinctively since the beginning of the protectorate, of depicting the Ottoman ruler in primarily negative terms and instead try to portray him as a ruler manipulated first by the British and then by the Germans, for their own interests that, of course, were at variance with those of the umma. A second French objective in stressing this interpretation was to discredit the activities of German-backed Islamist organizations that had emerged in the early 1900s with the aim of undermining France's position throughout the Maghrib. Even during World War I, with France and the Ottoman Empire at war, Resident General Alapetite warned of the negative reaction a Quai d'Orsay proposal to bestow the title of caliph on the Moroccan sultan would provoke in Tunisia, partially because Tunisians disliked Mawlay Yousef, but more important because they continued to harbor a sincere attachment to the Ottoman ruler.[16]

The acquiescence of the bulk of the 'ulama to French rule, as the Young Tunisians proceeded down a path that increasingly challenged French policy and ultimately evolved into an anti-French nationalist movement, marginalized the conservative religious leaders, leaving them no role in the political events that shaped Tunisia's history in the interwar era and opening them to charges of collaboration that minimized their influence even after independence. A few 'ulama did manifest their disapproval of such a relationship, however, by abandoning Tunisia for a life of self-imposed exile in Ottoman lands. It could be argued that the havens available for such disillusioned Muslims were more or less confined to the Ottoman Empire, making its selection a matter of necessity rather than of choice. Yet, the past history of popular Tunisian emotional attachment to the empire and the enthusiasm with which many of these exiles launched into activities linking their homeland with the empire suggest that, for most of them, it was specifically in Ottoman territory that they wished to reside.

Among the most prominent of this early wave of exiles were Salah Sharif and Ismail Sfaihi, two conservative 'ulama with connections to the Zitouna mosque-university.[17] Sfaihi had followed the somewhat unusual course of concealing his true views, perhaps in the hope of attaining a position in which he might exercise the power to change some of what he did not like. He began his career at Zitouna in 1885, but also taught Arabic at the Western-oriented Sadiqi College. The longtime (1883–1908) Director of Public Education in the protectorate, Louis Machuel, took Sfaihi under his wing, naming him to a series of administrative posts and, in 1896, to the directorship of the capital's most prestigious Arabic-language teacher-training institute. Only after securing appointment to the post of Hanafi qadi in the following year did Sfaihi begin openly criticizing protectorate policy that, at this point, still favored the Young Tunisians. In 1906, he left Tunis for Damascus, but moved on to Istanbul in 1908. Salah Sharif's conservatism, on the other hand, was never in doubt. He departed for Istanbul in 1906, ending seven years of service on the Zitouna faculty, during which time he had helped to obstruct any meaningful changes at the mosque-university through his work on its reform committee. Once in the Mashriq, Sfaihi and Sharif linked up with the small Tunisian, and more substantial Algerian, communities already there.[18]

Despite their unreconstructed views on Islam—Sharif, for example, publicly engaged in a running battle with Rashid Rida over articles appearing in Al-Manar—neither man showed any interest in the efforts of reactionaries, among them theology students, some of whose views replicated those of their conservative colleagues and former students at Zitouna, to reverse the 1908 Young Turk revolution. In fact, they collaborated with the Young Turk leadership, whose interest in pan-Islam, if not in the powers of the sultan-caliph, appeared to hold out the last hope of diminishing the influence of the French, and of

Frenchified Tunisians, in their homeland. Both Sfaihi and Sharif participated in the work of Al-Jama'a al-Khairiyya al-Islamiyya (The Islamic Welfare Society) in Istanbul, an organization with which they were undoubtedly already familiar, since a branch had been operating in Tunis since 1905. They also founded, in 1910, an Association Fraternelle d'Aide et de Soutien Moral entre les Algériens et les Tunisiens in the Ottoman capital, with branches in provincial centers, such as Damascus, where there were significant Maghribi communities. In the next year, Sharif accompanied Enver Bey to Tripolitania to rally opposition to the Italian invasion. He also hoped to galvanize the popular Islamic sentiment of his fellow Tunisians, spurring them to action against their own, and their neighbors', European occupiers. Sharif well understood the power of Islam as a motivating factor among his countrymen, but it may have surprised him to learn that, since his departure from Tunisia, the Young Tunisians themselves had begun very skillfully to employ the symbolism of Islam to marshal support.[19]

The suffocation of the Young Tunisian movement in 1912 brought new Tunisian exiles to the Ottoman Empire. Because these new arrivals shared with Sfaihi, Sharif, and the earlier emigrants the desire to circumscribe French influence in Tunisia, they joined them in a variety of undertakings designed to secure an Ottoman victory in World War I. Within the empire, these included the dissemination of anti-French propaganda in Syria and efforts to raise a Turkish force to attack Tripolitania and Tunisia. In Germany, Sharif and others occupied themselves with attempts to persuade French Muslim troops to desert or, if they had already been made prisoners or war, to come over to the Ottoman side, and with a second campaign tried to calm the fears of the German public that the concept of jihad might ultimately be turned against the Muslims' wartime allies.[20]

But the Young Tunisians harbored a quite distinctive vision of the Tunisia they hoped would materialize in the wake of a French defeat. Theirs would be a society molded by the concepts of Islamic reformism, not Islamic conservatism, and one that was open to the adaptation of desirable and useful Western social, economic, and political values. The 'ulama who had succumbed to French blandishments were discredited; those who, like Sfaihi and Sharif, felt compelled to make the hijra to the Muslim-ruled Ottoman Empire, may have preserved their Islamic principles intact, but they gravely diminished their prospects for influencing the politico-religious situation in post-war Tunisia. Among the 'ulama, only the reformists, who traced their intellectual heritage to the likes of Khair al-Din and 'Abduh and who had joined forces with the Young Tunisians, survived.

In the company of the residue of the Young Tunisian movement, these reformist 'ulama, the most notable of whom was 'Abd al-'Aziz al-Thaalbi, formed the nucleus of the Dustur Party that emerged after World War I. By then, the Ottoman Empire was, of course, gone; the Ottoman card no longer had any value. But the model provided by the empire of a Muslim state resisting Western control, and the inspirational value of its symbols, especially the caliphate, remained alive among many Tunisians. Dusturians applauded Turkish resistance to the Allies' plans to divide Anatolia among themselves, as they had dismembered the Arab provinces of the empire, although had they been able to foresee the end results of Mustafa Kemal's policies, they might well have been more circumspect.[21] For people such as al-Thaalbi, the abolition of the Ottoman caliphate in 1924 eradicated the last vestiges of transnational Muslim leadership, the emotional value of which had remained of great consequence even as its real power and influence had almost entirely dissipated.[22]

Al-Thaalbi's circumstances allowed him to devote considerable attention to this issue. He had left Tunisia in 1923, anticipating his arrest in a French crackdown on political activists. In July 1924, he attended the Islamic Congress convened by Sharif Hussein of Mecca in the hope of securing the assembled Muslim notables' recognition of his claim to the now vacant caliphate. But al-Thaalbi and many other reformists, with Rashid Rida in their vanguard, had lost faith in the Sharif, whose rebellion against Istanbul during the war seemed, in retrospect, only to have weakened the Ottoman state and paved the way for the European domination of the Mashriq. The Tunisian 'alim played an important role in mobilizing the successful opposition to Hussein's plan. His unwillingness to support Hussein subsequently earned al-Thaalbi an invitation to the General Islamic Congress for the Caliphate, convened by the al-Azhar 'ulama in 1926 with the implicit agenda of arranging the appointment of Egypt's King Fuad to the office of caliph. Once again, however, al-Thaalbi acted as a spoiler and the congress failed to achieve the desired results. Although realistic hopes of resurrecting a viable caliphate were fading, al-Thaalbi continued to immerse himself in other Islamist questions. In 1931, he traveled to Jerusalem to participate in the General Islamic Congress of 1931, whose goal was to generate Muslim support for the Palestinians in their confrontation with Zionism.[23]

In the meantime, in Tunisia, brash newcomers to the political scene were on the verge of shouldering aside the Dustur leadership, and the lessons of Tunisian history were not lost on these Westernized, secular Neo-Dusturians. They expedited their ascent by coming to the defense of Islamic values and appropriating Islamic symbols. So dexterously did they combine these tactics with their adhesion to liberalism and their introduction of Western concepts of political party organization, that by the time al-Thaalbi returned to the country in 1937, he appeared, to all but a few die-hard Dustur supporters, as a political dinosaur.

Ironically, just as the Tunisian rebels of 1864 and 1881—Khair al-Din, Sfaihi, Sharif, and al-Thaalbi—had turned, in their search for guidance, almost instinctively toward the Ottoman heartlands, the Neo-Dustur leadership, while not consciously imitating events in Turkey, had certainly embarked on a path of unabashed modernization and Westernization that offered clear parallels with the Kemalist experiment in Turkey.[24] It was the legacy of the caliphate's abolition, not the legacy of the caliphate itself, that the Neo-Dustur emulated. The party had easily co-opted Islamic values for its own advancement, in large part because the *'ulama* had become so weak, either by virtue of their earlier submission to the French or their loss of contact with the reality of Tunisian developments, that they could not thwart that tactic. An awareness of the ensuing six decades of Tunisian history might well lead one to conclude that in adopting this approach, Neo-Dustur leaders lost sight of ordinary Tunisians' genuine and earnest commitment to Islam—an oversight for which a high price may yet have to be paid by their political heirs.

NOTES

1. Tunisia's relationship with the Ottoman Empire prior to 1881 is outlined in François Arnoulet, "Les rapports tuniso-ottomans de 1848 à 1881 d'après les documents diplomatiques," *Revue de l'Occident Musulman et de la Méditerranée*, vol. 47 (1988): 143-52. An overview of Ottoman policy following the inauguration of the protectorate is Abdurrahmane Çayci, *La question tunisienne et la politique ottomane (1881–1913)* (Istanbul: Edebiyat Fakültesi Matbaasi, 1963). For Ahmad Bey and the Ottoman Empire, see L. Carl Brown, *The Tunisia of Ahmad Bey* (Princeton, NJ: Princeton University Press, 1974), pp. 237–41.

2. Mezri Bdira, *Relations internationales et sous-développement: La Tunisie, 1857–1864* (Stockholm: Almqvist and Wiksell International, 1978), pp. 141–42.

3. On Ahmad Bey's reforms, see Brown, op. cit., 261–312; on his successors' endeavors, see Bdira, op. cit., 51–56 and 72–79.
4. The best account of the revolt is Bice Slama, *L'Insurrection de 1864 en Tunisie* (Tunis: Maison Tunisienne de l'Edition, 1967). On the official Ottoman position and the funding of the beylical government, see pp. 59–60 and 101. A somewhat different perspective on the revolt is offered by Jean Ganiage, *Les origines du protectorat français en Tunisie* (Paris: Presses Universitaires de France, 1959), pp. 217–86.
5. Khair al-Din's views and career are discussed in the introduction to his *The Surest Path: The Political Treatise of a Nineteenth Century Muslim Statesman*, L. Carl Brown, trans. (Cambridge: Harvard University Press, 1967), pp. 29–36. For the Tunisian's attitude about the Ottoman Empire, see pp. 57–58.
6. On Abdul-Hamid's tactics, see Jacob Landau, *The Politics of Pan-Islam: Ideology and Organization* (Oxford: Clarendon Press, 1990), pp. 40–42. A contemporary account is Gabriel Charmes, "La situation de la Turquie," *Revue des Deux Mondes*, vol. 47 (October 15, 1881): 721–61 and vol. 49 (February 15, 1882): 833–69. André Martel, *Les confins saharo-tripolitains de la Tunisie (1881–1911)*, 2 vols. (Paris: Presses Universitaires de France, 1965), vol. 1, pp. 212 and 223 discusses these incidents within the broader framework of international responses to French actions in Tunisia.
7. Good descriptions of the Tunisian resistance include Martel, op. cit., vol. 1, pp. 238–81; and Hachemi Karoui and Ali Mahjoubi, *Quand le soleil s'est levé à l'ouest: Tunisie 1881 — Impérialisme et résistance* (Tunis: Cérès Productions, 1983), pp. 93–125. Portions of the latter are summarized in Hachmi [sic] Karoui, "La résistance populaire à l'occupation française (1881) chez les élites tunisiennes: Désaveu et oubli," *Connaissances du Maghreb: Sciences sociales et colonisation*, Jean-Claude Vatin, ed. (Paris: Centre National de la Recherche Scientifique, 1984), pp. 401–21. An especially useful article for establishing a comparative framework is Mohamed Hédi Chérif, "Les mouvements paysans dans la Tunisie du XIXème siècle," *Revue de l'Occident Musulman et de la Méditerranée*, vol. 30 (1980): 21–55.
8. Martel, op. cit., vol. 1, 290. A discussion of the number of refugees appears in Karoui and Mahjoubi, op. cit., 145–48.
9. Karoui and Mahjoubi, op. cit., 143. Martel, op. cit., vol. 1, 269–74 reviews Ottoman policy regarding Tunisia during early 1882 more extensively. The Ottomans did build up their military strength in Tripolitania, but never to the point of seriously threatening French forces across the frontier. Nevertheless, Landau, op. cit., 42, judges the sultan's policy in Tripolitania a "step forward in the foreign relations of Pan-Islam."
10. Karoui and Mahjoubi, op. cit., 164. See also Richard A. Macken, "The Indigenous Reaction to the French Protectorate in Tunisia, 1881–1900," unpublished Ph.D. diss., Princeton University, 1973, p. 78.
11. Arnold Green, "Political Attitudes and Activities of the Ulama in the Liberal Age: Tunisia as an Exceptional Case," *International Journal of Middle East Studies*, vol. 7 (1976): 232, notes a rare deviation from this norm in the case of two Gabès members of the 'ulama class in 1881, but suggests that their brotherhood and tribal affiliations may have accounted for their unusual behavior.
12. His works include *The Tunisian Ulama, 1873–1915: Social Structure and Response to Ideological Currents* (Leiden: Brill, 1978); "The Tunisian Ulama and the Establishment of the French Protectorate, 1881–1882," *Revue d'Histoire Maghrébine*, vol. 1 (1974): 14–25; "French Islamic Policy in Tunisia," ibid., vol. 3 (1975): 517; and "A Comparative Historical Analysis of the Ulama and the State in Egypt and Tunisia," *Revue de l'Occident Musulman et de la Méditerranée*, vol. 29 (1980): 31–54.

13. These visits, and their impact on Tunisians, are discussed in Moncef Chenoufi, "Les deux séjours de Muhammad Abduh en Tunisie et leurs incidents sur le réformisme," Les Cahiers de Tunisie, vol. 16 (1968): 57–96.

14. Green, "A Comparative Historical Analysis," 44.

15. On the Young Tunisian movement, see Taoufik Ayadi, Mouvement réformiste et mouvements populaires à Tunis (1900–1912) (Tunis: Université de Tunis, 1986).

16. Green, "French Islamic Policy," 14–15.

17. The following sketches of these two men's Tunisian careers are drawn from Pierre Bardin, Algériens et Tunisiens dans l'Empire Ottoman de 1848 à 1914 (Paris: Centre National de la Recherche Scientifique, 1979), pp. 190–92.

18. On this earlier group of Maghribi immigrants, see Bardin, op. cit., 146–58 and Béchir Tlili, "Au seuil du nationalisme tunisien: Documents inédits sur le panislamisme au Maghreb, 1919–1923," Africa [Rome], vol. 28, no. 2 (1973): 220.

19. For their part, the Young Turks had no doubts about either the strength of Islamic sentiments in Tunisia or where those sentiments were directed. An official report in 1911 stressed that "the masses [in Tunisia] look ardently to Istanbul [for support]." Cited in Bardin, op. cit., 233. Bardin also discusses the activities of Sfaihi and Sharif following their departure from Tunis, 193–95, as does Tlili, op. cit., 222, n. 4.

20. On the World War I period, see Tlili, op. cit., 222 and 229; and Peter Heine, "Salih ash-Sharif at-Tunisi: A North African Nationalist in Berlin during the First World War," Revue de l'Occident Musulman et de la Méditerranée, no. 33 (1982): 89–95. For an account of southern Tunisia and Tripolitania in the course of the war, see Mahmoud Abdelmoula, Jihad et colonialisme: La Tunisie et la Tripolitaine (1914–1918) (Tunis: Editions Tiers-Monde, 1987).

21. Béchir Tlili, "Problématique des processus de formation des faits nationaux et des idéologies nationalistes dans le monde-islamo-méditerranéen de l'entre deux-guerres (1919–1930): L'Exemple de la Tunisie," Les Cahiers de Tunisie, vol. 21 (1973): 198–200 discusses the tendency of Arab nationalists to support the Kemalist venture in its early stages, but to conclude subsequently that the revolution in Turkey constituted a definitive breaking point between Turkey and the Arab-Islamic world. Although not yet the political activist he would later become, Habib Bourguiba, while living with his brother in Le Kef during 1920–1921, was "attuned to the great adventure of Ataturk." Sophie Bessis and Souhayr Belhassen, Bourguiba: À la conquête d'un destin, vol. 1 (Paris: Jeunes Afriques Livres, 1988), p. 29.

22. At the time of the abolition of the caliphate, Tunisia was the only North African territory in which the caliph's name continued to figure in the khutba. Afrique Française, vol. 34 (March 1924): 157.

23. Al-Thaalbi's involvement in these events is outlined in Martin Kramer, Islam Assembled: The Advent of the Muslim Congresses (New York: Columbia University Press, 1986), pp. 84–85, 98–101, and 132–37.

24. Habib Bourguiba occasionally expressed reservations about the speed with which Ataturk had transformed his country or his relentless refusal to compromise with its traditional institutions. Even then, however, he did not question the Turkish ruler's ultimate goals. See, as examples, his remarks quoted in Derek Hopwood, Habib Bourguiba of Tunisia: The Tragedy of Longevity (New York: St. Martin's Press, 1992), p. 84; and in Sophie Bessis and Souhayr Belhassen, Bourguiba: Un si long règne, vol. 2 (Paris: Jeune Afrique Livres, 1989), p. 81.

⊚ **3** ⊚

A Rereading of Islamic Texts in the Maghrib in the Nineteenth and Early Twentieth Centuries: Secular Themes or Religious Reformism?

Khalifa Chater

INTRODUCTION

The nineteenth century was an era of trial for the Maghrib. The Exmouth expedition was launched in 1816 against Algeria, Tunisia, and Tripolitania; Algiers was occupied in 1830; Tunisia was invaded in 1881; and the century witnessed the beginning of the process that would end in the occupation of Morocco in 1912. In 1815, the Maghrib was moving into its precolonial era, brought on by demonstrations of force that would eventually impose the European order. The regencies were forced into a situation of dependency in fact if not in law, obliged to submit and to recognize the established power.

In the cry of despair of Hussein Dey, the era was "the end of the world, the age of decline. All those who are in charge of Muslim affairs must be on the alert, ready instantly to react to the assaults of the whole Christian nation." This excerpt from a letter from Hussein Dey of Algiers to Hussein Bey of Tunis in 1824 defines the context and reveals the stakes of the reforms that were undertaken.[1] Whether imposed by the powers or elaborated as resistance responses, the reforms were part of a new interaction between foreign dictates and internal dynamics.

In order to deal with the new situation, the changing times and the demands of temporal morality, the rulers resorted to *fatwas* issued by *'ulama* to legitimate their actions and especially the innovations that they envisioned.[2] The partisans of *islah* (reform)—which in the Maghrib scarcely dealt with theology or worship, but rather with the political, social, and juridical applications of the *shari'a*—based their visions and their various reform plans on new analyses of sacred texts. In this privileged moment of the nineteenth century, characterized by intense *ijtihad* activity, Muslim humanism moved toward a reexamination of its politico-ethical system and a revision of its ideal-types. This approach disturbed and shocked the dominant religious establishment, which was little inclined to admit innovation, rereadings, or the reopening of settled issues. The age of decline, together with the cultural autarky that characterized it, had reinforced traditional approaches that became absolute dogma in the Muslim world.

The new awareness on the part of an enthusiastic and determined elite minority, which called into question the traditional consensual vision, transformed the internal dynamics of North African politics. Their awareness should be seen within the framework of an attraction-repulsion response to Europe, which was perceived simultaneously as a force of aggression and "the realm of lights" (the Enlightenment). The initiatives to revise and call into question well-established norms and values were part of a determined movement to read and reinterpret religious texts, and incontestably represented a renaissance in Muslim thought. They clearly showed Western secular influences, and thus actual, if not formal, secular tendencies. The study of this large collection of state *fatwas*, whose growth was quite exceptional, will permit an analysis of the reform dynamic and its different ideological threads.

I. THE ALGERIAN ORDEAL, THE FATWAS AND THE NEW PRINCIPLES OF LEGITIMACY

The capitulation of the Dey of Algiers on July 5, 1830, and the defection of the Regency's Ottoman authorities made the quest for a new government the order of the day. This government would need to be legitimated. The *bay'a*[3] of Tlemcen, the emergence of 'Abd al-Qadir's state, and the affirmation of the authority of the Ahmad Bey of Constantine were ratified and justified by *fiqh* discourse or actual *fatwas*.

A) The Bay'a of Tlemcen (1830)

A delegation of notables of Tlemcen presented themselves, on August 20, 1830, to the Sharifian governor of Oujda to announce their allegiance (*bay'a*) to the Moroccan sultan and to ask him to designate a governor for their province. In the face of the sultan's reticence, based on *fatwas* of the *'ulama* of Fez, whom he had consulted,[4] the Tlemcenians drew up a counter-*fatwa* to refute the reasons invoked and to legitimate this measure of "public safety."[5] The *fatwa* begins by calling into question the Fez arguments:

> (1) The inhabitants of Tlemcen are not bound by any *bay'a* to the Ottoman sultan; [but] only by a simple formality, or nominal affirmation; (2) The governor of Algiers exercised power through the use of force without respecting the requirements of religion. Divine will, which accords stays to oppressors before the inexorable sanction, provoked his fall, for [the Dey of Algiers] was an oppressor, unjust with the believers. Neither did he recognize the authority of the sultan nor execute the orders of the sultan. This is witnessed by his refusal to take into account the instructions of the sultan relative to the resolution of the conflict with the Christians by the payment of a fine; (3) [Ottoman authority] were it really corroborated by a *bay'a* which obligated us, would hardly constitute an argument, given the distance from our regency especially because information attests that the sultan is preoccupied by his own security and the defense of his throne, and is incapable of assuring the defense of his closest provinces. He was therefore incapable of assuring our defense as is witnessed in the occupation of Egypt and of Syria by Christians for more than five years.[6]

This *fatwa* is based on the facts in evidence, and an examination of the objective situation in Algeria. It examines the nature of the relations with the Ottoman sultan, who is called the imam and not the caliph, which constitutes a serious diminution of his titles, a banalization of his office. It also emphasizes the political necessity of integrating an Ottoman province into the Sharifian kingdom. A new principle affirmed by the *fatwa*, the defection puts the legitimacy of the established power structure in question and authorizes the installation of a new authority, "since waiting for [hypothetical] aid brings catastrophe while the situation engenders great threats."[7] Political opportunism dominates. It allows the *ahl al-hal wal-'aqd* (those who have the power to bind and unbind, the *'ulama* and the notables) to remove, as a final solution, those who can no longer govern, and to name new governors. During this exceptional period, these notables would exercise de facto sovereignty, in order to achieve the transfer of power to persons selected by them.

In the end, the Moroccan sultan accepted the *bay'a* of Tlemcen, named a representative, and deployed troops to support the new government.[8] The gravity of the situation, the opposition of the Kouloughis, and the support that was accorded them by French troops explain the Moroccan retreat toward the end of the month of Ramadan 1246 (March 14, 1831).

B) Constantine and the Tunisian Alternative (1830–31)

The Bey of Tunis took the initiative to write to the inhabitants of the Province of Constantine proposing that they accept Tunisian sovereignty in order to escape French colonial designs. The Franco-Tunisian diplomatic negotiations relative to this affair do not concern us here.[9] Let us limit ourselves to the *fatwa* letter from the Bey of Tunis to the *'ulama* and the notables of the Beylik of Constantine, written by the *'alim-bashkatib* (minister) Ibn Abi Dhiaf,[10] who attempted to validate a transfer of power.

> Since the events that Algeria underwent, according to the will of God, you have been in complete anarchy, exposed to the whims of the strongest, living in insecurity, incapable of resisting. Your continued presence in this state will provoke the dispersal of the word of the Muslims and the defeat of a Muslim nation. You are not in a position to resist the French military. It is therefore your duty to join with us and to abandon combat.[11]

The *fatwa* was based on an argument for the public interest of Muslims, on an evaluation of power relationships, and, therefore, on criteria of political expediency. The *shari'a* arguments were presented in their general outlines: the peril that threatens a "Muslim *umma*," the unity of Muslims as "a single structure" and the necessity of not "exposing oneself to an inexorable danger."[12] All flowed from the area of *fiqh* discourse and from the principles and expressions of the Sunna.

The response of the *diwan* of Constantine affirmed its support for Ahmad Bey and stressed "the dependency of both the Beylik of Constantine and the Beylik of Tunis on the caliph at Istanbul, the

Sultan Mahmud."[13] The Ottoman argument was therefore used differently by the inhabitants of Tlemcen and Constantine, according to the differing circumstances. In Tlemcen the choice was dictated by the political void and by the tribal and Arab foundations of its resistance. In Constantine, on the other hand, the resistance authority was of Ottoman origins. It was therefore normal that Constantine should value the prestigious title of caliph-sultan upon which its power was founded.

C) The Bay'a-Fatwa Foundation of 'Abd al-Qadir's State

The *bay'a* of 'Abd al-Qadir took place, in the course of a meeting of anti-French tribes, on November 27, 1832 in Gheris, in eastern Algeria. At a gathering under the tree of Dourdara, the traditional place of consultation for the tribes, a proposal was made by the assembled sharifs, *'ulama*, and tribal notables to the Sharif Mohieddine that he take power or designate his son 'Abd al-Qadir to lead the nascent jihad state.[14] The *bay'a* of 'Abd al-Qadir was significant, according to specialists, because it followed the example of the Prophet, since the *bay'a al-radhwan*, the "oath of satisfaction," which was immortalized by a Qur'anic verse, took place under the Umm-Ghailan tree during the battle of al-Houdeybiya.[15]

The text of the *bay'a-fatwa*[16] stressed the following arguments: (1) The investiture of an imam is a religious necessity in order to ensure the security of persons and property. The Prophet said, "God defends by authority what He does not defend by the Qur'an"; (2) This need is more evident during "this era of falsehood" of the Christian invasion of Muslim regions, of anarchy and of dispersion, and in the absence of a guide for the jihad; (3) The choice of the *ahl al-hal wal-'aqd* fell upon Mohieddine and then upon his son 'Abd al-Qadir. When his father declined, they pledged fealty to 'Abd al-Qadir, without his having asked for this charge.

This was an exceptional *bay'a*, since it implied exit from the Ottoman community, considered until then as the holder of legitimate power, and founded an Algerian power by associating the Arab and Berber populations and privileging the tribes. The power of 'Abd al-Qadir was, therefore, justified by Muslim principles of ethics derived from the Sunna to deal with a situation of historic difficulty.[17]

II. FATWAS, RAISON D'ÉTAT, AND SITUATION

Faced by the occupation of Algeria, the jihad state of 'Abd al-Qadir, and the growing dependency of Morocco and Tunisia, the established authorities and the 'ulama followed an approach of raison d'état, stressing the "ethics of responsibility,"[18] rather than simple accommodation vis-à-vis the power structure.

A) The Creation of Nizami Armies

The creation of a nizami, European-style army to face European threats raised controversy in North Africa. The creation of the Ottoman nizam al-jadid army of 1793 threatened the position of the Janissaries, who were pillars of the established order, and brought on a revolt by them and the 'ulama that overthrew Sultan Selim III in 1808. His son, Mahmud II, returned to the task and, in 1826, re-created a nizami army, which was legitimated this time by a fatwa in proper form. The intervening experience of Muhammad Ali of Egypt with such military reforms was decisive in showing their value.

Did the creation of nizami armies in the Maghrib necessarily have to be legitimized? Originally founded solely in pursuit of jihad, 'Abd al-Qadir's state considered the creation of a nizami army as a necessity and did not feel the need to legitimize its institution. 'Abd al-Qadir's mobilization discourse and the texts of military laws that he drafted confine themselves to the facts of the situation.[19]

In Tunisia, the justification for the creation of a modern army was pursued after the fact by sending a mission to Turkey in May 1831, supposedly to ask authorization to create a nizami army.[20] In fact, the creation of the nizami army had been initiated in January of the same year.

In Morocco, the nizam question aroused a considerable movement of opinion and fed lively discussions among the 'ulama.[21] The response fatwa of Mahdi Ben Souda dated 28 Ramadan 1276 (April 20, 1860)[22] is a model of the genre. Its argument builds upon the need to oppose the systematic condemnation of innovation: (1) Not all innovations are illicit since "gunpowder did not exist in the time of the Prophet, but nevertheless the Muslims used it as soon as it was invented; certainly it is an innovation, but a praiseworthy one"; (2) "The duty of the imam includes constant readiness for any eventuality . . . [the nizam] is today an addition to the power available to Muslims when confronted by Christians. Everything that is available is at the same time obligatory; therefore the nizam is an obligation for each Muslim."

The author cites affirmations of good sense, contextual needs, and examples of victories won by *nizam* armies of both enemy Christians and Muslims (in Egypt, Syria, and in Tunis, but curiously omitting the Ottoman state), in addition to Qur'anic verses and *hadiths*. The *fatwa* is mostly a study of expediency, an evaluation of situation. The rereading of the religious texts is designed to legitimate, by means of arguments in the Qur'an and the Sunna, the norms that emerge from a new context.

B) The Fatwas on the Conduct of 'Abd al-Qadir's War

'Abd al-Qadir's signing of the Treaty of Tafna with Bugeaud in 1837 aroused strong opposition. Was it licit to make peace or conclude a truce with the enemy and to stop the jihad? The maternal uncle of 'Abd al-Qadir delivered a long juridico-religious explanation in a famous *khutba-fatwa*. According to this document, the pursuit of war, when the enemy is in a position of superior strength, is equivalent "to exposing oneself to inexorable peril." The author recalled the terms of a *hadith* that condemned this policy and showed that this choice actually gave the advantage to the enemy. To justify the treaty, he also referred to a second *hadith* that stipulated that "the preservation of a single Muslim [from death] is preferable to the taking of an enemy fortress. Those who oppose this initiative of the imam," he concluded, "lose both houses [the present life and that of the hereafter]."

The conduct of the war raised the problem of punishment of collaborators, of those who shirked jihad, and of those who refused to pay the *zakat* (Qur'anic alms) or the *mawna* (war tax).

In March 1837, 'Abd al-Qadir, who had been called upon to impose sanctions and sometimes death sentences, consulted the *'ulama* of Egypt and of Fez to learn the position of the *shari'a*.[23] The *fatwa* of Fez *'alim* Hassan Ali Ben 'Abd al-Salam Mdides al-Tassouli, which was drawn up on 10 Rabi' al-Awal 1253 (June 14, 1837), was an academic exercise, laying out in a traditional manner the nuanced positions of the different schools.[24] Al-Tassouli justified, with a great many citations from *fiqh* treatises, the punishment of spies, of deserters, of accomplices of evildoers, and of all those who defected, including those who did not pay the war tax. Concerning the delicate question of the legitimacy of the Treaty of Tafna, al-Tassouli judged that "truce with the enemy is permissible if the enemy is not in an offensive mode. Otherwise jihad is a personal duty." Interestingly enough, the 'alim relativized his judgments by affirming that "necessity dictates its imperatives" and that in any case, "the eyewitness sees what the absent one does not."[25]

It has been argued that al-Tassouli took into account "the political implications of the questions posed and was thinking of the interest of the makhzan the whole time." But the interpretation of Abdullah Laroui, who believes that al-Tassouli instituted or reinforced what he calls "makhzan ideology,"[26] seems excessive. Al-Tassouli remains traditional in his approach. It seems to this author that what appears as compromise, accommodation, or ideologically based analysis, is actually based on the contemporaneous theses of the principal legal schools. It seems clear, in fact, that the Sunna logically validates political expediency even under conditions of jihad.

In order to deal with the tribes who had rallied to the colonial authorities, 'Abd al-Qadir consulted the qadi of Fez before attacking them. "How should those who have submitted to the infidel enemy and who have joined his troops be viewed? Are they apostates? How should their women be viewed? Should one demand their repentance, execute them, or reduce them to slavery? What attitude should be adopted toward their children? What attitude should be adopted with respect to the Ibadi Kharijites?"[27]

The answering fatwa of qadi 'Abd al-Hadi Ben Abdallah Husseini, dated 1 Muharram 1256 (March 5, 1840) referred to the history of the first caliphs and drew from examples in the Andalusian time of trial to show that the fiqh schools were not unanimous in considering Muslims who rally to Christians as apostates. But even if they were apostates, it would be forbidden to seize their wives and children. He demonstrated the same tolerant attitude with regard to the Kharijites: "They cannot be considered as infidels." The fatwa categorically rejected the laws of war, which 'Abd al-Qadir proposed to use against those who rejected his authority, and forbade him to demand contributions other than the zakat from the inhabitants. The fatwa studied the questions in the absolute, without taking into account the wishes of 'Abd al-Qadir. It forbade any leeway or any "circumstantial" measures.

C) The Raison d'État Fatwas in Morocco

In order to improve state finances, the Moroccan Sultan in 1860 proposed some new taxes, on whose legality he decided to consult the 'ulama. The majority of the 'ulama avoided taking positions.[28] Ali al-

Soussi al-Semlali (d. 1893), one of the rare *'ulama* to respond to the query in drawing up a *fatwa*, invoked raison d'état and the demands of the situation.[29] He based his argument on the notion of "the indisputable interests" and "current interests not mentioned by the *shari'a*." According to al-Soussi, the *mawna* used for the good of religion and of life belonged to this category of current interests. Al-Soussi cited as justification the needs of Moroccan society in its hour of peril.

III. THE TUNISIAN REFORM FATWAS

The Tunisian reformers of the nineteenth century were, in their own way, practitioners of *ijtihad*. They invested the *fatwa* with a mission of progress and emancipation. A few examples of this *fatwa* literature that was so rich in nineteenth-century Tunisia are discussed here.

With the abolition of slavery between 1842 and 1846, the Regency of Tunis inaugurated an era of reforms. The letter of Ahmad Bey[30] to the *shari'a*, dated January 26, 1846 and drawn up by *bashkatib* Ibn Abi Dhiaf, was a *fatwa*. The juridico-religious argument[31] pointed out that slavery was an object of controversy among the *'ulama*, that those who treated their slaves according to the *shari'a* were rare if not nonexistent, and that the laws of the *shari'a* actively encouraged manumission. In highlighting the liberation agenda in Islam, the author placed himself within the spirit of the law, if not the letter.

The Dibaja (1844) of Mahmoud Kabadou was a veritable manifesto in favor of reforms, of progress, and of borrowing from the West. This Tunisian man of letters affirmed that "wisdom is the goal of the believer. He looks for it where he can find it." In support of his reformist thesis, the author cited the famous Qur'anic verse: "Are those who know and those who do not know equal?"[32]

The work of Khair al-Din, *Necessary Reforms in the Muslim States* (*Aqwam al-masalik fi ma'rifat ahwal al-mamalik*) (1867), adopted the methodology of the *fatwa*.[33] Qur'anic verses, *hadiths*, and examples drawn from the Sunna were advanced in support of his reforming theses, which pointed to contradictions in the arguments by opponents of the Tanzimat, and cited European progress founded on justice and the sciences, the necessity of consulting the *shari'a*, the destructive effects of despotism, and man's natural affinity with liberty. A reading of Ottoman and European history allowed him to defend his ideology and provided the basis for his methodology of implementation: "The one who recalls these two remarks, that the Islamic *shari'a* is intended to ensure happiness in both lives [present and future], and that [good] organization in the present life strengthens religion, observes with sorrow that certain *'ulama,* who should take into consideration the situation of the times, neglect the study of facts both internal and external. They do not have a full understanding of the relevant conditions and this constitutes the greatest of handicaps."[34]

The colonization of the Maghribi countries caused North Africans to lose the initiative and forced them to adopt defensive stances. By reinforcing their faith in tradition, and in reacting to the initiatives of evangelists, they sought to defend an Islam under attack. The treatise of 'Abd al-'Aziz al-Thaalbi in 1905, which was coauthored by al-Hadi Seba'i and César Bénattar (this Judeo-Muslim alliance was already in place), emphasized "the liberal spirit of the Qur'an," which was the title of the work.[35] Adopting the style of a *fatwa,* the book grounded its defense of Islam in a rereading of the history of the Muhammadan state, highlighting the liberating facts and deeds of the Prophet and the first caliphs.

The conclusions drawn from the preceding were the following: Women should have their faces uncovered, should not be shut in at home, should not be kept hidden from view, and should be educated and have a decent and honest bearing.[36]

When it is realized that 'Abd al-'Aziz al-Thaalbi was the founder of the Dustur and that he embodied the movement—pejoratively called antique by the newer elites who took over the direction of the Neo-Dustur—it is possible to understand the roots of *ijtihad* modernity. In 1930, this *ijtihad* modernity favoring the emancipation of women was defended with boldness and temerity by the Zitouna sheikh Tahar Haddad, author of the work *Our Women in the Shari'a and in Society (Imra'atuna fil-shari'a wal-mujtama').* This Tunisian thinker, who adopted the same methodology and the same strategy of treatise *fatwas* as the reformers, shook the Tunisian intelligentsia during the new era, that of the national struggle.

The Essential and the Transient

One must take into consideration the important and obvious difference between the founding principles of Islam—its dogma and essence—immutable principles such as belief in the oneness of God, ethics, justice, and equality among human beings and the contextual givens such as local human situations and mind-sets rooted in the pre-Islamic era . . . [In these latter cases], positions taken concerning their preservation or their modification are valid as long as these situations persist, but they become invalid as soon as the context changes. I cite the example of slaves, of concubines, of polygamy, which do not come from Islam.

To know if a question comes from the essence of Islam or not, one must ask oneself: Is it part of the founding principles of Islam?[37]

CONCLUSION

In the course of the precolonial era, the composition of *fatwas* was mostly a response to the demands of the new circumstances, aimed at consolidating existing regimes and allowing them, through fiscal measures and military reforms, to enhance their potential for resistance. More rarely, the government initiated reforms in the spirit of the liberal vision celebrated by the modernist reformers. The *fatwas* were founded on Qur'anic texts, *hadiths*, and legal treatises of the main schools. There were traditional *fatwas*, which dealt in absolutes according to the "ethics of conviction" of their authors. There were also enlightened *fatwas*, which dealt with new questions, analyzing their dimensions "from the point of view of *fiqh* and *shari'a* law, of judgment and politics, and of understanding of divine acts and their analysis," such as were laid out by the Moroccan academic and historian al-Naciri.[38]

The argument that the specific situation facing North Africans had to be evaluated in its spiritual and temporal context defined this new approach. Amongst audacious *'ulama*, *ijtihad* was again the order of the day. The evaluative methods and terms of reference of this *ijtihad* integrated temporal data. Along these lines, the approach of Khair al-Din offered one instance of an argument in favor of reforms that stressed religious principles and maintained that it was both the prerogative and duty of the *'ulama* to reach judgments by taking into account the present situation and the givens of its context.[39] The separation of the political and the religious was, therefore, not an issue in the thought of the reformers.

Political dynamics explained the quest for *fatwas* and their principal logic. In Ali Merad's words, Islam as such, therefore, seemed to recede as a "principle of movement,"[40] in spite of the limiting cases of jihad in the origins of 'Abd al-Qadir's state. "Raison d'état" explained most of the reactions of the regencies during the course of the era of dependency and struggle. The modern *fatwas* analyzed here referred both to spiritual and temporal givens, and never overshadowed the religious givens, even in the most hardy of the reforms.

What explains the retreat of the *'ulama* from the issuance of legal opinions when important consultations came up? The *'ulama* of Tunis, who were asked by the government to participate in the commission establishing the Fundamental Pact of 1857, withdrew from the proceedings, saying that it would be possible to "consult them and obtain written responses each time that a question of *fiqh* arose."[41] They also asserted that questions about general policy and the affairs of the country were not their business. Invited in 1860 to study whether the proposition of the sultan to institute taxes was well-founded, the Moroccan *'ulama* responded that "our master possesses the books which permit him to decide that question himself."[42] This attitude of the *'ulama* of Fez and Tunis is explained more easily by withdrawal or abdication than by a desire to separate the political and religious.

Political leaders were more likely to call into the establishment *'ulama* who were up to date with the situations involved, more understanding of political dynamics, and, sometimes, more favorable to the reform philosophy. The common *'ulama* became marginalized, reinforced their traditional positions, and withdrew effectively from the decision-making centers. "Neutralization of religious forces [through] centralism,"[43] the triumph of *makhzan* ideology, and the undermining or abdication of members of the traditional schools all helped the power structure to ensure a certain monopoly of *fatwas* and to erect an effective barrier between the religious and the secular.

Were these developments part of a process of secularization? In the emergence of a group of "legalists in the exclusive service of the state," Abdullah Laroui believes he "detects a stumbling laicization movement."[44] But the *fatwas* were linked to a specific historic culture, representing a distinctive Muslim humanism, and a well normalized politico-ethical system. Laicism, on the other hand, develops in a completely different context, in which society becomes its own reference. The *fatwas* themselves affirmed that legitimacy relied upon the domain of the sacred, of the divine, and of normative religious models.

Historically, the Islamic states limited the interventions of government to questions of sovereignty, public order, and very serious matters. The ongoing religious affairs and the everyday questions were dealt with by the imams, the *qadis,* and the *'alim* professors. All of this induced a de facto separation, which normative discourse, legal treatises, and Muslim governmental ethics do not formally recognize. The essential *fatwas*, which concerned vital questions, were within the range of matters of which governors believed they could directly take charge.

The abdication of the *'ulama*, with the exception of the establishment that religious officials associated with the power structure, left the political arena open. It contributed to making this implicit secularization, or at least ethic of responsibility, a fact. But laicism and secularization were never affirmed or claimed.

In Egypt, the work of Ali 'Abd al-Raziq, published in 1925, was the founding discourse on secularism: "The caliphate, justice, and the other governmental functions," he said, "are not religious charges. They are quite simply political charges . . . confided to our care so that one may use judgments of reason, the experiences of peoples, and political rules. In the same way, religion does not concern the organization of armies, the urbanism of cities and ports, or the organization of government."[45]

Nothing similar existed in the Maghrib in the nineteenth and early twentieth centuries, when secularism was hardly mentioned as an ideology. There existed programs of state consolidation and of modernization that were clearly grounded in lay or secular themes but that were spontaneous and unrecognized as such. The context in which they were articulated is best described as one of religious reformism.

Notes

1. Letter from Hussein Bey of Tunis, July 28, 1824. See Chater, *Dépendance et mutations précoloniales: La Régence de Tunis de 1815 à 1857* (Tunis, Publications de l'Université, 1984), p. 211.

2. See Chater, "Islam et réformes politiques dans la Tunisie du XIXe siècle" in *Maghreb Review*, vol. 13, no. 1–2 (1988): 77–83.

3. The *bay'a* is a presentation of an oath of recognition of authority, and therefore an act of allegiance.

4. The sultan consulted the *'ulama* of Fez and asked them to draw up *fatwas* on the question. The majority recommended that he reject this *bay'a*. The *fatwa* of Tlemcen rejects the arguments of the Fez *fatwas* and justifies the *bay'a*. See Ahmad al-Naciri, *Al-Istiksaa fi akhbar al-maghrib al-aqsa*, Jaffar al-Naciri and Mohamed al-Naciri, eds. (Casablanca: Dar al-Kutub, 1956), book III–9, p. 27.

5. This *fatwa* letter was published by al-Naciri, ibid., 27–29.

6. Personal translation of the *fatwa*.

7. Al-Naciri, ibid., 28–29.

8. Al-Naciri, ibid., 30–32.
9. See Chater, *Dépendance et mutations précoloniales*, op. cit., 374–420.
10. Ibn Abi Dhiaf (vulgo Ben Dhiaf), *Ithaf ahl al-zaman fi akhbar muluk tunis wa ahd al-aman* 8 vols. (Tunis: Kitabat al-Dawla li-Shu'un al-Thaqafiyya, 1963–1965), book 3, p. 175.
11. See Chater, *Dépendance et mutations précoloniales*, op. cit., 410–11.
12. Ibid.
13. See the text of the letter in Muhamad Larbi Zbiri, *Mudhakkarat Ahmad Bey* (Algiers: SNED, 1973), pp. 21–23.
14. See Muhammad Ibn 'Abd al-Qadir al-Jaza'iri, *Touhfat al-za'ir fi tarikh al-jaza'ir wal-amir 'Abd al-Qadir*, Mamdouh Haqqi, ed., second ed. (Beirut: Dar al-Yaqdha, 1964), p. 155.
15. Ibid., 156.
16. See the text of the *bay'a*, ibid., 157–59.
17. The texts of the second *bay'a* and the *fatwa* letters of support use the same arguments. Ibid., 159–65.
18. Max Weber with reason disagrees with these two positions: both the existence of an "ethics of conviction," which takes positions in the absolute, and the existence of an "ethics of responsibility." Max Weber, *Le savant et le politique* (Paris: Plon, 1963), pp. 172–73. Raymond Aron notes that "the morality of the man of action is truly one of responsibility."
19. See Muhammad Ibn 'Abd al-Qadir al-Jaza'iri, *Touhfat al-za'ir*, op. cit., 191–205.
20. Ibn Abi Dhiaf, *Ithaf ahl al-zaman*, op. cit., 178.
21. Abdallah Laroui evokes the rich discussion that this question aroused. See Abdallah Laroui, *Les origines sociales et culturelles du nationalisme marocain (1830–1912)* (Paris: Maspero, 1977), pp. 272–84.
22. Laroui presents the principal arguments of this response in his analysis. See Laroui, op. cit., 280–281.
23. The letter of 'Abd al-Qadir is published by Al-Naciri, op. cit., 45–46; and Muhammad Ibn 'Abd al-Qadir al-Jaza'iri, *Touhfat al-za'ir.*, op. cit., 316–17.
24. The *fatwa* is published in its entirety by Muhamad Ibn 'Abd al-Qadir al-Jaza'iri, *Touhfat al-za'ir*, op. cit., 318–29.
25. Ibid., chapter 4, 325.
26. See Laroui, op. cit., 266–71.
27. The letter of 'Abd al-Qadir is published in its entirety by Muhamad Ibn 'Abd al-Qadir al-Jaza'iri, *Touhfat al-za'ir.*, op. cit., 384–86.
28. See Laroui, op. cit., 294.
29. See al-Soussi's analysis of the *fatwa* in Ahmad Amari, "*Nadhariat al-tahdith wal-muwajahat min khilal al-Simali*," *Actes du colloque réformisme et société marocaine au XIXème siècle* (Rabat: Publications Faculté des Lettres, 1986), pp. 91–111.
30. See the text in Ibn Abi Dhiaf, op. cit., 87–88.
31. This question was studied in Chater, "Islam et réformes politiques dans la Tunisie du XIXème siècle," *Maghreb Review*, vol. 13, no. 1–2 (1988): 77–83.
32. Ibid., 78–79.
33. Khair al-Din al-Tunisi, *Réformes nécessaires aux états musulmans; Aqwam al-masalik*, Moncef Chennoufi, ed. (Tunis: MTE, 1972), 331 pages.
34. Ibid., 82–83.
35. César Bénattar, al-Hadi Seba'i, and 'Abd al-'Aziz al-Thaalbi, *L'Esprit libéral du Coran* (Paris: Ernest Leroux, 1905), 100 pages.
36. Ibid., 19.

37. Personal translation of Tahar Haddad, *Imra'atuna fil-shari'a wal-mujtama'*, second ed. (Tunis: MTE, 1972), pp. 22–23.
38. Al-Naciri defines his methodology, his *ijtihad* viewpoint, in the introduction of a *fatwa* dated January 10, 1887. See al-Naciri, op. cit., 184–99.
39. Khair al-Din, op. cit., 82–83.
40. Ali Merad, "L'Idéologisation de L'Islam dans le monde musulman contemporain" in *Islam et politique au Maghreb*, Ernest Gellner and Jean-Claude Vatin, eds. (Paris: CNRS, 1981), pp. 151–60.
41. See Ibn Abi Dhiaf, *Ithaf ahl al-zaman.*, op. cit., book 4, 248.
42. See Laroui, op. cit., 294.
43. See Mohamed Mansour, "Les oulémas et le makhzen, dans le Maroc pré-colonial," in *Le Maroc actuel, une modernisation au miroir de la tradition* (France: IREMAM, 1992), pp. 3–15, especially p. 15.
44. See Laroui, op. cit., 301.
45. Ali 'Abd al-Raziq, *Al-Islam wa usul al-hukm* (Beirut: Maktabat al-Hayat Editions, 1965), 245 pages. See the conclusion on p. 201.

⊚ **4** ⊚

Salafis and Modernists in the Moroccan Nationalist Movement

Mohamed El Mansour

Three major factors have made Islam a dominant feature of Moroccan political life. First, ever since Morocco achieved statehood and became an independent entity in the eighth century, Islam has been the cement joining Moroccans together. Islam was the only common factor able to bridge the gap among different ethnic and linguistic Moroccan communities, particularly Arabs and Berbers. Second, the geographical location of Morocco at Islam's far western frontier meant that the jihadist drive remained a powerful element in the country's destiny. Furthering the cause of Islam was a strong rallying principle behind the emergence of the great Moroccan empires. When expansion was no longer possible after the fifteenth century, resistance against the Christian threat kept the jihadist spirit alive. The third factor that enhanced the religious character of the country was the monarchical institution, which was always identified with Islam. From the time of the first Islamic dynasty of the Idrisids (the eighth through the tenth centuries) the monarchy made religion its main legitimizing theme, and used it continuously in efforts to rally the different social communities. Even before the coming to power of the Sharifian dynasties in the sixteenth century, the monarchy was seen as a religious institution with the power to unite the Moroccans and make them one nation.

SECULARIST TEMPTATIONS

Religion played a preponderant role in Moroccan society but this did not mean that there were no cleavages between Islamic theory and government practice. It became clear to the *'ulama,* for instance, particularly during the nineteenth century, that the *shari'a* had ceased to be the only reference in the government of the country. Nonreligious taxes had become a fact of life that few *'ulama* contested, while the abandonment of jihad and the increasing intercourse with the Christians required the state to make various concessions and accept many practices that were seen as contrary to religion. At the beginning of the twentieth century, the *'ulama* were no longer a monolithic conservative group acting as guardians of the *shari'a* and rejecting nonreligious models of government. Perhaps the best illustration of this change of mind was "the constitutionalist movement" witnessed by the country during the first decade of the twentieth century.

Around 1900, the state of Morocco was on the verge of collapse and could be best described as a crumbling edifice that European colonialist ambitions threatened from all sides. The state (*makhzan*) was powerless to check these designs, especially at a time when internal rebellions created a chaotic situation preventing any hope of recovery within the traditional political structures. This did not mean that the intellectual elite faced the crisis with lethargy. Though limited in scope and doomed to failure in the end, a liberal current of thought emerged, proposing new ideas to save the country and preserve its independence.

What was the nature of this liberal current of thought? Did it really reflect the concerns of the Moroccan intellectual elite of the time? The leading nationalist 'Allal al-Fasi (d. 1974) speaks about a genuine constitutionalist movement, the first of its kind. Had it succeeded, he thought, it would have reformed the Moroccan state and prevented the colonial takeover.

In fact, this "constitutional movement" was mainly the work of a few Syrian émigrés who coordinated their efforts with a group of enlightened scholars in Fez.[1] By the turn of the twentieth century, the Moroccan elite looked increasingly toward the Middle East as a source of inspiration and assistance. For instance, the *makhzan* made attempts to bring Ottoman military instructors in the place of the European ones, but the European powers, and France in particular, thwarted such attempts. Ideas of pan-Islamism and pan-Arabism, however, made their way from the Middle East through a number of Moroccan *'ulama,* such as Abu Shu'ayb al-Dukkali, Ali Znibar, and Muhammad Ibn 'Abd al-Kabir al-Kattani, and also through the Arabic press.

The main achievements of this constitutional movement consisted in the publication in 1907 of the first Arabic newspaper in Tangier and the elaboration of a project for a constitution that was addressed to the sultan in 1908. In fact, at least two newspapers were founded between 1907 and 1909 by Syrians. They served essentially to relay Middle Eastern constitutional ideas. The most important was *Lisan al-Maghrib,* which was published by Arthur and Faraj Allah Nimmur upon the invitation of the *makhzan.* It was in this paper that the two Syrian brothers published a project for a constitution. This project was not the first one, since two years earlier another Syrian by the name of 'Abd al-Karim Murad (d. 1928) presented a constitution proposal to Sultan Mawlay 'Abd al-'Aziz.[2] The other newspaper, *Al-Fajr,* was founded by the Lebanese Ni'mat Allah al-Dahdah in 1908 and was supposed to reflect the views of the Moroccan government. The educated elite also became acquainted with a number of Egyptian publications, such as *Al-Manar, Al-Ahram, Al-Mu'ayyad,* and others, but was not always aware of the liberal or secular content of some of them. Ideological differences between religious and secular tendencies as they existed in the Middle East were unknown in this part of the Maghrib. Moroccan *'ulama* accepted pan-Arab and pan-Islamic ideas as a whole without being able to discern the ideological differences that reflected a heterogeneous Middle Eastern reality. As a result, many secular ideas were assimilated at least by a few enlightened individuals. 'Allal al-Fasi claims that the Syrian émigrés were not alone but were joined by a group of scholars from Fez who founded the Fez "Association of Union and Progress,"[3] a name that clearly reflects an admiration for the Young Turks movement. A member of this association, 'Allal al-Fasi's uncle, affirmed that this association also took part in the elaboration of the constitution project published by *Lisan al-Maghrib.*[4]

The ideas 'Allal al-Fasi attributed to the *Lisan al-Maghrib* group show a strong secular tendency and a great sympathy with the reformist movements in the Middle East and in Turkey in particular. It is worth noting that the publication of the constitution project came only a few months after the constitutional revolution of the Young Turks.[5] The Arab press of Tangier and the presence of a group of Middle Easterners in Morocco allowed the Moroccan-educated elite to follow closely the news of the Ottoman constitutional movement.

This movement raised hopes among a group of young Moroccans that perhaps Muslim peoples could meet the challenge by relying on their own capabilities to reform their society and stave off the menace of European domination.

It is not clear how much of the literature produced by the *Lisan al-Maghrib* group reflects the convictions of Moroccan intellectuals, but it is undeniable that the exposure of these intellectuals to a political language imported from the Middle East had an impact on the political discourse of the Moroccan *'ulama*. Describing the despotism of Mawlay 'Abd al-'Aziz, 'Abd al-Hay al-Kattani wrote in 1908: "To trust the nation means that you should believe in its ability to think and act. Such a thing could not even be conceived by 'Abd al-'Aziz, who believed that all the authority was his and that his power over men was unlimited and absolute."[6] The impact is also clear in the conditional *bay'a* by which the *'ulama* of Fez proclaimed Mawlay 'Abd al-Hafid in 1907[7] as well as in the discussion that preceded it and in which Muhammad Ibn 'Abd al-Kabir al-Kattani insisted on a *majlis al-shura* as one of the conditions to proclaim the new sultan.[8]

The views expressed in the columns of *Lisan al-Maghrib* clearly reflected the principles of liberal constitutionalists. The root of evil was seen in the conjunction of "ignorance and despotism." Salvation was to be found in education, on the one hand, and in constitutional government, on the other. Reference was also made to the freedom of thought and action without which the nation's energies could not be mobilized and oriented effectively to achieve reform and progress.[9] The guiding ideal was not the Islamic state of any time or place but "the present civilized nations of the world, both Muslim and Christian,"[10] which have acceded to the rank of great nations through the curbing of despotism. The obsession of the time was Japan, "that rising sun of Asia which forty years ago was at the rear of nations, but now it figures among the great nations after it realized an amazing victory over one of the most powerful countries of the world [Russia]. Closer is the splendid revolution that took place in the sublime state of Turkey after His Majesty Amir al-Mu'minin granted a constitution to his people and ordered the convening of a parliament. May we take him as an example to serve and reform our country."[11]

The appeal was addressed to Mawlay 'Abd al-Hafid, the new sultan proclaimed at the end of 1907 in replacement of Mawlay 'Abd al-'Aziz, who was removed because of his incompetence in dealing with the European threat. The *Lisan al-Maghrib* group continued to press for a constitution and produced a project that it hoped would be adopted by the new sultan. Here again, the ideological inspiration was essentially liberal. While making Islam the state religion, the constitution project proposed that freedom of worship should be guaranteed and that all creeds should be treated equally. Freedom of expression, individual liberties, and equality of all before the law were also affirmed. More important was the concept of popular sovereignty. The project made the *muntada al-shura* or parliament the source of all authority since "its opinion is above every other opinion."[12]

What was the relevance of these ideas to the Moroccan elite? Did these ideas really reflect the concerns of Moroccan *'ulama* on the eve of the collapse of Morocco to European imperialism?

This whole "constitutional movement," despite its portrayal by nationalist leaders as a protonationalism, remained marginal and limited to a few Moroccan intellectuals. It is not even certain that these young Moroccan scholars played any significant role either as columnists in *Lisan al-Maghrib* or as coauthors of the constitution project that appeared in the same periodical. The political language used in both cases was too modern and secularist for the Qarawiyin *'ulama.* Terms such as despotism, progress, and freedom of expression, had not yet made their way into their vocabulary, at least not on a wide scale. Therefore, it is very probable, as Abdallah Laroui points out, that Moroccan *'ulama* at this particular phase were making use of Middle Eastern modern discourse as a cover for their grievances against the *makhzan* and as a means of demanding their rehabilitation in their role of consultants of the sultan, a role they had no longer been able to fulfill since the Moroccan sovereigns had become increasingly dependent on the advice of the Europeans.[13] In other words, the *'ulama* were reclaiming the institution of *shura,* not as it was understood by Middle Eastern reformists, but rather in its traditional sense in the Morocco of old. In this sense, the constitutional movement could be turned into nothing more than a form of protest against the increasing marginalization of the *'ulama* by the *makhzan.*

In the end, Mawlay 'Abd al-Hafid not only disregarded the constitutional demands of the *Lisan al-Maghrib* group but took effective measures to end its activities. French officials, it seems, were able to convince the sultan of the harmful effects that a constitution would have on his authority. As a result, an order was issued in May 1909 to ban *Lisan al-Maghrib* and to deport the Nimmur brothers.[14] To the secularist program of the *Lisan al-Maghrib* group, Mawlay 'Abd al-Hafid opposed a *salafi* alternative that would allow the *makhzan* to keep the initiative of reform and orient it in a way that would preserve the traditional interest of the ruling dynasty and its allies.

THE POWER OF SALAFI IDEOLOGY

The "Young Moroccans" who contributed to the elaboration of the liberal constitution project of 1908 were not numerous and had apparently no or little influence within the traditional scholarly elite. The majority of *'ulama* either did not understand their language or did not share their liberal orientation. These *'ulama* were imbued with traditional Moroccan culture and remained insensitive to a language that seemed to reflect the concerns of the Middle East region rather than their own particular concerns. Behind the failure of the constitutionalist movement there lay two main factors. One was the hegemony of religious ideology, which prevented the religious scholars from supporting the movement, except perhaps as a tactical tool in their opposition to a *makhzan* that failed to defend the country while denying them any way in the management of state affairs. The second factor lay in the emergence, with the proclamation of Mawlay 'Abd al-Hafid, of an official *salafiyya* through which this sultan wanted to reassert the leadership and authority of the weakened 'Alawi state. In the long run, *salafiyya* as an ideology of Islamic revivalism was in a better position to meet the traditional aspirations of both the 'ulama and the monarchy. It provided a common ground on which both could meet to preserve and perpetuate the traditional system.

In Morocco, as in some countries on the fringes of the Islamic world, Islam served as the principal medium of national cohesion. While in many Middle Eastern countries Arabism offered a means of prevailing over religious differences, in Morocco this secular concept failed to appeal to the majority of the population. Historically, it was Islam and not any other ideology that served as the primordial mobilizing force. Throughout Moroccan history, the most significant movements of protest and resistance have had a religious character. Moreover, Morocco by virtue of its separate history and political independence from the rest of the Arab world developed a separate identity of its own. That identity was strengthened by the religious character of the monarchy. As a result, secularist solutions had little chance of being adopted, even if they tempted some figures of the nationalist movement.

The closing down of *Lisan al-Maghrib* in 1909 and the establishment of the French protectorate in 1912 did not mean the abandonment of secular options altogether. In fact, up until 1930 there was still much admiration for secularizing experiences, such as those of Japan and Turkey. Muhammad Ibn al-Hassan al-Wazzani (d. 1978), one of the leading nationalists, wrote in his memoirs that during the 1920s he and young people of his age had a great admiration for the Young Turk movement and especially the constitutional ideas of Midhat Pasha (d. 1844).[15] Al-Wazzani also speaks of Kemal Ataturk as "the great leader" whose victory showed the way to the Islamic peoples.[16] "Moroccans, like other Muslims," wrote al-Wazzani, "considered the Turkish war of liberation as their own . . . [This war] imbued them with a nationalist spirit . . . and sowed in them the seeds of renaissance and freedom."[17]

The great leader of the Rif war (1921–26), Muhammad Ibn 'Abd al-Karim al-Khattabi (d. 1963), also acknowledged the influence that the Kemalist revolution had on him. "I admired the political course followed by Turkey," he declared. "The Islamic countries cannot achieve independence unless they free themselves from religious fanaticism and follow the path of the European peoples."[18]

Clearly, al-Khattabi was more imbued with Western ideals of progress and republicanism than he was with *salafi* ideas advanced by nationalist leaders, such as 'Allal al-Fasi.[19] Apart from his declared convictions mentioned above, the institutions he created and the reforms he introduced during his short rule reflected a clear modernizing inclination. This can be seen in the name of "republic" he chose for the Rifi political entity in 1923. The "Rifi Republic" was also provided with a council of representatives (*majlis al-umma*), even if this council remained essentially tribal in its composition and without much power.[20]

However, the Rifi republican experience was short-lived. The main cause of its collapse, as al-Khattabi himself acknowledged, was the power of religion and his failure to use it as a mobilizing tool. Being aware that the leaders of the religious brotherhoods were his worst enemies, al-Khattabi regretted later that he had not used religion enough as a means of combatting his opponents.[21] The *salafi* Egyptian newspaper *Al-Manar*, which published an interview with al-Khattabi, sharply criticized the Rifi leader's admiration for Turkey's secular experience. *Al-Manar* also disapproved of his attempts to minimize the importance of religious bonds, which he wanted to replace with those of national loyalty (*al-jam'iyya al-wataniyya*).[22] Al-Khattabi's "errors" constituted perhaps the most important lesson that the young Moroccan nationalist learned from the short-lived Rifi experience.

According to 'Allal al-Fasi, the success of *salafi* ideology in Morocco was largely due to French colonial policy. In fact, since the beginning of the protectorate, it was clear to the educated elite that French policy was directed against Islam through the manipulation of those who spoke in its name—the Sufi brotherhoods. The Berber policy, which was aimed at reducing the sphere of the *shari'a,* was put into effect well before 1930,[23] and was officialized in 1914.[24] The French also made it a principle to seek the support of the religious orders whenever possible and Lyautey used leaders of religious centers or *zawaya* on a large scale to further his "pacification policy."[25]

This French colonial policy induced the *'ulama* to play a greater role in political life and turned early *salafis,* such as Abu Shu'ayb al-Dukkali and Muhammad Ibn al-'Arbi al-'Alawi, into active militants against what they regarded as the corrupt Islam of the religious brotherhoods. What differentiates Moroccan *salafis* from their counterparts in the Middle East is the active role played by the former in public life. Not only did they attack degenerate Sufi practices; they roved through the country to spread their message and put it into practice whenever possible.[26]

Moroccan *salafiyya* was not only militant in the sense of playing an active role against corrupt Islam; it was also militant in its resistance to the colonizer. The French authorities realized that the scope of the *salafi* action went far beyond the religious brotherhoods and that the ultimate target was the French protectorate itself. Religion and nationalism in Morocco went hand in hand. "It is a fact," wrote 'Allal al-Fasi, "that the fusion of the *salafi* doctrine with the nationalist cause in Morocco was profitable both to the *salafiyya* and to nationalism. We can also affirm that the method followed in Morocco resulted in the success of the *salafiyya* to a degree not attained even in the country of Muhammad 'Abduh and Jamal al-Din al-Afghani."[27]

What 'Allal al-Fasi meant by the success of the *salafiyya* was probably its power of mobilization. Moroccan society in the 1920s was essentially molded by popular Sufism, and Islam was still perceived by the large masses through the perspective of the religious brotherhoods. These brotherhoods could not be successfully fought outside religion, and the method followed by the *salafi* nationalists was in the line of the Qarawiyin *fuqaha'* who had behind them a long tradition of fighting religious deviations. No other method could have been of any efficacy. Nationalist arguments of a secularist type would have been no match for the well entrenched power of the *zawaya* and the unlucky experience of Muhammad Ibn 'Abd al-Karim al-Khattabi was there to prove it. The ascendancy of Sufi ideology over the people was such that even the nationalists themselves, whether *salafis* or modernists, had to speak the language of the *zawaya* and adopt their organizational structure. In fact, the first nationalist organization founded shortly after the *zahir* (decree) of 1930 was given the name of *zawiya*, while the circle of sympathizers was called *ta'ifa*.[28] Robert Rézette, who studied Moroccan political parties during the protectorate period, also noted that the terminology used by the nationalists was partly borrowed from the *zawaya*. Thus 'Allal al-Fasi was known in the countryside as the *shaykh* while his followers were referred to as the *ikhwan* or the *'allaliyin*.[29]

One might argue that many nationalists were modernists with a Western education. They were not imbued with *salafi* ideas, and perhaps the emphasis on religion was nothing more than a tactical choice. There is certainly some truth in this argument: What the nationalists needed most at this stage of their movement was a mobilizing cause that appealed to all Moroccans. Religion was the only field in which the nation felt secure from French reprisals since, in principle and by virtue of the protectorate treaty, the French authorities were supposed to keep away from anything that concerned religion. The *salafiyya* thus seemed to provide a shield against persecution by the French authorities while serving as an extremely powerful means of popular mobilization. Even the young modernists, whose convictions were largely based on Western ideals, realized the effectiveness of the *salafiyya* as a mobilizing device and, therefore, used its discourse when addressing the people.[30] These young modernists, who were to a large extent cultural aliens in their society, could only mobilize the masses with *salafi* arguments. They espoused a "tactical nationalism" with a strong *salafi* coloring, but as the nationalist movement gained ground, the *salafi* character progressively lost its importance.

MONARCHICAL SALAFIYYA

But was *salafiyya* just a tactic? Did it not offer a genuine means—perhaps the only means—of conciliating religion with modernity or tradition with the new reality imposed by the West? *Salafiyya* was exercised not only by the *'ulama* as guardians of the *shari'a* but also by sultans by virtue of their religious prerogatives. Since the eighteenth century at least, with Sidi Muhammad Ibn Abdallah (1757–90) and Mawlay Sulayman (1792–1822), the 'Alawi sultans had become increasingly involved with issues of religious reform. Mawlay Sulayman showed some sympathy with the Wahhabi doctrine and manifested a firm determination to eradicate unorthodox Sufi practices.[31] Significantly enough, one of his *khutab* (sermons) was printed by the nationalists during the 1930s and widely used in their campaign against the French-supported *zawaya*.[32] At the beginning of the 20th century, Mawlay 'Abd al-Hafid also identified himself with the ideas of the *salafiyya*. He wrote a pamphlet against the Tijani *tariqa* and repressed the Kattani *zawiya* in Fez.

Thus, *salafiyya*, or Sunnism as it used to be known in the Moroccan religious tradition, were old concerns of Moroccan sultans, who shared it with the *'ulama*. After 1912, colonial attacks on the *shari'a* and the limitations the French imposed on the juridical prerogatives of the sultan paved the way for an alliance between the two. Both were directly threatened and both felt it was their duty to preserve the country's Islamic identity and ensure the survival of the Islamic tradition.

The *salafi* nationalists have often been accused by the more liberal wing of having given the monarchy a far greater role in the nationalist struggle than it deserved, thus strengthening its despotic character. Clearly, at the end of the nationalist struggle, the monarchy was stronger than ever, while in other countries, such as Tunisia, the institution was so weakened and marginalized during the colonial period that it ceased to exist after independence. But did the *salafi* nationalists have any other option? Perhaps one could say that the nationalists needed the monarchy to further their cause as much as this one needed their support. In Morocco, the monarchy was a religious institution and not just a political one. The sultan was the spiritual leader of the Islamic community and his affiliation with the Prophet's house made him a highly venerated person. His religious prestige, even during the colonial period, was enormous, a fact that made him the symbol of Morocco's Islamic identity, unity, and sovereignty. Therefore, the *salafi* nationalists, by opting for the religious alternative, could not possibly thrust aside the sultan. Even the modernists who showed a strong republican inclination could not disregard the institution of the monarchy, for it stood for the continuity of Morocco. Their hope was to use the sultan's prestige in the same way that they used religion to resist colonial policies and draw popular support.

The monarchy felt equally threatened by the French encroachment on the domain of the *shari'a*. It became clear after the departure of

Lyautey in 1925 that the real power tended to be in the hands of the French resident general, while the sultan was no more than a "machine à *zahirs*." The Berber policy, which culminated in the *zahir* of 1930, was seen by the monarchy as a direct threat to its own existence as much as it was to national unity. Thus, the conditions were ripe for the union, or reunion, of the Qarawiyin and the court. *Salafi* ideology offered the most suitable basis for this alliance and the two parties could resume their past collaboration with a view to ensuring the continuity of Morocco's Islamic culture and traditional system of government.

TRADITIONALISTS AND MODERNISTS

As the Moroccan nationalist movement affirmed itself, the value of the *salafi* ideology progressively lost its importance. Many young liberals, such as Muhammad Ibn al-Hassan al-Wazzani, saw the use of the *salafi* discourse as a tactic to allow the movement to take root and mobilize popular sympathy, while they themselves looked toward Western political models. For traditionalists, such as 'Allal al-Fasi, however, the *salafiyya* was more than a tactical program; it was a comprehensive doctrine in which Muslims should find solutions to all their concerns. Differences soon erupted between the two wings of the movement, leading to the constitution of two competing political parties, one led by a Qarawiyin *'alim* and the other by the first Moroccan graduate of the Paris Institut des Sciences Politiques.

The basic question that confronted nationalists in Morocco and elsewhere in the Islamic world was how to conciliate Islam and modernity. How could Muslims adapt to a civilization imposed by the West while maintaining a national identity that was essentially Islamic? Two main trends emerged within the Moroccan nationalist movement during the 1930s. The nationalist campaign against the religious brotherhoods in the 1920s and the Berber *zahir* in the early 1930s had favored the cohabitation of all tendencies and submerged the ideological differences within the movement. For a time the *salafi* discourse seemed to answer the needs of the movement because all tendencies realized the advantages they could draw from it. However, as the nationalist agitation against the French Berber policy lost its fervor, dissensions between two main tendencies erupted to the surface and led to the creation of two distinct political organizations. While 'Allal al-Fasi considered the central issue to be how to modernize Islam, al-Wazzani estimated that it was, rather, how to Islamize modernity.

Both continued to use the *salafi* discourse, but their ideological references and their political conceptions greatly differed. It should be made clear, however, that although al-Fasi and al-Wazzani belonged to two different schools of thought, one being *salafi* and the other more secularist, the parties that gathered around them were not homogeneous and traditionalists or modernists could be found on both sides. Since both leaders continued to recruit *'ulama* and use the *salafi* language, it was not always easy for potential members to discern the exact ideological differences between the two. In any case, personal affinities always played a role in political affiliation.[33] However, many *'ulama* members of al-Wazzani's party (the Parti Démocratique de l'Indépendance), left the party after they discovered its nonreligious orientation.[34]

The ideological differences between the two nationalist currents were apparent in their respective approaches to basic issues, of which two will be examined here as examples: the relation between state and religion; and the issue of authority and the exercise of political power.

I. State and Religion

Clearly, the ideological and political references for someone like al-Wazzani are found in Western liberal thought. He is the archetype of the Westernized intellectual or what the French protectorate authorities called the *évolué*. Throughout his writings, most of which were in French, his arguments were basically drawn from Western political thought, even though they were dressed in an Islamic cover to make them acceptable to his audience and to stay within the religious norms of society.

Although he did not make it explicit, al-Wazzani made several arguments that favored a separation between religion and state. In principle, he argued, Islam did not allow for any form of clergy, so that a theocratic state would be unacceptable.[35] Interestingly, his position regarding this issue was very similar to that of the Egyptian Ali 'Abd al-Raziq whom he admired.[36] Al-Wazzani also defended the thesis that the Prophet's prophethood cannot be inherited and that his prophetic mission ceased to exist with his death. Neither the caliph nor even the *'ulama* can claim spiritual power. None of them, for instance, can alter the *shari'a*; otherwise, he argues, there would be a repetition of the Shi'a error according to which the imam inherits the prerogatives of the Prophet.[37] All the *'ulama* can do when society is confronted with a new situation is to exercise *ijtihad*, which has no spiritual quality.

Another aspect of al-Wazzani's secularism was his opposition to the intervention of "men of religion" into politics. "Religion has its men and so does politics. Because God has given man one heart only he can never manage both at the same time."[38] If al-Wazzani consented during the nationalist campaign against the Berber *zahir* to the use of religion for political purposes he nevertheless later expressed his opposition to the politicization of the *salafiyya*. Al-Wazzani maintained that the *salafiyya* was a religious movement and not a political one. By turning a religious doctrine into a political movement, he thought 'Allal al-Fasi and his colleagues were transforming the *salafiyya* into "a clerical organization," which was no different from the religious brotherhoods the nationalists were fighting.[39] To the question whether Islam as a religion should shape the Moroccan political system, al-Wazzani answered in the negative. He frequently invoked the Prophet's *hadith,* "There can be no priesthood in Islam," to back his argument. Islam does not impose any specific form of government and religion does not provide any particular prescription for the state apart from the general principles of justice, the preservation of individual rights and liberties, and the necessity of consultation in the running of public affairs.[40] These principles were universal, he maintained, and should be the goal of every government. It was up to the community of Muslims to use the "right of *ijtihad*" to determine the political system that was best suited to their needs.[41] The principles of the *shari'a* were the principles of every good government. It could not be invoked to justify despotic or outmoded forms of government. Morocco, he thought, must take the path that was followed by other nations, Oriental or Western, Muslim or otherwise.[42]

The secularist character of al-Wazzani's thought was especially manifest in the program of the party he founded in 1937. In that year the National Movement party made public a "Charter of National Rights," which was another version of the French "Déclaration des Droits de l'Homme et du Citoyen." The aim was to endow the nationalist movement with a document that secures "sacred rights and basic liberties." What is striking is that this program makes no reference to Islam or Islamic values and could very well be the political program of any Western liberal party.[43]

On the other hand, 'Allal al-Fasi, as a traditional religious scholar, could not conceive of a system in which religion and state would be set apart. "Religion in an Islamic state," he wrote, "cannot be separated from politics, since the two are like twins."[44] Al-Fasi spoke about an

"Islamic state," which is already significant as far as his ideological references are concerned. The ultimate goal of the nationalist movement, believed al-Fasi, should be "the establishment of a Moroccan state based on the principles of Islam."[45] The state that al-Fasi had in view was an Islamic one in which the *shari'a* was the law that governed all aspects of life and in which the supreme constitution was the Qur'an.[46]

'Allal al-Fasi rejected secularism in all its aspects. Secular nationalism, for instance, was unacceptable and al-Fasi deeply regretted that a number of political movements in the Middle East had drifted away from Islam to take a secularist turn.[47] Al-Fasi conceived of true Arab nationalism as closely associated with Islam.[48] Purely secular nationalism would be based on racial affiliation, and that would be an unacceptable form of racism (*'unsuriyya*).[49] To the concept of *qawmiyya* strongly defended by al-Wazzani, 'Allal al-Fasi opposed the unity of the "Islamic *umma*," which forms "a political entity regardless of geographical boundaries."[50]

2. Sovereignty and the Bases of Political Power

Al-Wazzani and 'Allal al-Fasi also had different starting points for their political theory. For one, the *shari'a* served as a basic point of reference, while for the other it was the ideals of the French Revolution.

Al-Wazzani's writings refer constantly to the ideas of Western liberal thought. His political concepts are essentially those of the Enlightenment. He was fascinated by the French Revolution and its ideals, and even conceived of Islam as a great revolution that announced the principles of fraternity, equality, justice, and freedom.[51] For al-Wazzani, these were the real pillars of Islam, and should be the pillars of every Islamic government.

When al-Wazzani referred to the *shari'a,* it was mainly to justify his liberal opinion. The *shari'a* was not considered to be the source of political legitimacy or the legal reference to which society should return for its worldly concerns. The *shari'a,* he argued, defined the guidelines and set the principles that should govern every political system, namely those of justice, *shura* (consultation), and freedom. The way to reach these goals was to be defined by the people and their representatives through the exercise of *shura.* "It is the right of Muslims," he wrote, "to adapt their system of government according to the needs of their time by adopting a constitution which would serve as the basic law for their political system."[52]

Although al-Wazzani did not deny the role of the *shari'a* in government, he considered the people to be the source of "national sovereignty."[53] The fact that a ruler abided by the rulings of the *shari'a* did not dispense him from consulting the people and those who speak in their name because the *umma* is the source of every authority.[54] The *bay'a* was a covenant between the ruler and the people, a contract implying rights and obligations for both parties. Once the *khalifa* or sultan was proclaimed he became "the first servant of the community,"[55] and ruled according to the opinion of the *ahl al-shura* or those representing the *umma*.[56]

Political power, therefore, was conceived by al-Wazzani as being essentially a delegation of authority by the people in favor of the ruler. This delegation took the form of *bay'a* in Islam, but the people remained the real repositories of political power. The implication of such a premise is twofold: First, the delegation of power was neither total nor absolute; the *shura,* a word that for al-Wazzani is synonymous with democracy, implied the right of popular control. Secondly, this delegation was not permanent. The *ahl al-shura* could withdraw the right from the ruler if the interest of the community so required. Al-Wazzani presented the deposition of Mawlay 'Abd al-'Aziz and the proclamation of his brother Mawlay 'Abd al-Hafid in 1907 as a perfect example of the exercise of the people's sovereignty.[57] By virtue of the same principle, al-Wazzani believed that popular sovereignty was best exercised through the elective process. "Political leadership," he wrote, "cannot rest on heredity or appointment."[58] His ideal was the republican system, which he thought was the system adopted by the Muslim community during the first thirty years following the death of the Prophet.[59] In the case of Morocco, al-Wazzani was in favor of a "liberal constitutional monarchy" in which the powers of the king would be limited. In fact, one of the basic features of al-Wazzani's political movement during the colonial era was its insistence on democracy and the need to define the king's prerogatives. For him the struggle for democracy as guaranteed by a constitutional monarchy was as important as the struggle for independence, as was reflected in the name of the party he founded in 1944 (Hizb al-Shura wal-Istiqlal as opposed to 'Allal al-Fasi's Hizb al-Istiqlal). As a result, al-Wazzani's party never showed much fervor for the monarchy, a fact that explains the lack of warmth in its relations with the palace.[60]

'Allal al-Fasi, on the other hand, aimed at building a modern Islamic state. His political theory was geared toward the adaptation of the *shari'a* to the needs of modern society. 'Allal al-Fasi argued that God had already regulated life for us and that the Qur'an was the supreme constitution that no human constitution could contradict. While al-Wazzani's reference to the *shari'a* was selective, and obviously intended to justify his liberal options, al-Fasi was sincere in his adherence to Islamic values and principles. He believed that, as divine law, the *shari'a* was well-suited to all times, including ours.[61] Moreover, al-Fasi argued that the rule of the *shari'a* should be extended to cover all aspects of our life.[62]

Unlike al-Wazzani, 'Allal al-Fasi believed that popular sovereignty was not unlimited and had to be exercised within the limits set by the *shari'a*: "Original sovereignty," according to him, "belongs to God."[63] Al-Fasi distinguished between two different concepts, that of "sovereignty" (*hukm*), which belonged to God, and that of "authority" (*sulta*), which was exercised by man. Thus he conciliated the theory of *al-hakimiyya*, as propounded by al-Mawdudi or Sayyid Qutb, and the modern concept of sovereignty.[64] "The Muslim people" are sovereign but only as far as the popular will did not contradict the rulings of the *shari'a*.[65]

The fact that the two men relied on two different definitions of the concept of sovereignty, one secular and the other religious, led them to different attitudes concerning political authority. While al-Wazzani insisted on democratic guarantees with particular vigor, al-Fasi seemed to be less concerned about the risks of absolutism on the part of the monarchy. During the struggle for independence, al-Fasi and his party believed that the issue of political power and how it should be regulated was irrelevant. Al-Wazzani's party was even accused of diverting attention from the real struggle, that of independence, to a secondary one, that of democracy. The divergence was not as superficial as it might seem; it reflected the different attitudes of a Westernized liberal who was almost a republican, and of an *'alim* who saw in the monarchy "a symbol of Morocco's unity and continuity," and a guarantee for the survival of the traditional order.

CONCLUSION

When Morocco became independent in 1956, the Istiqlal Party and the monarchy were the great victors of the nationalist struggle. On the morrow of independence, at least 90 percent of Moroccans belonged to al-Fasi's party or sympathized with it.

This did not, however, mean that *salafiyya* developed into a practicable party doctrine for the Istiqlal Party despite the efforts of 'Allal al-Fasi. In 1947, al-Fasi regretted that most liberation movements in the Arab world had ended up with the establishment of secular regimes. "The movements which emerged in the Arab world following the *salafi* revival were unfortunately secular and greatly influenced by the ideas of the French Revolution. . . . Thus we can say that *salafism* fails every time it leaves the theoretical level to the practical one."[66] The Istiqlal Party itself was the scene of major internal changes. The real leadership of the party fell into the hands of modernists, even though al-Fasi continued to act as the party's theoretician. While the *salafiyya* continued to be the source of ideological inspiration for the party's theoreticians, effective leadership was exercised more and more by the Istiqlal's modernists. However, the real victor of the nationalist struggle was the monarchy, which assumed a leading role in the modernization of independent Morocco while preserving its traditional culture.

Notes

1. 'Allal al-Fasi, *Al-Dimuqratiya wa kifah al-sha'b* (Democracy and the Struggle of the People) (Rabat: 1990), p. 109; Muhammad al-Manuni, *Mazahir yaqazat al-maghrib al-hadith* (Casablanca: 1985), vol. 2, p. 361.
2. See text in al-Manuni, op. cit., vol. 2, 432–44. There is even a much earlier constitutional project in the form of a reform proposal (*mudhakkira*) submitted to Mawlay 'Abd al-'Aziz by Abdallah Ibn Sa'id al-Salawi in 1901. See text in al-Manuni, op. cit., vol. 2, pp. 130-35.
3. Al-Manuni, op. cit., vol. 2, 361; 'Allal al-Fasi, *Al-Dimuqratiya,* 29.
4. Ibid.
5. The project was published in October and November 1908. 'Allal al-Fasi, *Al-Dimuqratiya,* 35.
6. Abdallah Laroui, *Les origines du nationalisme marocain, 1830-1912* (Paris: François Maspéro, 1977), p. 381.
7. The *bay'a* was written on January 5, 1907. See text in al-Manuni, op. cit., vol. 2, pp. 349–53.
8. Ibid., 345.
9. 'Allal al-Fasi, *Al-Harakat al-istiqlaliyya fil-maghrib al-'arabi* (The Independence Movement in the Arab Maghrib) (Tangier: n.d.), pp. 98–99.
10. Ibid., 99.
11. Ibid.
12. Al-Fasi, *Al-Dimuqratiya,* 125.
13. Laroui wrote: "Il semble peu douteux que le constitutionnalisme laïcisant servit essentiellement à moderniser la formulation de l'opposition des *'alims* qui luttaient depuis un demi-siècle contre le despotisme grandissant du sultan et son mépris pour la *shura.*" *Les Origines,* 381.

14. Al-Fasi, *Al-Dimuqratiya*, 40.
15. Muhammad Ibn al-Hassan al-Wazzani, *Hayat wa jihad* (Life and Jihad) (Beirut: 1882), vol. I, pp. 334–35.
16. Ibid., 336.
17. Ibid.
18. Quoted by Laroui in *Esquisses historiques* (Casablanca: 1992), p. 111.
19. See for instance 'Allal al-Fasi's claim concerning Muhammad Ibn 'Abd al-Karim's *salafism* in *Al-Harakat*, 118–19. As Laroui noted, the *salafi* image of Ibn 'Abd al-Karim as depicted in the nationalist literature does not necessarily reflect the real convictions of the Rifi leader. See *Esquisses historiques*, 112–14.
20. C.R. Pennell, *A Country with a Government and a Flag (The Rif War in Morocco, 1921–1926)* (Cambridgeshire, England: MENAS Press, 1986), p. 128.
21. In this sense al-Khattabi's failure served as a lesson for the young Moroccan nationalists in their action against the Berber *zahir* and the religious brotherhoods.
22. See al-Khattabi's interview with *Al-Manar* in Pennel, op. cit., 257–59.
23. Robin Bidwell, *Morocco Under Colonial Rule* (London: Frank Cass, 1973), p. 265.
24. The *zahir* of 1914 stated: "Les tribus dites de coûtume berbére sont et demeureront régies et administrées selon leurs lois et coutûmes propres sous le contrôle des autorités [françaises]." Quoted by Bidwell, op. cit., 273.
25. Bidwell, op. cit., 128–54.
26. 'Allal al-Fasi mentions that the early *salafiyya* used to travel around the country to destroy idols or uproot trees that were venerated by the common people. See *Al-Harakat*, 133.
27. Al-Fasi, *Al-Harakat*, 134.
28. Al-Wazzani, *Hayat wa jihad*, vol. 3, 298–304.
29. Robert Rézette, *Les partis politiques marocains* (Paris: Armand Colin, 1955), pp. 282–83.
30. In fact, those who studied Moroccan nationalism did not fail to underline the role of leadership played by the Westernized elite. See John P. Halstead, *Rebirth of a Nation* (Cambridge, Mass.: Harvard University Center for Middle Eastern Studies, 1969), p. 196.
31. See Mohamed El Mansour, *Morocco in the Reign of Mawlay Sulayman* (Cambridgeshire, England: Menas Press, 1990).
32. This *khutba* was also presented to the sultan in support of a petition by the *'ulama* demanding a ban on the activities of the Sufi brotherhoods.
33. Rézette, op. cit., 287.
34. The best example is that of Idris al-Kattani who left al-Wazzani's party in 1958 in protest against the secular orientation of its political program. Al-Kattani explained the reasons of his action in a book he published in the same year (*Al-Maghrib al-muslim didda al-ladiniyya* [Casablanca: 1958]).
35. Al-Wazzani, *Hayat wa jihad*, vol. I, 316.
36. For al-Wazzani, the Egyptian *'alim* Ali 'Abd al-Raziq was "one of the great reformist *'ulama* of al-Azhar" who wrote "a daring book" to demonstrate that the caliphate cannot be assimilated with any form of priesthood. See *Hayat wa jihad*, vol. I, 316.
37. Al-Wazzani, *Al-Islam wal-dawla* (Islam and the State) (Beirut: 1987), p. 21.
38. Al-Wazzani, *Hayat wa jihad*, vol. I, 326.
39. Ibid., 324, 326. Muhammad 'Abduh, argues al-Wazzani, was a *salafi* whose sole concern was religious reform without any ambition to play a political role.
40. Al-Wazzani, *Harb al-qalam* (Beirut: 1981), vol. I, 182.
41. Ibid., 181.

42. Al-Wazzani, *Harb al-qalam* vol. 1, 74; *Hayat wa jihad,* vol. 1, 326.
43. Al-Wazzani, *Hayat wa jihad,* vol. 5, 59.
44. 'Allal al-Fasi, *Masqasid al-shari'a al-islamiyya* (Casablanca: 1963), p. 216.
45. 'Allal al-Fasi, *Manhaj al-istiqlaliya* (Rabat, 1962), p. 45.
46. Al-Fasi, *Masqasid,* 215.
47. Al-Fasi, "*Al-Haraka al-salafiyya fil-maghrib*" (The *Salafi* Movement in the Maghrib), lecture delivered in Cairo in 1947 and published in *Durus fil-haraka al-salafiyya (Studies of the Salafi Movement)* (Casablanca: 1986), pp. 141–42.
48. Al-Fasi, *Manhaj al-istiqlaliyya,* 46.
49. Al-Fasi, *Al-Harakat,* 136.
50. Al-Fasi, *Masqasid,* 217.
51. Al-Wazzani, *Al-Islam wal-dawla,* 127.
52. Al-Wazzani, *Harb al-qalam,* vol. 1, 182.
53. Al-Wazzani, *Hayat wa jihad,* vol. 5, 59.
54. Al-Wazzani, *Al-Islam wal-dawla,* 126.
55. Ibid., 98.
56. Al-Wazzani, *Harb al-qalam,* vol. 1, 13.
57. Al-Wazzani, *Al-Islam wal-dawla,* 126.
58. Ibid., 101.
59. R. Rézette, op. cit., 162.
60. 'Allal al-Fasi, *Difa' 'an al-shari'a* (Defending the *Shari'a*) (Rabat: 1966), p. 138.
61. Ibid., 231.
62. Al-Fasi, *Masqasid,* 211.
63. Ibid., 215.
64. Ibid., 216.
65. Al-Fasi, *Al-Harakat,* 199.
66. Al-Fasi, "*Al-Haraka al-salafiyya fil-maghrib,*" 142.

◉ **5** ◉

Continuities and Discontinuities in the Algerian Confrontation with Europe

John Ruedy

For the first twenty-five years of Algerian independence most specialists viewed Algeria largely through the prism of its political order, which, being explicitly secular, was easily approachable in political and sociological vocabularies generated in the Western academies. Even scholars specifically focusing on Islam in the Maghrib tended, during most of the 1980s, to see Islamism in Algeria as the least developed and the least coherent of the region's Islamic movements.[1] The striking successes of the Islamists after the explosion of October 1988, however, and particularly their sweeping victories in the elections of June 1990 and December 1991, caught most analysts off-guard.

While the strength of the Islamist movements in the 1990s can be cogently explained in a variety of ways, I will argue, in the pages that follow, that the recent emergence of Islam as a major political force represents a surfacing of contradictions in the Algerian experience that have existed for centuries. These contradictions are primarily cultural and political in nature, but they are related to geography, as well.

Literature on intra-Islamic conflict in the eighteenth and nineteenth centuries is filled with the attempts of millenarian or other renewal movements that arose in many hinterlands or peripheries to challenge the political and cultural dominion of the urban centers. The Wahhabis of the Najd, the Fara'idis of Bengal, the Babis of Iran, the Mahdists of the Sudan, and the Sanusiyya of Cyrenaica are but a few examples of this dynamic.[2]

There are many Algerias geographically, but this study focuses on two in particular: the Mediterranean coastal zone and the interior zone. There exist significant continuities from one of these zones to the other in terms of physical interpenetration and in terms of economic base, life-styles, and worldview. But there are also contrasts, many of which are considerably more striking. The coastal zone has always found itself interacting with a broader Mediterranean world. Well-being there has depended upon a multiplicity of economic exchanges and political relationships with non-Arab and/or non-Muslim peoples. Along with these relations has come cultural interaction that conferred upon the coastal cities considerable ethnic diversity and a relatively cosmopolitan outlook.[3] During the nineteenth and twentieth centuries that cultural connection brought with it the European notion of secularism and the objective adjustments in human relations and institutions that are its reflection.

The hinterland communities, on the other hand, were historically more self-sufficient economically, more self-contained socially and politically, and more conservative culturally. From the point of view of culture, understood in the anthropological rather than in the high sense, it would not be unreasonable to argue that the interior represented the core of Algerian society and the Mediterranean coast its periphery. But politically, the relationship is the opposite. Political power since Ottoman times and continuing through the colonial period to the present has centered upon and been largely monopolized by the coastal cities, whether they are culturally peripheral or not. Those cities have also been the centers of the official religious establishment, home to many of the best-educated men in the country and the mosques, schools, and courts over which they presided.

For its part, the interior has spent much of the past five hundred years and particularly the last two hundred trying to neutralize the impact of the political and military power that emanated from the coast. Much of the discourse in which the interior's opposition was framed was an alternative religious discourse of mysticism and Sufism articulated by local marabouts and by the sheikhs of the religious orders that spread across the Maghrib in the eighteenth and nineteenth centuries.[4]

The last forty years of Ottoman rule in Algeria were times of enormous turmoil, in which one Sufi order after another led the hinterland in opposing Ottoman attempts to consolidate their military control and intensify fiscal extraction in the countryside.[5] When the French invaded the country in 1830, Ottoman resistance around Algiers collapsed in weeks; within months it collapsed at other Turkish outposts. But Algerian resistance to France in the interior continued tenaciously for forty-one years. Between 1830 and 1871, there was only one year—1861—in which the colonial authorities did not confront major military opposition in one region of Algeria or another.[6] An early phase of that resistance was led by Ahmad Bey of Constantine, who mobilized local *jawad* (tribal leaders) in the name of Islamic legitimacy to resist French attempts to establish a protectorate over their province. Subsequently, the heart of the resistance moved westward to the lands controlled by 'Abd al-Qadir, sheikh of the western branch of the Qadiriyya order, whose headquarters were at Mascara. With his defeat and imprisonment in 1847, millenarian and other religious revolts emanating from mountain and desert regions succeeded each other for decades. In the forties, fifties, and sixties, Algeria saw the appearance of one *mahdi* after another proclaiming the apocalypse and the impending millennium. The last major attempt to throw off colonial rule exploded in the Kabylie mountains in 1871, where the revolt was declared a jihad by the venerable sheikh of the Rahmaniyya order. It was put down and gradually armed resistance sputtered out. In the meantime, *colons* were appropriating the bulk of the rich landed resources that had been the economic base of precolonial society, and with the disappearance of the land, the kinship-based social system and the traditional tribal hierarchies collapsed.

For about a generation Algeria was eerily silent. Then, in the years before World War I, new voices protesting the colonial conditions began to be heard. But these were no longer the voices of country people, and, if they invoked Islam at all, they invoked it in a cultural sense to distinguish native Algerians from European Algerians. These were city voices speaking almost exclusively in French and demanding not the world of the Qur'an, the Sunna, or of the local holy man but the world envisioned by European thinkers—Voltaire, Rousseau, Auguste Comte. Out of the cataclysmic destructuring of traditional Algerian society, there had emerged small new middle and professional classes, largely the product of French schools, who were interacting on a regular basis with the *colon* establishment. At first assimilationists and later liberal nationalists, these men were overwhelmingly secular in outlook, and they adopted to varying degrees the life-styles of Europe and hoped to rebuild Algeria in accordance with liberal models flowing from the Enlightenment and from the experiences of nineteenth-century Europe.[7]

Competing with the liberals in the years before and after World War II were the followers of the more radical Messali Hadj in the Étoile Nord-Africaine, the Parti du Peuple Algérien, and the Mouvement pour le Triomphe des Libertés Démocratiques (MTLD). Issued from the urban proletariat that was another product of France's destructuring of rural tribal society, the Messalists, like the liberal middle classes, also protested the colonial situation in discourse learned from France. But this discourse was a discourse learned in the streets of Paris rather than in French *lycées, collèges,* and universities. It was also informed by the early nurturing of the French Communist Party and of the CGT, from which it learned about Marx, Engels, and class conflict.[8] A third urban discourse, which emerged by degrees during the first half of the twentieth century, was the Islamic reform movement in the tradition of Muhammad 'Abduh, who visited Algeria in 1905. Smaller than either the liberal or radical movements in terms of the popular support it was able to mobilize, the reform movement is thought by most analysts to have played a critical role in the crystallization of Algerian nationalism by insisting upon the historical and cultural specificity of the Algerian personality at a time when many liberals seemed to favor a process of progressive Gallicization and when radicals appeared suspended between class warfare and Algerian national solidarity.

It was Ahmad Tawfiq al-Madani, one of the charter members of the Association of Algerian Muslim 'Ulama, who, in the preface to his *Kitab al-jaza'ir,* appeals to his readers to adopt in word and deed the slogan "Islam is my religion; Arabic is my language; Algeria is my fatherland." It was 'Abd al-Hamid Ben Badis, founder of the association, who in response to Ferhat Abbas's affirmation of *la patrie française,* wrote

> We, for our part, have searched through the pages of history and we have also examined the present. We have come to the conclusion that the Algerian nation was formed and does exist as all other nations on earth were formed and do exist. Moreover, this nation has its history, defined by innumerable great events; it has its linguistic and religious unity, it has its own culture, its traditions, and its customs both good and bad, as do all the other nations.
>
> Therefore, this Algerian Muslim nation is not France; it is not possible that it be France; it does not want to become France; and even if it wished, it could not be France.[9]

While it is undoubtedly correct to emphasize the ideological contribution of the reformists to the development of Algerian nationalism, it is quite possible that contribution owes more to the uses the secular nationalists made of their ideas than to their substantive contributions at organizational or tactical levels. If at the time of the Muslim Congress of 1936, it appeared that the *'ulama* were ready to take an active role in the emerging nationalist coalition, by the end of the decade most had backed off from such participation. Ben Badis, himself, made it clear that the most important mission of the movement was cultural. It involved purging Algerian Islam of heterodox accretions, winning back youth who had strayed too far into the morally questionable paths laid out by Europeans, and encouraging religious and Arabic language instruction. The reformists, in fact, devoted at least as much attention to the struggle against mystic and Sufi Islam of the interior as they did against the secularizing influence of French culture. Without wishing to overstate the case, it also appears that the Algerian *islah* movement, like its predecessors and contemporaries farther east, may, in fact, have been more deeply influenced by secular thought than many of its members were aware of or were willing to admit.

At the political level, Ben Badis made a clear distinction between what he called *jinsiyya qawmiyya* or ethnic nationalism, on the one hand, and *jinsiyya siyasiyya,* political nationalism, on the other. Ethnic nationalism, which defines culture, religion, and values, is by far the more important concept. Political nationalism is almost external. Two peoples such as the French and the Algerian can beneficially share political nationality so long as each respects the ethnic nationality of the other.[10] It seems clear that the mainstream of reformist Islam, continuing in the well established tradition of orthodox Muslim establishments in Algeria and elsewhere, was willing to accept a de facto separation of the religious and the political. It was content to coexist with the French political reality, as the official religious establishment was then doing and as the *'ulama* had coexisted with the Turkish establishment long before the French conquest.

Only a small part of Algerian society lived in the cities, however. By the eve of the Algerian revolution, fully 85 percent of the Muslim population still lived in the countryside. The French military had destroyed the resistance there in the nineteenth century. But the mechanisms that had drawn significant elements of the urban population into the French world were scarcely operative in the countryside. Given the village setting and the agricultural workplace, few opportunities for acculturation to French ways existed for Algerian peasants. Nor was the French school a significant institution in most interior jurisdictions. In 1954 only 12.75 percent of Algerian children of elementary age attended school and the great majority of these were city children. Ninety-one percent of Algerians, including the overwhelming majority of peasants, were illiterate.[11]

With the exception of certain classes in hinterland cities of the interior like Constantine, Sétif, and Tlemcen, the interior remained largely outside France's cultural orbit. In that interior, through military action or through cooptation of leaderships, most of the great *tariqas* had been dramatically reduced in influence. Many marabouts were weakened by colonial co-optation or by the attacks of the reformist *'ulama*. But Islam—popular, effective Islam—remained nevertheless for interior Algeria, which was most of Algeria, the principal means of self-identification, the source of values, and ultimately, its principal refuge from the alien peoples, laws, values, and tongues that dominated the country.[12]

The Algerian Revolution that began on November 1, 1954, was instigated by secular militants split off from the MTLD, but these managed by 1956 to build a leadership coalition of radicals, liberals, and Islamic reformists. The revolution they presided over was one whose explicit goal was the vindication of Algeria as an Arabo-Islamic society. Yet the affirmation of Arabism and Islam was made by men of European thought and education, usually in the French language, and in terms of paradigms alien to the experience of the great majority of the Algerian people. For the bulk of these urban leaders, the Islam affirmed was a cultural Islam, an essential element of national identity. For most it was not a way of life, not a way of restructuring society, and certainly not a political system. With the *mujahidin*, however, the peasant foot soldiers of the revolution, Islamic values and observances were focal. FLN cells were strictly separated by gender. Persons guilty of illicit sexual encounters could be and sometimes were executed. In order to minimize the incidence of illicit sex, guerilla leaders would stand in for absent fathers or brothers in facilitating marriages of militants. Performance of prayer and observance of the Ramadan fast and other religious duties were rigorously enforced. As *mujahidin* poured into the cities during the heady summer of 1962, women alone on the streets were intimidated. A woman discovered in the company of a male other than a relative was liable to be hurried off to a forced marriage or jailed if she refused.[13]

Independence saw a brief, unseemly struggle for power between rural commanders and the secular leaderships of the FLN and the military. It saw a somewhat longer struggle between liberal nationalists more or less representing the middle and professional classes and the socialists and other radicals more or less representing the lower middle and proletarian strata. But eventually the latter won and the Democratic and Popular Republic of Algeria guided officially by a single party but with the national army as guarantor, embarked upon an ambitious development path whose central features were state planning, state decision-making, and state capitalism. Constitutions overwhelmingly approved by popular plebiscites in 1963 and 1976 contained guarantees of civil and political rights analogous to those found in most Western systems, even going to far as to guarantee these rights regardless of gender, which many Western constitutions did not.

The language of these constitutions and of most other political documents was overwhelmingly populistic. Everything was done in the name of the people and for the good of the people. Yet, the predominantly rural masses, overwhelmingly illiterate, and deeply steeped in the popular Islam of the countryside, seem rarely to have understood the causes the elites propounded in their names. After independence, peasants showed enormous enthusiasm for building and repairing mosques and *zawaya*, but very little for the various infrastructural and other community projects for which local government and party officials tried to mobilize them. By the 1970s, the volunteer brigades dispatched to the countryside to further the agrarian reform met with widespread resistance not only because of objections to specific goals and programs but because they were perceived as representing Marxist and atheist values and aberrant life-styles.[14]

During the first years of independence members of the 'ulama establishment, particularly those of the reformist strain that, by rallying to the FLN in 1956, had come out of the war with enhanced status, strove to expand and strengthen the Islamic components of government programs and to move toward that authentically Arab and Islamic society for which the war had nominally been fought. In response, presidents Ben Bella and Boumediene appeared more frequently at public religious observances and presided over multiple mosque dedications. They also increased budgets for religious building. In 1964, Ben Bella began the slow process of Arabizing education, a process that, in Algeria, was firmly associated in most minds with the affirmation of Islam. Arabization of the educational system was essentially completed twenty-three years later, in 1987.[15] In 1964, Ben Bella instituted religious education in the public schools.[16] Most importantly, the government successfully co-opted the majority of the reformist 'ulama, giving them charge of both the Religious Affairs and Original Education ministries but limiting their ability to affect broader policy formulation.[17] In co-opting the 'ulama, the state followed in the tradition of the deys, the French governors general, and that of scores of regimes elsewhere in the Muslim world over the centuries. In 1964, Ben Bella authorized the creating of the Qiyam (Values) Association, charged, as its name implies, with the cultural revivification of Islam. Al-Qiyam played a significant role in lobbying for Islamic issues in the educational, linguistic, and cultural spheres, but, when it stepped into the political arena by protesting the 1966 execution in Egypt of Sayyid Qutb of the Muslim Brotherhood, it was dissolved.[18] With the notable exception of men such as Muhammad Sahnoun and 'Abd al-Latif Soltani, the spokesmen for the Islamic reform tradition in the end made their peace with the FLN regime and embraced the rhetoric of Islamic socialism.[19]

The co-optation of the reformists, whom Berque had called Islamic Jacobins, left the leadership of the pro-active branch of Islam open and the challenge was taken up by men generally called Islamists. What were the origins of these Islamists? It would be an oversimplification to argue that all came from the same social strata. Given the widespread dissatisfaction with the outcomes of post-independence period, individuals from many strata and situations have rallied to the Islamist banners. These include a significant contingent of small and middle sized entrepreneurs and landholders who were never happy with socialism. They also include graduates from science faculties whose educations included little if any exposure to Western thought and ideology, as well as graduates of education faculties, unhappy with the exclusiveness and the priorities of French-style education. They also include former officials of the regime itself who grew disillusioned with its shortcomings. But the great majority of Islamist militants are young men from the Arabic-speaking regions of the interior who have arrived in the big cities during the past fifteen years and have been sorely disappointed with their welcome there.

During the Ottoman and colonial periods, Algerians had migrated continuously from the interior to the coastal cities. While not all migrants adapted easily to the Mediterranean coastal environment, most managed to accommodate in one form or another. Acculturation

was accomplished through a variety of mechanisms. The most important of these were absorption into the Western-ordered economic system—its labor market, its business environment, its professions;
residence in Europe; work in government; socialization with secularized neighbors; service in the French army; learning the French language; and, particularly, attendance at French schools.

Theoretically, as urbanization progressed after independence,
Mediterranean Algeria could have continued to absorb and socialize
interior populations indefinitely. But the ability to do so depended
upon two critical factors. One was the rate of migration and the other
was the resources with which to provide the social and economic
infrastructures upon which the effectiveness of the acculturative
mechanisms depended. Neither condition prevailed. Rural-urban
migration had been accelerating significantly since World War I. But
it exploded at the moment of independence because of interior dislo-
cations brought on by French counter-revolutionary tactics. The pressure to migrate toward the cities was complemented by the pull of vast
vacant urban spaces created by the summary departure of the *colons*
during 1962. Rural-urban migration slowed briefly after 1963 and
then accelerated again. Between 1954, when the War of Independence
broke out, and 1990, the Muslim urban population increased by a factor of eight, from 1,399,000 to 11,344,000. The great bulk of this
increase was in Algiers and two or three other cities.

TABLE 5.1
Urban Population (000s)

1906*	1926*	1936*	1954*	1965	1975	1985	1990
342	508	722	1,399	4,486	6,460	9,251	11,344

*Muslim population only[20]

By the 1970s and the 1980s, Algeria's population was increasing at
more than 3 percent annually and the age structure was sloping dramatically toward the dependent ages, with the median age in 1990 at
17.51 years. At the same time, Algeria was experiencing enormous difficulties generating the economic growth necessary to provide for the
needs of this population. Annual growth of GDP, which was 5.2 percent
in 1984, slipped to 0.6 percent by 1986 and -2.7 percent by 1988.[21]

The devastating outcomes were due partly to misconceived investment strategies and partly to the inefficiencies of the dominant public sector, but were exacerbated by the 70 percent drop in oil prices that occurred between 1985 and 1986, prices that had only recovered half of their losses in real terms by the early 1990s. Even during the exuberant growth years of the 1970s and early 1980s, investment strategy favored heavy industry located in the cities, leaving the agricultural sector to stagnate and in many cases to regress. Young, inadequately educated peasants streamed to the cities in search of jobs. There they encountered a system dominated by French-speaking elites who were the principal beneficiaries of the Algerian Revolution. These elites continued to propound a populist rhetoric, but were incapable of providing the children of the interior with the benefits they and many of their own children enjoyed.

The vanguard of militant Islam in Algeria is peopled by young men between the ages of fifteen and thirty. The increase in the size of this cohort in the past generation has been spectacular. It grew from 1.15 million in 1965 to 1.44 million in 1970; to 1.88 million in 1975; to 2.41 million in 1980; to 2.98 million in 1985; and to 3.62 million in 1990.[22] The voice of this cohort was first heard in the late 1970s within the Arabic-speaking sections of the universities. These sections, where enrollment was typically dominated by young men of rural origin, who had proceeded through the newly created Arabic-language tracks of the educational system, viewed with dismay the privileged position of contemporaries issued from the French or bilingual tracks. They also expressed strong resentment that the most lucrative career opportunities were reserved for the Francophones, who, in the great majority, were the children of parents with roots in these urban Mediterranean zones or of the Berber-speaking Kabylie. Not surprisingly, much of the protest the Arabized youth aimed at the privileged targeted the latter's Marxist or liberal ideologies, their secular worldviews, and their Westernized life-styles.[23]

At least as important as the dysfunctional university system in swelling the ranks of the alienated, was the inability of the primary, middle, and secondary levels of education to measure up to expectations. The Algerian educational system was a steeply pitched pyramid that, in 1989, was attempting to educate 6,390,000 young Algerians. Because access to each of the three levels was dependent upon success in the preceding, there were, in that year, 5,610,000 pupils at the primary level but only 780,000 in the middle and secondary levels. Even so, access to secondary school, the indispensable prerequisite to university admission, on which hopes of any sort of professional career depended, actually led to the university for only a small fraction of secondary students. Many failed along the way. But those who completed their three years of studies faced the formidable baccalaureate examination at the end. During the 1980s, 75 percent to 82 percent of students sitting for this test failed. During the same period, 400,000 to 500,000 students annually were being rejected from other levels of the school system.[24] In sum, the Algerian educational system, which consumed about 10 percent of GDP annually and which should have become the main vehicle for acculturating the newly arrived to the system the elites had erected, was rejecting far more of the candidates for that acculturation than it was accepting.

A good proportion of the rejects joined the dangerously swelling ranks of the unemployed. Estimates of the Algerian unemployment rate for 1988 and 1989 were between 25 percent and 28 percent, with underemployment and inappropriate employment exacerbating the problem by a factor of as much as 33 percent. In these circumstances, according to Ahmed Rouadjia, it was a rapidly expanding network of unofficial and official mosques that emerged to provide support and a degree of dignity for the young rejects from the schools and the workplace. According to official figures there were, in 1986, some 6,000 operative mosques in the country and 1,055 under construction. But official reports probably counted about half of the actual number of mosques. Since the middle 1970s, in fact, Algerians had been erecting mosques without permits in all the major cities. Sometimes their builders and congregations applied after the fact for permits, but sometimes they did not. Large numbers of these mosques were erected in the poor neighborhoods, the public housing developments, and the peripheral shantytowns that were the main habitats of the newly arrived country folk and of the rejected young.[25] Here they were ministered to by followers of 'Abd al-Latif Soltani or Muhammad Sahnoun, by young clerics trained in the Arab East, familiar with the thought of Muslim Brotherhood leaders, by imams coming out of Arabized tracks of the university, themselves wounded by the cavalier rejection of the secularized elites. It was from these mosques that the frontal assault of popular Islam upon the secular regime was launched in the 1980s by young Muslims who only a few years before had lived in the villages of the interior.

The author does not claim to have demonstrated beyond doubt the hypothesis he laid out at the beginning, that current conflict in Algeria between the secular and the Islamic is but a new phase of an ongoing struggle between Mediterranean and interior Algeria. The hypothesis could be validated to a considerable extent, for instance, by analyzing by district the polling data from the 1990 and 1991 Algerian elections to confirm impressions that the strongest Islamist support in fact developed in the neighborhoods of the newest urbanites, the unemployed, and the school rejects. It would also be useful to examine a sampling of the religious discourse occurring in the mosques of these neighborhoods in order to compare the relationship of that discourse to that of the traditional countryside. It nevertheless seems probable, on the basis of considerable data presented, that the hypothesis proposed will stand. At the very least, it is worthy of further investigation.

Notes

1. François Burgat, *L'Islamisme au Maghreb: La voix du sud (Tunisie, Algérie, Libye, Maroc)* (Paris: Karthala, 1988), pp. 143–44.

2. Nikki Keddie, *Roots of Revolution: An Interpretive History of Modern Iran* (New Haven and London: Yale University Press, 1981); Edward Evans-Pritchard, *The Sanussi of Cyrenaica* (Oxford: Oxford University Press, 1954).

3. Pierre Boyer, *La vie quotidienne à Alger à la veille de l'intervention française* (Paris: Hachette, 1963); Lucette Valensi, *Le Maghreb avant la prise d'Alger, 1770–1830* (Paris: Flammarion, 1969).

4. Jean-Claude Vatin, "Puissance d'état et résistances islamiques en Algérie, XIX-XX siècles: Approche méchanique," in *Islam et politique au Maghreb*, (Paris: CNRS, 1981), pp. 243–69 at 245–49; Louis Rinn, *Marabouts et khouan: Étude sur l'Islam en Algérie, avec une carte indiquant la marche, la situation et l'importance des ordres religieux musulmans* (Algiers: Jourdan, 1884); Emile Demerghem, *Les cultes des saints dans l'Islam maghrebin* (Paris: Gallimard, 1954).

5. John Ruedy, *Modern Algeria: The Origins and Development of a Nation* (Bloomington, Ind.: Indiana University Press, 1992), pp. 39–41; Charles-André Julien, *Histoire de l'Algérie contemporaine*, vol. 1, *La conquête et les débuts de la colonisation (1817-1871)* (Paris: Presses Universitaires de France, 1964), pp. 14–19.

6. Ruedy, op. cit., 55.

7. Charles-Robert Ageron, *Histoire de l'Algérie contemporaine*, vol. 2, *De l'insurrection de 1871 au déclenchement de la guerre de libération (1954)* (Paris: Presses Universitaires de France, 1964), pp. 232–319, 389–402, 433–66, 547–78, 602–18; Mahfoud Kaddache, *Histoire du nationalisme algérien: Question nationale et politique algérienne 1919–1951*, 2 vols., 2d ed. (Algiers: Société Nationale de l'Édition, 1982), passim; William B. Quandt, *Revolution and Political Leadership: Algeria, 1954–1968* (Cambridge, Mass.: MIT Press, 1969), pp. 24–42.

8. Charles-André Julien, *L'Afrique du Nord en marche: Nationalismes musulmans et souveraineté française*, 3d ed. (Paris: Julliard, 1972), pp. 106–10; Kaddache, op. cit., passim; Benjamin Stora, *Messali Hadj, pionnier du nationalisme algérien (1898-1974)* (Paris: Le Sycomore, 1982); Quandt, op. cit., 53–65.

9. Ali Merad, *Le réformisme musulman en Algérie de 1925 à 1940* (Paris: Mouton, 1967), pp. 398–99.

10. Ibid., 397–99.
11. Ruedy, op. cit., 126.
12. Vatin, op. cit., 251–52; Augustin Berque, *Écrits sur l'Algérie* (Aix-en Provence: Edisud, 1986), pp. 25–136; Jacques Berque, *Le Maghreb entre deux guerres,* 2d ed. (Paris: Éditions du Seuil, 1970), pp. 77–80.
13. Monique Gadant, *Islam et nationalisme en Algérie: D'Après "El Moudjahid" organ central du FLN de 1956 à 1962* (Paris: L'Harmattan, 1988), pp. 36, 41, 54.
14. Ahmed Rouadjia, *Les frères et la mosquée: Enquête sur le mouvement islamiste en Algérie* (Paris: Karthala, 1990), pp. 30–34.
15. Ruedy, op. cit., 228; Rouadjia, op. cit., 120.
16. Burgat, op. cit., 154.
17. Vatin, op. cit., 259–60; Abderrahim Lamchichi, *Islam et constestation au Maghreb* (Paris: L'Harmattan, 1989), pp. 147–50.
18. Lamchichi, op. cit., 154–55; Burgat, op. cit., 150–51.
19. Burgat, op. cit., 145–47; Lamchichi, op. cit., 154; Mustafa al-Ahnaf, Bernard Botiveau, and Franck Frégosi, *L'Algérie par ses islamistes* (Paris: Karthala, 1991), pp. 60–64.
20. Ruedy, op. cit., 121; Nathan Keyfitz and Wilhelm Flieges, *World Population Growth and Aging: Demographic Growth in the Late Twentieth Century* (Chicago and London: University of Chicago Press, 1990), p. 115.
21. Ruedy, op. cit., 247.
22. Keyfitz and Flieges, op. cit., 115.
23. John P. Entelis, *Algeria: The Revolution Institutionalized* (Boulder, Colo.: Westview, 1986), pp. 91–96; Rouadjia, op. cit., 112–27; Burgat, op. cit., 101.
24. Rouadjia, op. cit., 120–39.
25. Ibid., 77–95.

6

The Political and the Religious in the Modern History of the Maghrib

Abdelbaki Hermassi

The Maghrib, like the rest of the Islamic world, was already lagging in development when it entered the modern age. Its integration into the world system placed it even farther behind and made it more dependent. These and other conditions of the region's insertion into the modern world seriously affect both its political and cultural dynamics. On the one hand, the political and bureaucratic elites managed to impart a certain authority to the state system beginning in the nineteenth century; state authority was justified by the exigencies of survival and efficiency in the modern world. On the other hand, however, there arose cultural reactions tied to religious movements that were characterized more by resistance and protest than by adaptation. A dialectic emerged between a logic of adjustment and a logic of resistance that marked all the major stages of modern history, even though that dialectic took slightly different forms during the different stages leading from the precolonial period to the present.

One factor that is clear is the gradual secularization of the state, paralleled by an equally gradual decline in religious institutions and ideas.[1] These ideas bear less weight and less power as a basically lay system of ideas expands. But in spite of this, Islamic protest attempted to win back space in the cultural and judicial spheres, and the states made concessions to religion as they tried to gain symbolic legitimacy and to break up Islamist opposition.

ISLAMIC BROTHERHOODS AND COLONIZATION

During the nineteenth century, both before the arrival of the French and during their progressive expansion in North Africa, the religious brotherhoods were the main sources of resistance, which was characterized frequently by armed uprisings against the central power. In a context where political power was notable more for its diffusion than for concentration, it was the Sufi orders (*turuq*) that were the most evident in the religious and social spheres. Up to a certain point maraboutism, as these Sufi orders were collectively called, was capable of transcending local and tribal identities and providing security for rural and peripheral populations. Long before the organized opposition to foreign, Christian occupation, the Islamic brotherhoods were mobilizing protest against the established dynasties, especially by challenging the extension of the political and fiscal power of Algiers and Tunis and their outposts in the countryside. It is clearly impossible to understand the great revolts of Ali Ben Ghédahom in Tunisia in 1864, the campaign of Amir 'Abd al-Qadir from 1832 to 1838, or 'Abd al-Karim's Rif revolt of 1925 outside the distinct context of the multiple networks Sufism had created across North Africa—Qadiriyyas, Tijaniyyas, Darqawas, and Rahmaniyyas. These orders were capable of mediation and order in time of peace and of effective mobilization in times of conflict and war.[2] The central governments constantly had to defend themselves either by fighting the brotherhoods or by striking alliances with them. Ultimately, after multiple clashes, the governments emerged victorious. In the process, the brotherhoods had nevertheless weakened the governments and tied up their resources.

In a predominantly rural society where collective tribal organization was still intact, armed action by the religious orders presented an effective opposition to the colonial occupation. Referring to this kind of resistance, Charles Richard, a French officer, observed that it was this resistance that best typified the essential spirit of the society by bringing into the struggle the symbolism and ideology of religion. This form of opposition had its limits, however. It could not bypass particularist identities and loyalties sufficiently to shape maraboutism into a broad social movement capable of fighting the French system over the long haul. Brotherhood resistance therefore represented less an alternative state to that of the French than the potential of such a state. In its refusal to submit, the brotherhood attempted to deny the government's authority and perhaps to overthrow it, but not to replace it.

With the consolidation of central colonial power, the Sufi orders began playing a lesser role. While resistance continued, it was more dispersed. In fact, under the impact of the growing efficiency of the central administrative system, a new historical phase emerged. The Islam of the orders and *zawiyas* would cease to be the dominant form of religion. Maraboutism would end up bending under colonial pressure and its resistance would disappear. What followed would be a cultural shift—to Islam as refuge, as withdrawal, as closed off. In this regard the observations of Augustin Berque, developed by Jean-Claude Vatin, are of interest. These scholars hold that, after the orders stopped orchestrating armed resistance, they actually became more popular, attracted more members, and became more dynamic. It was within the framework of maraboutic Islam that the elaboration and diffusion of a new vulgate took place—that of adaptation/opposition to the French system, characterized by formulas of return to self and of negation by withdrawal.[3]

RELIGIOUS REFORMISM AND NATIONAL MOVEMENTS

Maraboutic Islam was tolerated by the colonial authorities because it had ended up accommodating the occupiers. But it would soon be rejected by the *salafiyya* reformist movement, which rose up against the cult of saints and magical and superstitious practices it did not consider an integral part of Islam.

The first confrontation would pit reformism against maraboutism. Making a return to orthodoxy and Islamic renewal their battle cry, the *'ulama* entered into a struggle with that which they considered the antithesis of their program—mysticism and the cult of saints, which they saw as driving Muslims away from God and into the arms of charlatans who were keeping society ignorant, backward, and pagan at the moment when it should face up to the power wielded by foreigners. It was necessary to lay out Islamic values and norms, and a political strategy capable of realistically dealing with the situation.

The reformist idea of purification of Islam proper is different from the apocalyptic purification preached by the *mahdis* of the millenarian movements. It is more in the nature of a theological and philosophical attempt at recapturing the true vocation of Islam, vehiculating appropriate responses to internal and external threats, and loosening the vice of intellectual and ideological blockages set by a tradition that had been disproved by history. Reformism stresses man's education and the reform of society. It does not pose many questions about the political framework within which it operates. In a sense, it continues the historic tradition of the *ulama,* who when faced with arbitrary power, often rent by discord and schism, opted to save that which they considered most essential—the Islamic nature of the community.

One must realize that the colonial reality greatly reduced the maneuvering room of the reformists. Everyone is familiar with the famous triptych of Sheikh 'Abd al-Hamid Ben Badis, founder of the Association of Algerian Muslim 'Ulama: "Arabic is our language; Islam is our religion; Algeria is our fatherland." But what has not been sufficiently observed is that this seeming intransigence on the cultural level was accompanied by great deficiency in political vision. The *ulama's* program was long elaborated within the framework of French law.

The vision of the reformists was founded in their function of teaching the Arabic language and in a religious magistrature that was extraordinarily elitist. A note presented by the Association of Algerian Muslim 'Ulama to the French authorities on August 15, 1944 stated that "the Muslim religion is an ensemble of rules and principles that must be applied as they are interpreted by the *ulama* (by whom we mean the true doctors of the faith), and not as they have been interpreted by the ignorant masses." Their main concerns centered on the family, marriage, and inheritance, which may explain that their central problem, that of Arabo-Muslim personality and identity, continues today to resonate and prolong itself in issues such as family code and civil status.

The same phenomenon was observable in Tunisia, where the Old Dustur, which campaigned against maraboutism in the name of Islamic renaissance, aligned itself with the colonialists by excluding the labor movement and approving in 1924 the dismantling of the Confédération Générale du Travail Tunisien, the first Arab and African union.

But during the same period, a confrontation of much greater political significance was developing, which would oppose nationalism or the nationalist movements to Islamic reformism. In Algeria the rhetoric of the Étoile Nord-Africaine and the Parti du Peuple Algérien had become uncompromising on the questions of independence and sovereignty, even though it remained more flexible at the level of cultural identity. These movements both converged with and diverged from the reformist *ulama.* The Islam they invoked was less formal, less rigorous, less elitist, and more popular. At the same time, their

Arabism was more political than historical, stressing the language of the masses, looking toward an idealized future characterized by the historical and social fact of an Algerian personality. This new direction considered national consciousness to be focused mainly on the future, since the most important issue was political—the accomplishment of independence through struggle. Historic in origin but in a state of continuing development, national personality is founded on other elements than the past. Nothing is sacred about that past.

Thus, after the brotherhoods, maraboutism, and the *salafiyya*, it would be nationalism's turn to define the stakes and nationalism did so with new vocabulary, forms of address, and terms of reference. In the case of Tunisia, the Neo-Dustur took the symbolic and organizational lead, speaking in the name of the people about a range of sacred values that included Islam. This was less the case in Algeria, where the '*ulama* had acquired an essentially religious legitimacy that no movement was able to dispute. In fact, when independence came in 1962, Algerian leaders took over as soon as they could the reformist cultural codes and orders left from the colonial period. Thus the state reaped the benefits of the reformists' intellectual and moral capital—their cultural "stock" —in order to assure its own legitimization.[4] In Morocco, the triumph of 'Allal al-Fasi over his detractors and over maraboutism and the brotherhoods lay at the theoretical level—in his ability to pour into the same mold both the *salafi* heritage and the Moroccan patrimony. But his victory redounded to the benefit of the *makhzan*, which put *salafiyya* in the service of political centralization and state conservation. This in turn generated tensions between the monarchy and political parties like the Istiqlal, which had led the independence movement.

THE NATIONAL STATE, TAMED ISLAM, AND THE ISLAMIST REACTION

The dominant trait of the postcolonial state was its takeover of Islam for use as political ideology. The rationalization of this action was as follows: since, early on, religious discourse had been used to rally the Muslim populations against the colonial occupier, what could be more logical than to mobilize everything, including religion, in the name of an even higher struggle, that of development. Certain leaders called this *al-jihad al-akbar*. State takeover, however, resulted in the nationalization of the religious sphere and the marginalization of the '*ulama*.

Certain Muslim scholars characterized this as *al-islam al-musta'annis,* or tamed Islam.

The new state foresaw the creation of a new, free, and egalitarian society through profound reform in values, customs, and tax distribution, which would mean radical changes in the traditional social structure. By dealing in such issues, the state entered forcefully into society, no longer content to be only its manager or security guard. Entering into the social order meant penetrating the domestic circle, which from time immemorial had been left to itself, even by the colonial state. The national state was going to project its action into the circle of family relations, the cornerstone or weltanschauung of Islam.

The state's strategy, as shown by Carmel Camillieri,[5] was to break the fabric of traditional society by taking away its monopoly of the cellular base. By changing family law, the state was reaching into the deepest and the most secret psycho-anthropological strata of society. It was imposing its own new constraints at the very time it was freeing the family from the older philosophical and traditional constraints. Government would take in hand areas concerning the individual previously controlled by custom or by lawyers of the Maliki school.

It was by frontally assaulting these old principles that the Tunisian Code of Personal Status (CSP) came to be viewed as a radical innovation unique in the Arab world that could not fail to unleash a number of reactions. The basic points of rupture are known. They included abolition of polygamy, requirement for individual consent to marriage, and the ending of unilateral male divorce. But more important than the emancipation of woman and her admission to legal access were the spirit of the reform and its willingness to confront tradition. In effect, the political elites had arrogated to themselves legislative authority in the most traditionally sensitive area. For once, sovereign reason and man's ability to elaborate law were affirmed with force over the traditional law of the *shari'a.*

The most important aspect of the CSP reforms was found in the symbols they promoted and the broad context within which they occurred. Their liberating effect was to proclaim the end of one era and one history and the beginning of another. The reforms demonstrated a will to do away with many things: *shari'a* courts were integrated into secular courts; confessional jurisdiction was abolished; *habous* (*waqf,* in the Arab East) were eliminated; the Zitouna University was dismantled; and astronomical calculations replaced lunar observation in setting lunar months and the dates of religious holidays. Several analysts have dealt with the resistance of the 'ulama and of traditional circles. But, resistance aside, it was clearly proven that when a regime is strong and enjoys broad popular legitimacy it can cause culture and religion to change decisively.[6]

In Tunisia, before and especially after the governmental change of 1987, the question of religious and legal reform was still being debated. Some, such as the member of parliament who exclaimed that, "after all, the CSP is not part of the heavenly books," hoped to reopen the question. But here the government spoke out and drew the line. President Ben Ali announced in March 1988 that the CSP and the status of women were irreversible accomplishments of the republican regime, twin victories for modernity. No law existed except the positive law of the state; nor could the substance of reforms be brought into question by other elements.

This policy was confirmed by the National Pact of November 7, 1988:

> The CSP and its complementary laws served after independence to bring about a series of reforms, the most important of which are the abolition of polygamy, the right of women to marry without consent of a guardian once she has reached the age of reason, and equality between men and women in divorce and its procedures. These reforms are aimed at freeing and emancipating women in conformity with an aspiration in our country that is founded upon a solid rule of *ijtihad* and on the objectives of the *shari'a*, thereby constituting proof of the vitality of Islam and its openness to the exigencies of change and of the era.
>
> The Tunisian state must watch over this rational policy, which proceeds from *ijtihad*, and work to see that *ijtihad* and rationality clearly impact upon education, religious institutions, and the news media.

It is evident that both the CSP and the National Pact have acquired an uncontested legitimacy in Tunisia. Islamist leaders themselves have had no choice but to adhere, at least verbally, to their dispositions. But at this level there is a more basic question that should be addressed. That is whether the political activism of the nationalists did not, in fact, provoke the creation of Islamism.

It is clear that Islamism, the most recent manifestation of religious resistance, is a reaction to rampant and abrupt secularization in Maghribi societies. In the view of traditionalists, the influence of Islam has long been declining. Even though the number of mosques has increased considerably, important issues seem always to be decided elsewhere and the 'ulama are considerably marginalized. Furthermore, the Arabic language, which has become the main language of instruction, still permits little mobility with relation to the Francophones. The entire social structure, in fact, has been affected by decades of massive urbanization, geographic mobility, and emigration to Europe. The rise of the middle classes has signaled the end of the old peasant order and consecrated a profound change in values, tastes, and lifestyles. Within the new value system, Islam occupies a reduced place. The effects of this change are traumatic both in Algeria and Tunisia. The most dramatic reaction against this process of accelerating modernization, with its accompanying rootlessness and inequality, has taken place in the name of Islam.

At the start, paradoxically, Islamist protest in the Maghribi countries did not arouse much concern. Some analysts even maintain that Islamist protest was actually encouraged as a counterweight to the leftist parties the establishments were trying to weaken, to get under control, or to re-integrate into the political process. But Islamist protest became dangerous at the point where its hostility ceased being directed against individuals and groups accused of deviating from Islamic norms and began targeting official Islam and the state itself. This was at a time (in the 1970s) when the state was becoming more vulnerable and was exhibiting signs of ideological fatigue and socio-economic bankruptcy.[7]

Let us examine the nature of these Islamist counterelites in comparison with preceding religious movements. In the first place the militants originate far outside clerical or traditionalist circles; instead they come from modern areas, such as normal schools, science departments, and urban areas. Secondly, in their discourse the political outweighs the religious: the Islamists speak more of Islamist "ideology" than of religion in the narrow sense; their task is to draw out of Islam a political model capable of competing with the grand ideologies of the West, especially with capitalism and socialism. They deal explicitly with the question of the state, the Islamic republic. Instead of wishing, like the 'ulama, to manage civil society, they aim at rebuilding society from the state down. Finally, their hostility is directed not only at the secular elites, but also at the 'ulama, relations with whom are characterized by mutual mistrust.

In a sense, the fundamentalism of the Islamists is more radical than that of the 'ulama. What they aim at is not a return to the shari'a as a means rather than an end, but the restructuring of political relations on the model of the first Muslim community. The juridical gives place to utopia, to millennialism, and to revolution. The reconstruction of society, which starts with a mythical model, leaves major space for this new "cleric," who is an intellectual. The distinction between the "intellectual" and the traditional "man of letters" is that the ultimate point of reference of the former is the state. Whether he is in opposition to it or not, his interlocutor remains the state, because his education in school, his political position, and even his place in society—usually that of a civil servant—presuppose the existence of the state. The 'alim on the other hand, is more likely to be indifferent to the state, because his points of reference are a body of thought and a body of people that are self-reproducing. His point of reference is the Muslim *umma*. This is why modernizing elites see Islamism as first and foremost a political threat.[8]

As noted above, some analysts hold that Bourguibism, with the excessiveness of its modernizing campaigns, created the Islamist reaction. But such an analysis may be too simple, because Algeria, which avoided open secularization, came up against an even more formidable Islamism. In fact, even though both Algeria and Tunisia broke with a tradition that remained enshrined in Morocco, each made different choices with regard to culture and society. The Tunisian leaders opted for a Tunisian identity, relegating to a second level both the Arab and Muslim identities. The Algerian authorities, in contrast, stressed the Arab and Muslim identity to the detriment of the Algerian.

Taking advantage of a reformist tradition going back to the nineteenth century, Tunisia's political elites were able to develop such a hegemonic position in the cultural and ideological domains that Islamists themselves were forced to line up behind these modernist choices. In Algeria, by contrast, Islamism has always benefited from the presence of representatives inside the FLN, such as Boualem Benhamouda, Ahmad Taleb, Beki Boualem, Abderrahmane Chibane, and Sheikh Hamani. The work of these individuals aimed at re-Islamizing society through the state. Their defining of the family institution in Islamic terms, their conception of the school and the educational system, their desire to prohibit any changes in the Arabic language, religion, and culture all link them to the activists of non-official Islam, including those who consider the new state as impious.

From 1965 onward, through political tradeoffs, the state/party in Algeria began to manage the national consciousness by utilizing religion. This ended up making religion the essential foundation—at least philosophically—of identity. In the political give and take, the winners were elements that favored a notion of Algerianness conceived as the monopoly of the main ideological systems of the state and especially the educational system, granting them—in the sense of Gramsci—a veritable cultural hegemony over society. There was a multiplication of transmission belts, along with the number of state/party mosques, which government, with real or feigned naiveté, thought it could use against the Islamists. The government also believed it could use against them the so-called modernism of certain "spiritual" allies, as in al-Ghazali, whose nearly daily speeches served only to strengthen Islamist ranks and legitimize their objectives.

The confrontation of the Islamists with government won over to them the victims of the agrarian reform movement from the 1970s. It also brought over *nouveaux riches,* who, following an old tradition, sought to legitimize their wealth by building mosques to honor the community, receiving honor themselves in return. After 1980 the Islamists, aided by the social crisis and political power plays, finally discovered the road to the popular classes; behind the religious face, political goals were hidden. Algerian Islamism appears to a scholar such as Muhammad Harbi to resemble a millenarian movement; its power of attraction and its lightning-like success can be explained by his hypotheses.

> Like the PPA-MTLD of 1946–1948, millenarian élan is characterized by its belief in the imminent rapid collapse of the system and by its belief in abrupt change resulting from a few quick thrusts, independently of any patient strategy for taking over power.
> In many of its traits, the Islamist progression recalls that of populist nationalism. It is thus rooted in an old tradition and is not the overwhelming new phenomenon that many perceive.[9]

The result of all of these processes, contributed to as much by the Islamist movements as by the different governments, is what might be called the ideologization of Islam, the shift of contemporary Muslim thought from the traditional theological field to an ideological field whose tendency is to formulate the content of Islam in terms of socioeconomic and political rather than spiritual norms and values. The result is a relativism and the submergence or even disappearance of properly religious values.

To the extent that government employs religious arguments, these are often factors of secondary importance in an overall strategy designed to reinforce the regime in the eyes of the masses and to sanctify principles of national cohesion centered on the political leaders. The official leaders as well as those of the opposition each exalt religious ideology and, in so doing, they both contribute to the ideologization of Islam. As this happens, Islam falls into the trap of ruse and reason and, according to Daryush Shayegan, "by standing up against the Satanic West, Islam Westernizes itself; wishing to spiritualize the world, it secularizes itself; and wishing to fight history, it becomes entirely sucked up in it."[10]

It thus happens that the majority of thinkers in the Islamic world are no longer sages or intellectuals in the proper sense of the term, but ideologues who are more preoccupied by expeditious action and solutions than by a particular view of reality. What they are looking for is readymade solutions for the problems of the world. The ideologue tries to impute to others the causes of his own failures; the scapegoats in his demonological pantheon are many: imperialism, colonialism, Zionism. In every case, his historical attitude is almost Manichean: the satanizing of the adversary and the idealization of the self.

It is not the intention of this analysis to advance a simplistic conception of the Maghrib as embodying conflict only between tradition and modernity or Islam and secularism. An attempt has been made to show the ways in which these societies have been dominated by contradictions resulting from the process of acculturation and development within a relationship of dependency. Therefore, rather than dealing with society in general, the present analysis has attempted to demonstrate that Maghribi societies were polarized around two types of elite, two conceptions of nationalism and social development. On the one side were elites open to the Western world, deeply acculturated and bent on promoting the development of their world according to global norms, and on the other were the more closed elites, more concerned with questions of identity, of societies dominated by the external, disposed to devote themselves to the discourse of cultural self-defense.

The Islamist protest of recent years has been so insistent that for the first time identity considerations are attempting to take precedence over those of development and modernity. Without exception, the Maghribi countries have sought to make ideological concessions in the area of re-Islamization at the same time as they have blocked every form of political participation. The game is thus complex, because, in spite of the concessions the state must make in order to win legitimacy from people and believers, fundamentalism is still in opposition and the secularism of the modern elites is still on the side of the state. The latter continues to direct prayers to honor the *din hanif* (the correct and authentic religion), but traditional Islam is directly implicated, as in Tunisia at the time of the CSP and indirectly by ruse in the other states.

The dispute that led Maghribi nationalists, communists, Bourguibists, and even Berberophones to share the same apprehensions regarding Islam and to align themselves with government recalls strangely another debate which was much in the news in Egypt in the period between the world wars and which pitted proponents of modernism such as Taha Hussein and Ali 'Abd al-Raziq against the *'ulama* of al-Azhar. The parallel is appropriate if one notes two differences. The first is that the current conflict no longer opposes modernists and *'ulama* but rises out of a cultural schism between two worldviews. The second is the involvement of whole sections of society in the opposition between prosperous middle classes within the system and other groups excluded or marginalized by the new growth.

It is worth stressing, however, that the rise of political Islam forced the modernizing elites to test their modernity and to develop, both in Tunisia and Algeria, a more explicitly secular discourse. The aspiration for institutional secularization centered in Tunisia on the defense of human rights. In Algeria it centered on the identity question and on the defense of cultural pluralism.

It should be noted that, unlike the Mashriq, where the question of religion and state was significant at an early stage, in the Maghrib it was not the object of specific discussion within the nationalist movements. It was still not addressed after independence when the states erected monopolies of religion and used Islam as a way of legitimizing the socioeconomic policies of successive regimes.[11] It has in fact been the political advance of Islamism that has forced a public debate on Islam and religion.

In Tunisia, the "lay" intelligentsia, long anesthetized by official reformism and by the monolithic stature of the dominant ideology, has had to enter into a debate that, until recently was either invisible or relegated to the background. This took place as the system liberalized and as the Islamist opposition affirmed itself. In Algeria, also, it was in the aftermath of the FIS victory in the June 1990 elections that the question of relations between Islam and the state gradually imposed itself upon the political class. Can it be concluded that the Maghribi intelligentsia today is sufficiently equipped to elaborate a theory of secularization appropriate to a Muslim milieu? The position of this writer on this question is close to that of the Egyptian philosopher Fouad Zakariya, who has observed the fact of a "negative secularism that knows what it does not want but is unable to unite around a positive objective."

Notes

1. Secularization is understood here as an intellectual and ideological process accompanying the modernization of society at the political and institutional levels. See Franck Fregosi, "Islam et État: Sécularisation ou laïcisation?" *Correspondances,* Institut de Recherche sur le Maghreb Contemporain, Tunis, no. 2, (January 1993): 11–14.

2. Michael Gilsenan, *Recognizing Islam: Religion and Society in the Modern Arab World* (New York: Pantheon Books, 1992).

3. Augustin Berque, "Les captans du divin: Marabouts, oulémas," *Revue des Deux Mondes,* vol. 43 (1951): 286–302; see also Jean-Claude Vatin, "Puissance d'état et résistances islamiques en Algérie, XIXe-XXe siècles: Approche méchanique," in *Religion et politique au Maghreb* (Paris: CNRS, 1979).

4. Jean-Claude Vatin, op. cit., 297.

5. Carmel Camillieri, "Famille et modernité en Tunisie," *Revue Tunisienne des Sciences Sociales,* no. 11 (October 1967): 27.

6. See the excellent pages of Yadh Ben Achour, *Politique, religion et droit dans le monde arabe* (Tunis: Cérès Productions and CETP, 1992).

7. For an analysis of the state crisis, see Abdelbaki Hermassi, *Société et état au Maghreb* (Beirut: Centre d'Études de l'Unité Arabe, 1987).

8. Olivier Roy, "Fondamentalisme, intégrisme, islamisme," in his book *Afghanistan, Islam et modernité* (Paris: Éditions du Seuil, 1985).

9. Mohamed Harbi, *L'Algérie et son destin: Croyants ou citoyens* (Paris: Arcantère Editions, 1992). See also Abdelhafidh Hamdi Chérif, "Les aventures de l'identité nationale," in *Naqd: Revue d'Études et de Critique,* Algiers, No. 2 (February–May 1992): 3–8.

10. Daryush Shayegan, "L'Islam et la modernité", colloquium on "Les familles musulmanes face à la modernité," University of Tunis, October 22–25, 1984, p. 9.

11. See the very important conclusions of Morroe Berger, *Islam in Egypt Today: Social and Political Aspects of Popular Religion* (Cambridge: Cambridge University Press, 1970).

II.

The Islamist Challenge

7

Islamism and Islamists: The Emergence of New Types of Politico-Religious Militants

Séverine Labat

S ince the interruption of the electoral process that saw the FIS win
a broad-based majority in the first round of legislative elections,[1]
Algeria has been the scene of bloody conflicts between militant
Islamists and the forces of order. The Algerian state has faced a politico-
religious opposition that was driven by the FIS during its three years
of legal existence but has subsequently been radicalized and partially
escaped its control.

Is it correct to see in the developing violence nothing but the last
convulsive gasps of a dying political Islamism whose failure spells certain disappearance? Or does it mean the resurgence, at the heart of
the Algerian Islamic movement, of a movement irreconcilably hostile
to the political and religious separation that is inherent to modern
nation-states?

With the advent of armed struggle, has the revolutionary option
replaced the participatory logic that the FIS formerly pursued? While
the FIS managed for a time to bring together the diverse factions of the
Islamic movement, and, to some extent, to pacify the more radical
forms of politico-religious expression, the experience of repression has
had the principal effect of accentuating the antagonisms between
evermore irreconcilable factions.

Applying the hypothesis of Pierre Bourdieu[2]—of a rivalry for monopoly on the means of salvation between a corps of religious people who are
repositories of dogmatic knowledge on the one hand, and lay clerics

who have access to the doctrinal corpus by means of rationalized knowledge on the other—it would be possible to hazard a rereading of the conflicts that now set the different factions of the politico-religious opposition in Algeria at odds with one another.

Unlike Egypt with al-Azhar University, Morocco with al-Qarawiyin University, or Tunisia with al-Zitouna University, the Algerian religious arena is notable for the absence of an autonomous and hierarchically organized clerical body. Management of the means of salvation has never been a monopoly in Algeria where the religious arena has been characterized by a multiplicity of competing and sometimes exclusive centers.

The newly independent Algerian state, at an early stage, set about building a civil religion in which nationalist ideology, colored with socialism, was assigned an historic weight more important than that of Islam.[3] However, under the influence of the Islamic wing of the power structure, and in order to set a counterweight to the nascent Islamist opposition, the Algerian state, following a Jacobin conception of Islam, fashioned an official Islam and an official clergy to compete with the body of independent 'ulama. Thus, under pressure from a religious opposition that attempted to organize into a class competing with the power elite, the state engaged in a process of Islamization that made it progressively renounce the options of revolutionary Algeria and offer to its adversaries assurances of "Islamness" that would profoundly alter the politico-religious landscape of the country. But this attempt was weak, and lacked legitimacy. It had no traditional basis of support, and the official clergy that was remunerated by the state and had not fulfilled the function of questioning the power structure became discredited. This allowed the adherents of Islamism to remain in charge of a religious arena in which a disparate political opposition was crystallizing.

It was thus through a profound destructuring of the traditional expressions of Islam, and within a framework of competition with official Islam, that the Islamist movement developed its first structures. The creation of the FIS in February 1989 was the result of an eclectic gathering of several more or less formal groups within the Algerian Islamist movement. Until the dissolution of the party in March 1992, different and sometimes conflicting concerns were expressed. Their common denominator lay in the aspiration for an Islamic state. However, this alliance was not able to fend off the problems generated by contradictory expectations both with respect to the state and to projects of the FIS itself.

A reading of the FIS program of March 7, 1989, is very illuminating in this regard. The different elements of the party, not having arrived at an understanding as to a precise plan, seem to have chosen a "least common denominator," as the only means of bringing them together. It is noteworthy that the debates that troubled the FIS were almost always over questions of strategy and not on the plan for society that the party intended to set out. It therefore functioned almost exclusively as a "revolutionary" party whose principal objective was the taking of power. Ideological quarrels were put off until power had been secured, and were never permitted to interfere with the quest for that power.

A HISTORY OF DIFFERENTIATION

The Algerian *salafiyya*, from *salaf* (meaning a pious tradition in the sense of fidelity to one's ancestors), was an eclectic movement. It had its roots in the work of Ibn Taymiyya[4] and Jamal al-Din al-Afghani[5] and in the experiences of the Islamic reformers 'Abduh and Rashid Rida as well as in the Association of Muslim 'Ulama of Ben Badis, which inspired the fathers of Algerian Islamism.

Salafiyya has the community of believers at the time of the Prophet and the first four caliphs as its political ideal. Its followers aspire explicitly to the restoration of the caliphate without ever having specified in what way this political organization would be reproducible. They reject the various contemporary political models, beginning with communism with which they have readily identified the Algerian regime.[6]

The Algerian *salafis*, apart from 'Abd al-Latif Soltani, have written little. Their political evolution can be followed through the writings of a few of them, which are in two reviews. The first is that of the Ministry of Religious Affairs, *Al-Asala*, which appeared between 1971 and 1981, and expressed different fundamentalist views. The other is the review *Al-Risala*, which appeared in 1980 and opened its columns to the most radical *salafis*.[7] One group of *salafis*, inside the official institutions such as the Ministry of Religious Affairs, joined with the government after Houari Boumediene's coup of June 1965. Their principal demands have been "the decolonization of Algerian history," Arabization, and the propagation of an Islamic morality viewed as the only "immunizing guarantee" capable of defending society from the corrupting influence of the West.

Unlike the Ben Badis "reformists," the Islamic wing of the power structure gave ideological substance to the call for a return to the sources of Islam. The discourse of these "state fundamentalists" contained a plan for society that they were asking the state to implement through its power of coercion. However, the resolutely socialist orientation taken by the state plunged them into a malaise from which they only emerged with the advent of President Chadli Benjedid.

Only with the nomination of Abdarrahmane Chibane as the head of the Ministry of Religion and the favorable orientation of the new government[8] did the most radical faction of the *salafiyya* recover influence. This is reflected in the writings of Abbassi Madani in the review *Al-Asala,* and those of Sheikh Sahnoun[9] in the review *Al-Risala.* A rapprochement began to take place between "state fundamentalism" and "protest fundamentalism," which ended in a radicalization of the *salafi* movement. Thereafter (and the Iranian revolution no doubt had a lot to do with this), demands for an Islamic state, inspired by the writings of the Pakistani Sayyid Abul Ala' al-Mawdudi and the Egyptian Sayyid Qutb, were at the heart of *salafi* propaganda. A pan-Islamist discourse at variance with the nationalism of the reformist *'ulama* was also developed.

As recalled by some of the founders of the FIS when they were pushed aside by it,[10] the party was founded upon *salafi* principles. This point, however, gave rise to much disagreement. The majority of founding members of the FIS in 1989 wanted to create a movement in the same vein as those that had formerly existed, with the sole exception that, owing to the new institutional arrangements, it was time to give up its clandestine character in order to be able to dominate the educational and social terrain. On the other hand, in the minds of Abbassi Madani and the young militants with whom he was allied, the objective was primarily to found a political party able to lead them to the gates of a power structure that they considered weakened and that would offer but token resistance.

It was on this point, independently of the differences in profile which will be examined later on, that the *salafis* differed from the new Islamist militants. These differences of approach explain, in large part, the dissension and expulsion that punctuated the party's three years of existence.

Algerian *salafiyya* includes a majority of preachers who received a traditional religious education parallel to a university education, mostly of the classical Arabic-speaking type. However, this grouping is far from homogeneous. It includes many "neofundamentalists" inspired by the Egyptian Muslim Brotherhood (Al-Ikhwan al-Muslimin) or by Saudi Wahhabism and inclined more toward preaching and social action than groupings like Al-Jama'a al-Islamiyya of Egypt, which tends toward radical and sometimes violent action.

Jaz'ara, the sobriquet denoting the "Algerianist" grouping of Algerian Islamism, is represented by its detractors as a sect of initiates with many variations who maintain ambiguous relations with the power structure. It is, in reality, an informal group composed of French-speaking university people with science degrees that was organized, under the intellectual patronage of Malek Bennabi,[11] within the Central Faculty of the University of Algiers.

It is mainly because of its elitist and secretive nature that the Jaz'ara has attracted the enmity of the *salafis*. The two groupings are not separated only by opposing strategic conceptions. The Jaz'arists are seen as "pragmatic" or "political." They consider the FIS as an instrument of political promotion while the *salafis* are more "ideological," and view the FIS as a means to spread the values of "true" Islam. The two groups are also separated by intellectual and social characteristics. The Central Faculty of Algiers University is considered the cradle of the Jaz'ara. During the 1970s and 1980s, it was the scene of numerous disturbances between Islamist students and leftist students, disturbances that reached a peak in November 1982.

It was in 1968 that, on the advice of Malek Bennabi, some French-speaking students undertook to establish a mosque within the faculty. The disciples of Bennabi published a review, *"Que sais-je de l'Islam"* and soon created for themselves a *majlis al-shura* or consultative council. Concerned by the absence of welcoming structures at the university, but also by the absence of outlets after graduation, the Arabic-speaking students wasted no time in joining them. But the university unrest did not appeal to the authorities, who later intervened strongly in 1971 against the National Algerian Students Union (UNEA), which although still independent, was accused of conspiring against the state. (Its general secretary from 1964 to 1965 later became the principal leader of the *majlis al-shura* of the mosque in the Central Faculty.)

In 1973, in the aftermath of a fire in the mosque, the Islamist students and the leftist students first confronted each other. It was shortly afterward that the *majlis al-shura*, the embryo of the future Jaz'ara, was created. Experiencing some success, the *majlis al-shura* transformed itself into an "Islamic association" and the other universities followed its example.

But it was the events that shook the Algiers university world in 1982 that first revealed the size of Islamism in the student audience.

Following a strike organized by the Arabophone students and joined by the Islamist students after the death of a young student on the campus of Algiers' Ben Aknoun University, the authorities decided to close the mosque of the Central Faculty. Thereupon Abbassi Madani, against the advice of the members of the *majlis al-shura* of the faculty, but joined by Sheikhs Sahnoun and Soltani, decided to organize a demonstration. Their protest took the form of a petition to the government containing fourteen points, including demands for the Arabization of education, the prohibition of alcohol, and the prohibition of mixing of the sexes. The authors of this platform were arrested, as were numerous Islamist students.

These events of November 1982 were a kind of birth certificate for the Jaz'ara. It began to organize around the former students of Malek Bennabi, as well as the new generations of students who had not known him[12] in order to counter the influence of Mahfoud Nahnah[13] in university circles. Its views were expressed notably through the publication, starting in June 1981, of a new review, *Al-Tadhkir* (The Recollection), which was outlawed in 1982 and that reappeared in 1989.

After refusing initially to participate in the creation of the FIS, the Jaz'ara joined the party after its capacity for mobilization made it seem an effective instrument for obtaining power. Thus, it is not surprising to find that numerous FIS candidates, elected at the time of the local elections of June 1990 and the legislative elections of December 1991, came from its ranks.

During its evolution, the FIS was afflicted by a struggle between the historic founders and the young militants who drove them from the leadership of the party. These tensions can best be understood through an analysis of three principal groups of leaders: the preachers' group, composed of a part of the historic founders of the FIS; the radical militants' group; and the Islamo-technocrats' group composed of those who seized control of the FIS during the summer of 1991.

The Preachers' Group

The pioneers of Algerian Islamism were mostly preachers who, when they pursued higher education, did so principally in the humanities. Among these university-educated preachers was the founder of the Al-Qiyam al-Islamiyya Association,[14] Tijani al-Hachemi, holder of a degree from the Faculty of Humanities of Bordeaux and teacher at the University of Rabat.

On the other hand, certain "fathers" of Islamism had only a strictly religious education taught in Arabic. This was the case with the other founders of Al-Qiyam. 'Abd al-Latif Soltani, born in 1902, after having learned the Qur'an in a *kuttab* (Qur'anic school), then in a *zawiya*, earned an advanced degree from the Zitouna in Tunis. Refusing to learn French as the language of the *kuffar* (infidels), Sheikh Soltani became an influential member of the Association of Algerian Muslim 'Ulama (1946) before becoming imam (1962) and teacher at the Ben Badis Institute, and then a secondary-school teacher, until his retirement in 1971. It was then that he published the works[15] that made him one of the principal inspirations of the Algerian Islamist movement. He was put under house arrest following the incidents at the Central Faculty in Algiers in 1982 and his funeral, in 1984, brought about a demonstration that attracted several thousand people.

Sheikh Omar Arbaoui, born in 1912, had the same type of profile. A former *zawiya* student and member of the Association of Algerian Muslim 'Ulama, Sheikh Arbaoui devoted himself to religious education and to the imamate. Ahmad Sahnoun also belonged to the generation educated by the Association of Sheikh Ben Badis. Put under house arrest until 1984 following the events of November 1982 at the Central Faculty, he was received by President Benjedid after the riots of October 1988. He founded the League of Islamic Da'wa in 1989. Mesbah Houidek, a member of Al-Qiyam, studied at Zitouna before running an educational establishment of the Association of Algerian Muslim 'Ulama. Like Sheikhs Sahnoun and Arbaoui, he got to know the French jails from his involvement with the nationalist camp. After independence, he attracted attention for his incendiary sermons at the al-Harach mosque in Algiers, which the authorities, despite multiple threats, never succeeded in stopping.[16]

Politically socialized in the cause of nationalism and the war of independence, these early militant Islamists, unlike the majority of members of the Association of Algerian Muslim 'Ulama, had not rallied to the FLN. Early on, they opposed a state whose orientations at independence appeared to them extremely distant from the admittedly nebulous objectives to which, they believed, the Algerian revolution had been committed.

In the same manner, certain founders of the FIS who experienced or participated in the war of liberation and spent longer or shorter periods in prison (notably in the connection with the "Bouyali affair"[17]) built up mosque clienteles during Algerian Islam's period of gestation. Their story is thus inseparable from the broader movement for construction of places of worship to which Ahmad Rouadjia has devoted a thesis and then a book.[18] Some of them limited themselves to da'wa (preaching) and social action; others were, for a time, tempted by more forceful action. But what they all had in common was being born between the years 1930 and 1940. They all belonged to the same generation as those who, within the FLN, contributed to the building of the new nation-state. Many received a Qur'anic education at zawiyas, madrasas, or at a religious institution of the Association of Algerian Muslim 'Ulama. When they pursued secondary studies, many graduated in literature or the least Arabophone curricula.

While the preachers' group can be partly identified with the salafiyya, certain individuals are more difficult to classify. Abbassi Madani was born in 1931 and received, in his childhood, a religious education of the traditional type. He was also socialized in the school of national-ism and participated in the war of liberation in the ranks of the MTLD (Movement for the Triumph of Democratic Liberties), then of the CRUA (Revolutionary Committee of Unity and Action). He fought with the FLN for many years. Like a number of the fathers of Algerian Islamism, he participated in the creation of Al-Qiyam and followed a preaching career that caused him to spend some time in prison as a result of the November 1982 events. However, his university educa-tion, during which he wrote a thèse de troisième cycle in the psy-chology of education, his mastery of foreign languages (besides French, he speaks English, which he learned during a stay in Great Britain between 1975 and 1978), as well as his political sense place him at the interface between salafiyya and Jaz'ara, a position that he has known how to use to deal with his adversaries.

A New Generation of Salafis: The Agents of Radicalization

The first armed resistance was launched under the direction of Mustafa Bouyali who, from 1981 to 1987, threw himself wholeheart-edly into armed struggle against the impious state in the name of jihad. The partisans of political violence have never since disarmed. Born out of confrontation with the state in its most tyrannical ver-sion,[19] radical Islamism feeds on a repression that it sees as intrinsic to the nation-state.

Radical militance was subdued during the years when the FIS dom-inated the politico-religious landscape. The radicalized militants of the

Islamist movement now monopolize the discourse of Algerian political Islam. The institutional and legal strategy of the FIS failed to overcome a system whose authoritarianism, dressed in the finery of democratization, was perceived as functioning exclusively in the service of a minority who were themselves the product of a single-party system. This could only encourage the return of armed struggle.

Thus, rather than an armed extension of the political strategy undertaken by the FIS until December 1991, the current tactics constitute an alternative approach to a nation-state whose existence is called into question. Jihad fits into a logic in which action is no longer judged on the basis of results, but in terms of its conformity to the cause that it is supposed to defend. There is a near absence of the main political leaders of the abolished party in the maquis and the armed groups. They are essentially composed of one-time Bouyalist militants who are opposed to the participationist strategy of the FIS and of new militant *salafis* re-Islamized by the FIS discourse, and have broken with the traditional forms of expression of political Islam since the interruption of the electoral process.

Because they were not pardoned by President Benjedid until November 1, 1989, the last Bouyalist militants played no part in the organization of the FIS. Set free at a time when the politico-religious landscape had changed, they never managed to recover the role of revolutionary avant-garde that their struggle beside Mustafa Bouyali conferred upon them. Very early they manifested their hostility to a leadership that sought to participate in the political system, and was little inclined toward the violent militance of the Bouyali group. Although they could not achieve autonomous political visibility because of the dominant position of the FIS, they never stopped criticizing the party and working to bring along the faithful of the mosques. First the strike of May-June 1991 and its ensuing repression, and then the interruption of the electoral process convinced them of the necessity to destroy the nation-state in order to replace it with an authentically Muslim community as a predecessor to a reunified *umma*. It is essentially the members of the second Bouyali group[20]— those who saw the most violent confrontations with the state—who are presently found in the armed groups.

The new generation of radicalized militants are trained by an avant-garde often composed of intellectuals from the FIS who have broken with the Islamist leadership because of its indecision when faced with state violence. One of them, a forty-year-old former officer, published a pamphlet in the first half of 1991 entitled *Civil Disobedience: Foundations, Objectives, Ways and Means of Action*, which was distributed in the mosques of the whole country before being outlawed. In it, he judges "democracy [to be] one of the means used to make the individual bend before his oppressors," while "the point of view of the majority cannot be taken into account." He also singles out liberalizing reforms for criticism, describing them as "mapped out by the Jews in order to destroy Algerian moral, economic, social, and military potential." For him, isolated opposition has no future, and it is necessary to resort to "the only solution, which consists of completely overturning the regime through popular struggle based on the principle of disobedience." Disobedience is an intermediate stage between political and military action; it fits within the logic of "gradual dissuasion," which proceeds along a path toward "direct conflict" when the break with the power structure is complete. Because of his positions, he was removed from the *majlis al-shura* of the FIS (the highest organ of the party) in July 1991, when the leadership of the party was oriented toward participation in legislative elections. He then went into hiding, and directs one of the maquis groups defying the government.

Another representative of this new type of radical militants is Ali Belhaj. A secondary-school teacher born in 1956, Ali Belhaj joined the Islamist movement in the 1970s. Close to the Bouyali group, he was arrested in 1983, and found guilty in 1985 by the State Security Court. Exultant, charismatic, and wildly violent in his speech, Ali Belhaj represents the "mystic"[21] tendency of Algerian Islamism. The *fatwas* that he sends out from his prison[22] will no doubt become the bases of the ideological corpus the radicals are building for themselves.

The radicals consist mostly of graduates from the Arabophone curriculae, the most ideologically hardened of whom were nourished on the works of Abdallah Azam[23] and Sayyid Qutb. These writers believed that it was impossible to build an Islamic state by starting with impious institutions. They proceeded to develop a militancy close to that of the radical Egyptian Al-Jama'a al-Islamiyya, as opposed to the "neo-Muslim Brothers," who are engaged in the Egyptian institutional game and whose activism is limited to preaching.[24] These radicals have suffered much professional disappointment because the education dispensed to them by the universities did not prepare them for the real job market. Since the events of May and June 1991 and after spending time in camps, they no longer expect anything from a system that has made them ideologically committed but socioeconomically impotent.

Repression, which heightens political consciousness and encourages the building of clandestine networks, has been a formative influence on the political development of these new militants. The great majority of those who were once confined to the camps have been arrested again. Among the militants are numerous Arabic-speaking primary and secondary school teachers acting as "independent imams," many low-level Arabic-speaking functionaries replaced by French-speaking personnel, several "bandits d'honneur" romantically converted to the sacred cause of Islam, and also deserters from the military whose career prospects were compromised by the promotion of more Westernized officers. Their socio-geographic origin can be found in the peripheral and marginal sectors of the Algerian society. Inhabitants of "non-cities," they develop new forms of collective behavior attested to by the diversity of their recruitment. In search of symbols to represent their anti-state attitudes, it is clear that they found in political Islam a system of meaning with an incomparable historic effectiveness. The majority of them were re-Islamized by the discourse of the FIS, though subsequently promoted a more radical worldview than that of the party during its period of legal existence.

Are these militants part of the same current as their "preacher" elders? They certainly do not correspond to Olivier Roy's definition of a "neofundamentalist"[25] group as one that has renounced any form of political action with respect to the state in favor of a commitment to a reislamization of society. Indeed, it is toward the nation-state, whose imported character they contest, that these new militants direct their action above all else. They also diverge radically from the "Islamo-technocrats" who are engaged in an "in-between" strategy to the extent that they do not tolerate any negotiation with the state they hope to overthrow.

Does this mean that they are the incarnation of the failure of political Islam, as Olivier Roy suggests?[26] Certainly the move to armed violence signals the failure of the attempt of the FIS to make Islam the dominant force in the Algerian political arena. Violence is the direct result of this failure. Nevertheless, the leadership of the ex-FIS continues to advance an eminently political Islam, which cannot a priori be declared to have no possibility of once again imposing itself on Algeria. The radical Islamists will likely be very politically visible in the near future. Repression is likely to produce the same effects as the Egyptian repression of 1965–1966, which brought great fame to the work of the most talented ideologue of the generation, Sayyid Qutb.

The Group of Islamo-Technocrats

Born in the 1950s, the Islamo-technocrats represent the first generation of graduates since independence.[27] With an almost exclusively scientific and Francophone education (because the sciences were more
successful than the humanities in resisting Arabization), they are
upwardly mobile members of a modern technological elite. Their
socialization into Islamism occurred during the years 1970 to 1980,
inside the universities, but not because of mosque preaching. They discovered militancy at a time when a part of the Islamist discourse was
already anchored and in some manner legitimized in the Algerian
politico-religious landscape. Among them can be found a number of
university faculty members, engineers, medical specialists, and
lawyers, some of whom have studied abroad, notably in France and the
United States.

Thus, a comparison of the background characteristics of the founding fathers who led the FIS until June 1991 with those of the leaders
who ousted them from the direction of the party in July 1991, makes
it clear that the renewal of the FIS leadership was the product of both
generational conflict and clan struggle.

Different Perceptions of the Algerian State

After independence, the question of the compatibility of Islam and
socialism was central to Algerian Islamist discourse and was especially
evident in the debates of the Al-Qiyam association. The veterans of
Islamism were opposed to any form of socialism from the outset, and
maintained this opposition while it was becoming the official doctrine
of the new state. This opposition was evident in the debates provoked
by the adoption of the national charter of 1976. But the new militants
in the FIS were different. They appeared on the political scene when
President Boumediene was putting the brakes on agrarian reform and
ridding himself of the burden of militant leftism in the universities.

The veterans of Islamism did not contest the existence of the nation-
state in itself, but rather objected to its historical framework and its
choice of socialism.

The preachers had always demanded a state that would inculcate
Islamic moral values and renounce the imported scourges of communism and secularism. An Islamic state, as they conceived it, could
accommodate any political form that had a certain degree of
Islamization injected into it. Their prison experiences had steered

them into a prudent view of the state and had convinced them of the invincibility of the Algerian state's repressive force and the necessity of limiting themselves to a progressive re-Islamization of the public and private arenas.

The new militants attained command positions within the Islamic movements and parties in a completely different way when the state, under President Benjedid, had begun to disengage itself from some sectors of the economy, and was trying to reduce its role as regulator. These young militants saw their influence begin to grow within the movement. In this period, the state, weakened by several decades of being the sole possessor of power, was no longer perceived as a force for repression.

While the early Islamists perceived the nation-state, which they had seen at its birth, as a repressive deviation from the ideals of 1954, the new militants viewed the state as the principal obstacle to their professional flowering. As Mohammed Boukhobza[28] notes, in Algeria "there is no market for competence because the conditions do not exist for the knowledge and recognition of competence. Promotions as well as disgraces are matters of chance and reinforce in the minds of interested parties the more or less arbitrary and unpredictable character of what happens to them." By being the cause of an "abnormal inversion of social hierarchies" through favoring the promotion of elements that otherwise would not have had that fortune, the state, as the principal provider of careers, was therefore perceived as the clearest hindrance to this group's professional ascent and its corollary—political participation. It was also perceived as functioning for the exclusive benefit of clients and not promoting any of the values leading to collective identity. This group was attracted to a resolutely Islamist discourse that addressed issues of identity, and proposed a "moral" and authentic model of state as opposed to the model imported after independence. These elites can be compared to the French-speaking elites of the 1930s who were pushed into the arms of the nationalists by the refusal of the colonial system to integrate them professionally or politically.

This group's perception of the state is that of a new elite competing with the power structure for control of the modernization process. This elite, which has strong technical and intellectual abilities, was refused the political role to which its training should entitle it, and entered into conflict with the Westernized state intelligentsia. As Nilufer Göle demonstrated in his works on the Islamist engineers in

Turkey,[29] there are modes of reappropriating Islam that allow elites of this kind to distinguish themselves from the power elite. In using a discourse that is both religious and technical, an elite of this kind also distances itself from the older leaders of the Islamist movement, who cease to be the sole means of access to the doctrinal corpus or the sole claimants to a legitimacy based on knowledge. The Algerian group distinguished itself singularly in this respect both from the older preachers and from the young militant *salafis* who developed a pan-Islamist and sometimes millenarian discourse. The tone of the Islamo-technocrats was clearly more nationalist with "Third World" overtones recalling the FLN discourse of the recent past.

The preachers' discourse focussed essentially on society and very little on the state. The Islamo-technocrats and the radical activists, however, developed a discourse which dealt both with society and with the state. But while the former chose a more "inside" form of action, in the hope of receiving posts of responsibility, the latter made a violent break with the state after the interruption of the electoral process.

A New Type of Politico-Religious Militancy

Another difference between the groups concerns their conceptions of the politico-religious struggle. The preachers are closer to the orientation of the Muslim Brotherhood in the use of *da'wa* or preaching as a tool for moralizing public life, and in a belief in gradual action.

The Islamo-technocrats, in contrast, opted for a more political and partisan struggle and, because of their short-term political ambitions, accorded little importance to the Brotherhood's theory of gradualism. They demanded to be integrated into the workings of power; they did not seek the installation of a theocratic state in which their own knowledge and authority would be called into question by a group of *'ulama* judging the legitimacy of their decisions. They opted for an electoral strategy that appealed to the people to decide between them and the state bourgeoisie.

This discourse represented a singular break with that of the new militant *salafis* who were engaged in a process of radicalization that was probably inspired by the example of the FLN between 1954 and 1962. These new *mujahidin* were resolutely opposed to the electoral strategy employed by the Jaz'ara, whose failure certainly convinced them that there was no salvation outside of the maquis.

Finally, unlike the preachers who saw the FIS as continuing the collective struggle they had started in secret, and unlike the new militant *salafis*, for whom violence continued to represent a means of capturing the state, the Jaz'arists considered the FIS to be a vehicle of individual political advancement. While the first group of preachers was essentially preoccupied with the moral rearmament of Algeria and left aside the question of the state and its conquest, the Islamist militants had turned Algerian Islamism into a new political force.

The Recomposition of the Politico-Religious Arena in Algeria

In the absence of a functioning clerical body on the Egyptian model, the Algerian preachers found themselves in competition with the lay clerics for the monopoly of the sacred. Because it is linked to cultural and symbolic resources that can be mobilized by many, the control of the sacred in Algeria no longer depends on the acquisition of formal religious education. Furthermore, the "natural" repositories of religious knowledge, in this case the preachers, are now in competition with the new militant *salafis* as well as with Islamo-technocrats who have been Islamized in the university setting. Thus, there is a need for more discriminating distinctions than the usual distinction between the religious and the political.

A parallel between the Algerian and Egyptian situations seems pertinent. In Algeria, as in Egypt,[30] it is possible to distinguish between two groups in terms of their age and social position, and their relations with the state.

On the one hand is the category of partisan Islamists composed of the group of preachers and the Islamo-technocrats. They both include the modern nation-state in their worldview. The preachers are aware of its importance in terms of its monopoly on force and the Islamo-technocrats—conscious of social position—are aware of the rules of the institutional game. The former are concerned with Islamizing the social order and defending the interests of a quasi-class of *'ulama*. The latter are concerned with integrating themselves into the workings of a power structure that they feel capable of running and perpetuating. This configuration is similar to that in Egypt where one section of the Muslim Brotherhood, together with Islamist intellectuals, is in a position of upward social mobility, and therefore participationist.

On the other hand, the radical Islamists present themselves as a complete alternative to a nation-state whose very existence they contest.

From a situation of social precariousness and blocked social mobility, often acting as "independent" imams, this group exercises its not inconsequential hold on the peripheral populations of the cities for whom it becomes "our" intellectuals. Thus, these agents of radicalization display the characteristics of the Weberian "proletarian intellectual." Unlike the "partisan Islamists," they do not want to reform the existing order by Islamizing it, but rather by substituting for it (to avoid chaos) a transcendent order of which they are the standard-bearers. This prophetic type of mission gives them a millenarian character that leads them, like certain militants of the Egyptian Al-Jama'a, to adopt a violent political praxis, comparable to that of revolutionary Marxists.

While there is a real divergence of approach and therefore of action between the Algerian "preachers" of the Ikhwan faction and the "Islamo-technocrats," it cannot be explained by the concepts of the 1970s. The two groups were active at all ends of the political and social spectrum. They were careful with their social action and with their political action. Both organized their actions within and against the nation-state, and both wanted to make popular mobilization the "strong arm" of their demands. The difference between them was the perception of one that the state can be "domesticated," while the other wished it to disappear.

Probably both groups will draw different lessons from the three years of legal existence of the FIS. The partisan Islamists seem to have a pessimistic view of their immediate future, judging that the FIS went too far and too fast. The preachers seem anxious to preserve their influence within the mosque system in order not to lose touch with a base of faithful who seem able to influence the religious orientation of the government. Similarly, the young technocrats who have come up through the ranks of the ex-FIS are aware that possibilities for dialogue remain in spite of everything. They manifest a prudence that hints of future dealings. On the other hand, it seems that the radical Islamists, who are against any return to dialogue with the "junta" in power, are taking refuge in a violently anti-state millenarianism.

Certainly the final accounting is yet to come, but while the brutality of repression at the moment validates the radical discourse, there is little doubt that with a calming of institutional violence, the latter could give way to a more conciliatory discourse.

The coalition or frontlike character of the FIS engendered an inability to manage internal contradictions and divergences. In effect, there is a great distance between the FIS embodied in Ali Belhaj, which is an expression of popular despair, and the FIS of Abbassi Madani, with his university-educated retinue. There is also great distance between a social movement assembling the new "wretched of the earth" and a political organization in the service of elite interests. A vehicle of collective salvation for the former and a tool for individual promotion for the latter, the FIS has been the point of intersection of very heterogeneous social and political demands. After the ordeal of dissolution and going into hiding, some might expect the rebirth of a union between a revolutionary proletariat (or the millennialists) and the "enlightened" intelligentsia. But this is far from sure.

In the face of compromise by the partisan Islamists with the *jahili* state, an Egyptian style of radicalization is more and more visible within one part of the Algerian Islamist movement. With the many attempts by the maquis to increase their attacks since winter 1992, there is no lack of evidence of a break between a "justification by ends," which judges action by its ability to realize its objectives and that is embodied by the partisan Islamists, and a "justification by values," which does not judge action by its immediate results but according to its conformity to the sacred cause of Islam of which radical Islamists would be heralds.

There are now two groups, whose divergences on the issues of the Algerian nation-state and the distinction between the religious and the political seem irreconcilable. In effect, the evolution of the partisan Islamists toward a recognition of the nation-state seems to represent implicit acceptance of a political order distinct from the divine. On the other hand, the "radical" faction of Algerian Islamism might be tempted to proclaim *takfir* against the apostate state. This faction would then insert itself into the tradition inaugurated by Kharijism, by Ibn Tayimiyya, by Wahhabism, and finally enriched by the eastern Islamists of politically redefining the borders of the *dar al-islam* in order to guard against the influence of the corrupting and secular West.

While partisan Islamism would institutionalize itself, the goal of radical Islamism would be destruction of the new Houbel.[31] If this hypothesis is correct, it would be tempting to suggest the existence of a sort of cyclical development of the expressions of Islamism, inasmuch as Algeria would repeat, with a certain time lag, the process of diversification observed in Egypt between the partisans of participation and the partisans of a total alternative to the nation-state.

Notes

1. In the first round of December 26, 1991, the FIS, with 47.27 percent of the votes, won 188 seats out of a total of 430.
2. See Pierre Bourdieu, "Genèse et structure du champ religieux," *Revue Française de Sociologie,* vol. 12, no. 2 (1971): 295–334.
3. On this subject see Mohammed Tozy, "Islam et État au Maghreb," *Monde Arabe Maghreb-Machrek,* no. 126 (1989): 25–46.
4. Ibn Taymiyya (1263–1328) denounced those Muslims who did not fulfill the duty of jihad against the Tartars.
5. In the nineteenth century he launched a call for revolt against colonialism and a return to the sources of Islam.
6. In this regard see 'Abd al-Latif Soltani, *"Al-Mazdaqiyya hiya asl al-ishtirakiyya"* (Mazdaqism is the Source of Socialism), (Morocco: 1974).
7. On the history of the review *Al-Asala* see Luc-Willy Deheuvels, *Islam et pensée contemporaine en Algérie: La revue Al-Asala* (1971–1981) (Paris: CNRS, 1991).
8. The reforms of President Benjedid, and notably the vote on the Family Code of 1984 and the National Charter of 1986, gave satisfaction on several points to the followers of Islamism.
9. Ahmad Sahnoun, one-time member of the Association of Algerian Muslim 'Ulama, is considered to be one of the "fathers" of Algerian Islamism. Arrested in 1982 on the occasion of the events at the Central Faculty in Algiers, he was put under house arrest until 1984. In 1989, he founded the Islamic Da'wa League in an unsuccessful attempt to federate the diverse Islamic tendencies.
10. At the Batna conference of July 1991, certain founders of the FIS were thrown out of the party's leadership, which devolved upon the young militants close to Abbassi Madani.
11. An electrical engineer, Bennabi (1905–1973) produced a considerable body of literature on the "conditions of the renaissance" of the Muslim world. Incorrectly considered to have been the principal inspiration for the Algerian Islamist movement, he nevertheless exercised a great influence over the young Islamist university people who came from the group at the Central Faculty in Algiers. For more details see Sadek Sallam, *L'Islam et les musulmans en France* (Paris: 1987).
12. In this respect, Jaz'ara shows similarities to the circles of former Anglo-Saxon students, to the extent that it seems that it was the difficulties in professional advancement by the former students of Bennabi that caused them to create a network of solidarity based on the heritage of the master.
13. Leader of the Algerian Muslim Brotherhood.
14. Founded in 1963, the association was suspended in 1966 following the protests it produced upon the execution of Sayyid Qutb, and then dissolved in 1970.
15. "Le mazdaqisme est l'origine du socialisme," "Les flèches de l'Islam," and "Pour la foi islamique."
16. See Aïssa Khelladi, *Algérie: Les islamistes face au pouvoir* (Algiers: ALFA, 1992).
17. Former mujahid of the war of liberation, Mustafa Bouyali established the first Islamist maquis between 1981 and 1987.
18. Ahmad Rouadjia, *Les frères et la mosquée: Enquête sur le mouvement islamiste en Algérie* (Paris: Karthala, 1990).
19. On this subject see Michel Seurat, *L'État de barbarie* (Paris: Éditions du Seuil, 1989).

20. Following a first wave of repression, the members of the first group were arrested in 1981 and 1982. It was consequently the members of the second group who maintained a guerilla organization until 1987 when Mustafa Bouyali died.

21. Quotation marks are used because the differentiation between Ikhwanism and Sufism is badly received in the Islamist movement.

22. He was arrested following the strike of May–June 1991.

23. A Palestinian fighting in the Afghanistan war, Abdallah Azam published works on jihad until his assassination in 1989 in Peshawar where he directed the recruitment office for Arab fighters.

24. Giles Kepel, Le Prophète et Pharaon: Les mouvements islamistes dans l'Egypte contemporaine (Paris: La Découverte, 1984).

25. Olivier Roy, "Le néofondamentalisme: Des Frères Musulmans au FIS algérien," Esprit (March–April 1992): 78–79 and "De l'islamisme révolutionaire au néofondamentalisme," Esprit (July-August 1990): 5–14.

26. Roy, op. cit.

27. It was a matter of training national cadres considered to be the avant-garde of socialist Algeria's "industrializing-industry" project of the 1970s. The effort in the realm of education raised the number of students registered at the Faculty from 2,800 in 1962–63 to 173,800 in 1987–88.

28. Mohammed Boukhobza, Octobre 1988: Evolution ou rupture? (Algiers: 1991).

29. Nilufer Göle, "Ingénieurs musulmans et étudiantes voilées en Turquie: Entre totalitarisme et l'individualisme," pp. 167–92, in Intellectuels et militants de l'Islam contemporain, under the direction of Giles Kepel and Yann Richard (Paris: Éditions du Seuil, 1990).

30. See Agathe Faraouët and Claude Guyomarch, "Islamisme ou islamismes: Les cas de l'Egypte et de l'Algérie," Les Cahiers de l'Orient (Spring 1992).

31. From the name of one of the idols of pre-Islamic Mecca. This is how some Algerians refer to the maqam al-shahid, an imposing monument erected in memory of the "martyrs" of the war of liberation.

Doctrinaire Economics and Political Opportunism in the Strategy of Algerian Islamism

Hugh Roberts

INTRODUCTION

Confronted with the startlingly rapid expansion of the Algerian Islamist movement between 1989 and 1991, many Western observers of Algeria tended to perceive the movement as engaged in a revolutionary challenge to the Algerian state, and to depict the opposition between the Islamists and the nation-state as all but total. The frequent invocation of a putative analogy with Iran was merely the most conspicuous symptom and an entirely natural corollary of this general tendency to interpret events in Algeria as a clash of absolutes. As part of this reading, the religious dimension of the Algerian state was almost entirely overlooked, and the state was presented as a secularist, if not already secular, state, when in fact it has never been either of these, notwithstanding repeated Islamist denunciations of *l'état impie*. In effect, substantial parts of Western commentary on Algeria merely took up and amplified the distortions of Islamist propaganda on this issue.[1]

There are numerous aspects of what has actually been happening in Algeria over the last few years that are difficult, if not impossible, to explain on the hypothesis that this absolutist reading of the relationship between the state and the Islamists is correct. One of these concerns the issue that was regularly presented as being at the heart of Algerian politics from 1988 onward, if not earlier, namely that of economic policy and the debate over proposals for "reform"—in reality, the radical transformation—of the economic structure of the country in the direction of laissez-faire private enterprise capitalism.

THE FIRST FACE OF THE PROBLEM

There are two striking aspects of the Algerian Islamist movement's position on this issue.

First, on the assumption that the movement was a mass movement that was bidding for, and possibly realistically aspiring to, state power in its own right, it was to be expected that it should have itself addressed the question of the economy and have developed positions of its own in respect of it. Yet in fact Algerian Islamism had virtually nothing to say about economic policy. Not only did it not have positions of its own, it did not even bother to canvass the kind of notion concerning properly "Islamic" banking and so forth that has been fashionable in international Islamist circles since the Iranian revolution. Moreover, this massive lacuna in the programmatic outlook of Algerian Islamism was most flagrant in the case of that element of the movement that was apparently the most dynamic, popular and politically ambitious, namely the Islamic Salvation Front (Front Islamique du Salut, FIS). While one might not be surprised to find small radical groupings on the political fringe neglecting to deal with the central economic issues that directly affect the mass of the electorate, it is natural to expect a party that is unmistakably cultivating a populist image and seeking to carve out a mass constituency for itself among the poorest and most deprived sections of the population to take care to address the "bread-and-butter" concerns of these voters, and to give a prominent place in its program to policies that at least claim to cater to these concerns. The FIS did nothing of the kind.[2]

Second, insofar as the FIS did take a position on the issue of economic reform, it explicitly and unequivocally supported it at the level of principle. It is certainly true that it did so without placing any real emphasis on this position, but its tacit support for the implementation of the government's reform program in practice was unmistakable.[3]

Now, whatever long-term benefits this program may have theoretically promised for ordinary Algerians, there can be no doubt that in the short run it imposed enormous burdens on the poor, and the urban poor above all. These burdens were a function of the increases in the prices of basic necessities as a consequence of the removal of government subsidies and price controls, and especially of the increase in unemployment as a consequence of the ending of government subsidies to unprofitable state sector enterprises and the privatization of many such enterprises. But they also arose in consequence of more general austerity measures that, by restricting imports of vital spare parts and raw materials and by depressing domestic demand, forced many enterprises in both public and private sectors to cut production and lay off workers, if not close down altogether.

Thus, at a time when Algeria's Islamists, regrouped for the most part in the FIS, were apparently bidding for power in conditions of unprecedented national economic crisis and controversy, they not only evacuated the entire debate over the future direction of the country's economic development but did so at the expense of the interests of the urban poor whom they were committed to mobilizing, by supporting the positions of the FLN government and party leadership in this debate, that is, the positions of those whom they were notionally committed to overthrowing.

This, it has to be said, is strange, indeed abnormal to the point of being bizarre in the extreme. What is normal is that a populist party seeking to stir up mass popular opposition to the party in power makes every effort to exploit every unpopular aspect of government policy. The FIS showed itself to be ruthlessly demagogic on all other issues, not in the least above putting its own ingenious spin on the realities of the matter where government religious policy, cultural policy, foreign policy, and so on were concerned. But the program of the FLN reformers was, uniquely, spared the kind of demagogic treatment it—more than any other—was crying out for.

This is one face of the problem, or enigma, with which we have to deal. The other face concerns the forces notionally committed to resisting an Islamist takeover in Algeria, namely the Chadli regime and especially its supposedly most "liberal" wing, the "Reformers" who came to unprecedented prominence after the riots of October 1988.

THE SECOND FACE OF THE PROBLEM

The leader of the reformers within the Chadli regime during this period was Mouloud Hamrouche, who had worked very closely with

Chadli as a key aide in the presidency until, on the recommendation of Hamrouche's patron and Chadli's close ally Abdelhamid Mehri,[4] Chadli appointed Hamrouche prime minister in September 1989. Hamrouche had overseen the team of backroom boys in the presidency that drew up detailed plans for economic liberalization and the move to a full market economy, and on taking over as prime minister he had made clear his new government's determination to press rapidly ahead with an extremely ambitious program of radical measures. As well as being identified with the most thorough-going economic liberalism, Hamrouche was also a supporter of close ties with France, and in particular a defender of the status of the French language in Algeria, which he went to far as to describe as "the second national language" of Algeria.[5]

One might have thought that a government headed by a politician so firmly associated with the principal economic and cultural preferences of the Westernized wing of the Algerian middle class and intelligentsia would have been unremittingly hostile to the Islamist movement and determined to prevent it from winning an electoral victory. Yet, as I have demonstrated in detail elsewhere, from September 1989 to June 1990 Hamrouche not only displayed an astonishing tolerance of the FIS's activities, including ones that, by their violence, clearly breached the law, but also went out of his way to bolster the FIS's electoral appeal and to sabotage the electoral appeal of his own party, the FLN.[6]

The case of Mouloud Hamrouche is by no means unique. Another leading figure whose political positions repay attention in this context is Abdelhamid Brahimi.

Brahimi was Chadli's prime minister from 1984 to 1988 and as such was one of the major political casualties of the 1988 riots. Long before Hamrouche rose to prominence, Brahimi had identified himself with the cause of economic liberalism, and his government had greatly accelerated the reform process (which had in fact begun in 1981),[7] presenting its commitment to economic liberalization as following logically from its recognition of the "scientific" character of liberal economic theory. Yet the same government that committed itself to bringing, via monetarist policies, a much needed element of "science" into Algeria's economic management (whence Brahimi's ironic popular sobriquet, "Brahimi La Science") also introduced a highly controversial Family Code that was clearly based on the *shari'a* and represented a massive concession to Islamist pressure and a correspondingly massive defeat for the Westernized wing of the Algerian intelligentsia. This was by no means the only time that a connection between economic liberalism and Islamist politics was to be made manifest in Brahimi's activity. In the spring of 1990, in the run-up to the local and regional elections of June 1990 that the FIS eventually swept, Brahimi suddenly emerged from the oblivion to which his fall after October 1988 had consigned him to announce that FLN corruption in government had cost the country $26 billion over the years, the equivalent of the entire debt burden, and this declaration was naturally seized on by the FIS and constituted a massive endorsement of the FIS's propaganda against its electoral rival, the FLN.[8]

There is reason to believe that Brahimi dropped this bombshell deliberately and that its purpose was indeed to assist the FIS, just as there is reason to believe that Mouloud Hamrouche was intent on facilitating a FIS victory in 1990.[9] Evidence of the closeness between the two men's political positions is found not only in their shared commitment to radical economic liberalism, but the fact that Hamrouche's government included Brahimi's brother.[10] The apparently bizarre behavior of Hamrouche and Brahimi is simply the most conspicuous aspect of the other face of the enigma we are addressing.

When we look at events in even just a little detail, we do not find an uncompromising, all-out, revolutionary Islamist onslaught on the state, nor an uncompromising resistance of this threat by the government of the day, as virtually all Western media coverage of the Algerian drama has suggested. On the contrary, we find an Islamist party giving significant support to a crucial aspect of the government's program, and the compliment being vigorously returned with senior figures within the government and the wider governing elite giving significant support to a crucial aspect of the Islamists' electoral strategy at the expense of their own party.

What has been going on?

AN APPROACH TO A SOLUTION

One side of the answer is that the mainstream of Algerian Islamism has never had a revolutionary attitude to the Algerian state in the sense of an uncompromising hostility to this state and its corollary, the determination to overthrow it. On the contrary, the Islamist movement has always sought to advance its cause *within* the framework of the Algerian state and, whenever its rhetoric has suggested a revolutionary ambition, its practice has invariably belied this. Because of this, the real, as opposed to apparent, strategy of the Islamist movement has always been a strategy of alliances. Thus, while the FIS's rhetoric denounced the actual Algerian state as *un état impie* run by *les voleurs du FLN* and counterposed to this the radiant vision of an Islamic republic, *dawla islamiyya*, its practice was another matter altogether. Far from adopting a revolutionary and correspondingly uncompromising practice of refusing to have anything to do with the actual state, the FIS persistently operated an unacknowledged alliance with some of the most powerful elements of the state, including those whose policies might reasonably be held responsible for the economic distress of the electors the Islamists were appealing to.[11]

This disposition of the Islamist movement to depend on strategic alliances with key elements of the state is one of the most important characteristics of the movement, and remains to be explained. But what also needs to be explained in respect to the FIS is the element of hypocrisy in its stance. The point is that the FIS represented an innovation in Algerian Islamism, not in its practice of a strategy of alliances, but precisely in its adoption of a revolutionary rhetoric that masked, and was substantially at odds with, this practice. Prior to the formation of the FIS, Algerian Islamism had not left itself open to the charge of political hypocrisy in the same way because it had taken care not to denounce the Algerian state as fundamentally illegitimate. But the FIS did condemn the Algerian state in these terms, and it is in virtue of this radicalization in Islamist rhetoric without a corresponding radicalization in actual strategy that we can describe the discourse of the FIS as hypocritical.

This element of hypocrisy was the expression in the FIS's discourse of the fundamentally opportunist character of its political strategy. And this opportunism was itself a two-faced affair. The adoption by the FIS of a populist strategy, which placed the mobilization of the urban poor at the center of the picture, and its adoption of an electoralist strategy, which placed the winning of local, regional, and national assembly seats at the center of the picture, led the party increasingly to depart from the tenets of Islamist orthodoxy in several major respects. By becoming popular and electoralist it became less pure. In its experiment with the FIS, Algerian Islamism compromised itself *par le bas et par le haut*—with the people and with the state at one and the same time. But it did so because it was congenitally inclined to do so, for reasons to which I shall return.

The other side of the solution to our enigma concerns the economic liberalizers, the reformers. It is not simply a matter of finding an explanation for an association of ideas that might seem incongruous. On the contrary, a case can be made for the view that the ideas of free market economics and the ideas of Islamic politics fit together reasonably well. For the purposes of this argument, I shall take this general case for granted. At most, however, it would offer an explanation of why intellectual advocates of free-market economics might be disposed to concede in theory the advantages of the Islamists' political project of an Islamic republic, and why Islamists should approve in theory the measures advocated by economic liberalizers. But, in the case that we are considering, far more dramatic matters are to be explained, namely the actual political positions taken on both sides in a context of extreme political crisis. Specifically, why should Hamrouche and Brahimi have acted to promote not merely Islamist ideas, but the electoral prospects of an Islamist political party mobilizing mass popular support on the basis of extreme hostility towards the state of which Hamrouche and Brahimi were senior figures?

It is my thesis that a major part of the answer to this is to be found in consideration of the fact that the advocacy of economic liberalization had undergone a decisive mutation since the mid-1980s, namely that it had become an ideological crusade in its own right, and one with which the Chadli presidency had become publicly identified in a way that marked a significant change in the character of this regime. These changes had enormous consequences in the political sphere, and the compromising of Algerian Islamism through the diverting of its energies into an essay in political opportunism was one of the most important of these. The first thing to be explained, then, is the rise of doctrinaire economics.

FROM COMMON SENSE TO CRUSADE: THE EVOLUTION OF CHADLISM

Although the Chadli regime initially presented itself as the heir to and faithful continuation of the socialist policies of its predecessor, the Boumediene regime, the approach it made a virtue of adopting was an avowedly pragmatic one, and the accent was placed on bluff common sense, realism, and practicality in what was clearly intended to be a contrast with the supposedly doctrinaire policies of the 1970s. It was in these terms that the tacit but unmistakable retreat from socialism was broached and rationalized in the early 1980s, and since the desirability of measures of economic liberalization was presented and canvassed in these uninflammatory terms, it was possible for the regime to secure a broad consensus in support of these measures within the power structure as a whole.

The contrast with the situation that obtained by the end of the 1980s, could hardly be greater. By the late 1980s the issue of liberal economic reform was no longer being presented by its supporters as a matter of pragmatism and common sense, but as an ideological crusade. And in prosecuting this crusade the reformers appeared to find it inconceivable that opponents of particular measures might have either valid (as in practical) arguments or honest motives on their side. This change in the outlook of the reformers, and the view they took (and ruthlessly promoted) of their critics, were only part of the changed picture. For another part was the position of Chadli himself. In sharp contrast to his personal political posture during his first five-year term from 1979 to 1983, by the late 1980s Chadli was an embattled president who no longer appeared to hold the position of impartial arbiter between factions, but was increasingly personally identified with a particular faction, the reformers, and engaged in a bitter, public, and apparently endless trial of strength with former major allies in the power structure.[12]

In short, the business of promoting liberal economic reform in Algeria had become an intensely doctrinaire matter, and the Chadli regime, instead of distancing itself from the reformers as their stance evolved from a pragmatic to a dogmatic affair, actually went the other way, and identified itself with doctrinaire economics in the most emphatic manner. A crucial feature of the situation that gave rise to the FIS and its political impact was thus the adoption by the regime of the doctrinaire mode of economic policy development.

For those outside Algeria who personally shared the ideological penchant of the Algerian reformers for doctrinaire economic liberalism, the adoption of this ideology by the Chadli regime could, of course, most satisfactorily be explained as no more than a belated conversion to the truth. For the rest of us it may be of interest to point out that the Chadli regime's plumping for doctrinaire economics almost exactly recalled the way in which the Boumediene regime became associated with doctrinaire economics of the socialist variety during the period of the so-called "révolution socialiste" (1972–1978), and that the reasons for this evolution were unquestionably political in the two cases.

The adoption of doctrinaire economics performed a series of political functions from the point of view of the Chadli presidency at a time when it was losing the support of important elements within the power structure on other issues.

First, the elevation of economic liberalization to the status of a crusade enabled Chadli and his allies to mobilize the enthusiasm of the younger generation of the intelligentsia on this issue in their own support; having originally sought legitimation from hoped-for success in delivering higher living standards through pragmatic economic management, the post-oil price slump Chadli presidency was now looking for new, ideological sources of legitimation; economic reform with a capital "R" got the younger intellectuals (technocrats, journalists, academics) on Chadli's side, a remarkable development in itself, and in the name of progress too.

Second, the investing of economic liberalization with the moral content of a crusade unquestionably performed legitimating functions for the essentially private-sector middle-class constituency to which Chadli and his allies primarily appealed. This constituency had been very much on the defensive during the 1970s, the target as often as not of official denunciations of "exploitation," "parasitism," "hoarding," "racketeering," and so forth. Now the boot was on the other foot, and Chadli was delivering something to someone at least.

Third, the crusade for reform enabled Chadli to play to the French and more generally the Western gallery with enormous effect, by posturing as the Algerian equivalent of Mikhail Gorbachev, and thus compensated the regime for its loss of popular support at home and of former powerful allies in the power structure, at least in the short term.[13]

Fourth, and most important beyond doubt, the crusade for reform had the effect—and without question also the purpose—of delegitimizing opposition to the Chadli regime from other elements in the power structure. Just as the opponents of Boumediene's socialism were liable to be labelled "les réactionnaires," "les pénuristes," and so forth, Chadli's critics in the era of the crusade for reform suddenly found themselves pilloried as "hard-liners," "caciques," "les barons du FLN," "la nomenklatura," and so on, whoever they were, whatever posts they occupied, and whatever it was that they actually stood for or objected to. It was here that the playing of the Western gallery was most explicit and most effective. Virtually without exception, Western commentary on Algeria has assumed that Chadli's opponents were opposed to him because they were opposed to his policies of economic reform. The possibility that they were branded as opponents of reform in virtue of being opposed to Chadli himself (for any of a wide variety of reasons, including entirely cogent ones) was never given serious consideration in either the Western media or Western academic commentary, but it is undoubtedly closer to the truth of the matter in many if not most cases.

Finally, of course, the cause of economic reform became the new orthodoxy, and those who pioneer a new orthodoxy can reasonably hope to maintain their leading position having done so. Economic reform became the sacred cause which no one dared to oppose openly, and in the name of which Chadli could hope to wrong-foot, silence, and eventually get rid of his enemies, whoever they were.

From the point of view of our overall argument, however, the chief interest of the Chadli regime's decisive plumping for *l'option capitaliste*[14] via reform is that the concomitant adoption of doctrinaire economics reflected the capture of not only government policy but also the presidential agenda as a whole by the younger generation of the technocracy.

THE ISLAH OF THE TECHNOCRATS

Fundamental to an understanding of the Algerian technocracy is the realization that the political sphere has been dominated by the military ever since 1962, and that the civilian politicians and especially the technocrats have accordingly been very junior partners in the successive provisional formulae for governing Algeria on which the men who command the army have periodically agreed among themselves. One cannot hope to appreciate the behavior and ideology of the technocracy without taking into account the dependent political positions of its individual members, the extent to which their careers depend on the patronage of powerful military figures, but also the narrowness in their political outlook that results from this client status and subaltern political role, their frustration at their dependent and limited situation and their resentful will to power over the less-educated but more unscrupulous, more cunning and more *political* power-brokers and maneuverers who make, frustrate, and break them, are all taken into account. For it is only if these are taken into account that it will be possible to understand why there has been such a strong tendency in the Algerian technocracy to opt for utopian blueprints and doctrinaire policies.

The utopian blueprint—whether the Plan, as in the socialist variant, or the model of the perfectly competitive market economy in the capitalist variant—is, of course, a form of *scripture*. And possession of an intellectual grasp of a complex doctrine (or, even better, a simple doctrine reserved for an elite of initiates by the arcane terminology in which it is expressed, and possessing endless secondary ramifications and applications) is often taken as a sign of possession of instruction, that is, genuine knowledge and an educated mind. Such considerations are central to the predicament of the technocrat in Algeria. The state is actually controlled by the men who control the guns, much as the Turkish regency was controlled. For the civilian figure with political ambitions, the political primacy of the military leaves open the role of *'alim* as a career option, and since the postcolonial Algerian state has been attempting to perform a vast number of functions never even dreamed of by its precolonial predecessor, and many of these functions presuppose for their performance a combination of specialized knowledge and the authority that goes with this, a secularized version of the *'alim*'s role has become available as a career option to thousands of Algerians.

In this sense, one is tempted to say that the technocrats are the real *'ulama* of the contemporary Algerian state. This is, of course, a provocative and unsatisfactory way of describing the matter, since it implies that the nominal *'ulama*—the senior functionaries of the Ministry of Religious Affairs, the directors of the Islamic institutes, the members of the Higher Islamic Council, and so on—are in some sense unreal or false. We need a different set of terms to do justice to the dichotomy in question. The distinction that Walter Bagehot made between what he called the "efficient" and the "dignified" elements of the English constitution meets the case to perfection.[15]

The Algerian state has two faces, one looking backward to the precolonial past and one looking forward to a futurist vision of national modernity. Since both faces are vital to it, and have to be taken care of, the state has two sets of *'ulama*. The first consists of the men of religion who are the *'ulama* of the "dignified" aspect of the state, the possessors of the traditional learning—*'ilm*—appropriate to the business of husbanding the legitimacy the state derives from its roots in history, cultural traditions, and the time-honored faith, in the name of which the policy choices of the state are legitimized on the ground that they are consistent with Algeria's personality ("to thine own self be true" being the catechism of every nationalism). The second set consists of the technocrats who are the *'ulama* of the "efficient" dimension of the state, the possessors of the rational knowledge—also *'ilm*—in the name of which the main socioeconomic choices are invariably further legitimized on the ground that they are *scientific* (Boumediene's scientific socialism, Brahimi La Science's scientific monetarism, and so on), when they have arguably been nothing of the sort. Indeed, it is precisely in their promotion of doctrinaire policies tending to the realization of utopian blueprints that the technocrats pretending to the new, secular *'ilm* have demonstrated how much this *'ilm* has to do with the impulses and functions of religion and how little to do with science.

Unlike the genuine, religious *'ulama* of the old regency, however, the technocrats have their being in an immeasurably more complex and above all unstable and insecure political environment, the Kafkaesque political universe of the FLN state.[16] The technocrat, the "efficient" *'alim*, is in this respect far worse off than his "dignified" counterpart in "religious affairs," because the former's functions are far less routine in character than the latter's, and the stakes involved in the state's economic choices are colossal, and competition for control of, or at least a hand in the management of, these decisions is intense. Unlike the "dignified" *'ulama,* who tend to inhabit a political backwater by comparison and to be relatively insulated from the vicissitudes of the Byzantine cut-and-thrust, the "efficient" *'ulama* are inclined to find themselves near the center of the arena of political faction fighting and maneuvering, and the frustrations but also the endless uncertainty and strain endured by the inhabitants of this environment make it natural that they should yearn for its reform. And what reform of this environment means in this context is above all its *simplification.*

It is probably for this reason as much as any other that certain technocrats who in the 1970s were enthusiastic supporters of Boumediene's "révolution socialiste" should in the late 1980s have emerged as leaders of the crusade for capitalist economic reform. Socialism or capitalism; quite frankly, either will do, so long as the process of establishing it involves a massive purge of the state power structure, a corresponding simplification and stabilization of the political environment and, above all, the emancipation of the technocracy from their demoralizing dependence on illiterate ex-*maquisards* or corrupt—or simply terrifying—powerbrokers in the military high command and thus, at last, their consecration as the men of learning and authority in the resulting political-economic order.

The Arabic term *islah* is used in Algeria to refer to the movement of Islamic reform organized from 1931 onward by the Association of Algerian Muslim 'Ulama of Sheikh 'Abd al-Hamid Ben Badis. (Because of Ben Badis's striking personality and leading role, the movement is also sometimes referred to by the specific term of the *badisiyya* in Algeria, as distinct from the generic term of *islah* that applied equally to parallel movements elsewhere, in Egypt, Tunisia, Morocco, and other places.) The central thrust of the Islamic reformers was to preach a return to the austere simplicities of scripturalist orthodoxy, and the twin targets of their assault were the vision of the French-oriented "assimilationists,"[17] who supposed that Algerian Muslims could find emancipation from colonial oppression through acceding to citizenship within the framework of the French Republic, and maraboutism, the cult of the saints, *murabtin*, on which a largely illiterate rural population, lacking direct access to God's will via scripture, depended for indirect, mediated access, *faute de mieux*. Both "assimilationism" and maraboutism were accused of *bid'a*, "blameworthy innovation," and maraboutism in particular was accused of the heretical superstition known as *shirk*, "associationism," that is, as Ernest Gellner has defined it, "the view that saints or the dead and other beings or objects can through association with God partake of his sacredness."[18]

The *islah* of the technocrats has not had any "assimilationists" to take issue with, for the very good reason that the technocratic reformers have been hand in glove with Paris and so have been their own "assimilationists." But it has certainly taken on a kind of counterpart to the old marabouts, namely party functionaries pretending to possession of knowledge and authority that, it is alleged, they do not in fact possess. Just as the charge of *shirk* was the stick used by the old *'ulama* to belabor the *murabtin* and stake their own claim to a monopoly of the religious field, so the discourse on corruption and the "barons of the FLN" has been used by the new *'ulama* of the technocracy to delegitimize those whose possession of power preempts and cramps their own.

Like the *murabtin*, the FLN has been mainly rural-based, as both the history of the war of national liberation and, more recently, the 1990 election results made clear.[19] Like Ben Badis and his colleagues, the new *'ulama* have been urban-based. Hamrouche and Brahimi, not to mention Hamrouche's patron Abdelhamid Mehri, are all from the urban society of the Constantinois. And like the first *islah*, the second *islah* has not been hostile to France in the political sphere, quite the contrary. But because what it has been preaching, monetarist economic liberalism, has had no nationally or locally legitimate cultural content unlike the Arabo-Islamic content of the Badisiyya's message it has itself been extremely vulnerable to delegitimization unless this shortcoming is compensated for.

The party functionaries whom (together with their allies in the administration and, for that matter, the army) the reformers have been out to destroy have been precisely that element disposed to employ a populist rhetoric and able to mobilize elements of a popular following; and it is they who have been the authors of the nationalistic counter-discourse by means of which they have sought to delegitimize the reformer wing of the technocracy as the ideological spokesmen of Hizb França, "the Party of France," France's fifth column.[20] On their own, the reformers had no defense against this charge, because it contained too much truth for comfort. They could not realistically hope to counter their critics' ploy of playing to the populist gallery with nationalist slogans. But the populist gallery matters in Algerian politics, and could not be left in the hands of the reformers' enemies indefinitely, if the reformers were ever to get anywhere. Which is where, in the reformers' view of things, the Islamists came in.

The adoption of doctrinaire economics thus translated the interests and impatience of the most ambitious elements of the technocracy in the first instance, and that of the Chadli presidency in the second instance. For Chadli, too, had unquestionably become frustrated and impatient with the political environment of the FLN state over which he presided, even more than Boumediene had before him. And just as Boumediene began to show signs of impatience, notably in a series of combative speeches in the summer of 1974[21] but also in his speech to the UGTA congress in early 1978, which launched the mobilization for the long-awaited Party Congress at which, it was rumored, "le grand nettoyage" would at last be undertaken, so too Chadli's impatience finally burst out in the extraordinary speech of September 19, 1988,[22] which gave the signal for the onset of the crisis that exploded in the riots a fortnight later.

In other words, the adoption by the Algerian presidency of the utopian blueprints and doctrinaire policies proffered by its technocrats has occurred when it can neither see light at the end of the tunnel nor endure life in the tunnel any longer, and has made up its mind to make a dash for it, by organizing a crusade against its former allies turned albatrosses and implicating public opinion in this crusade. Which, in the Chadli presidency's view of things, is where the Islamists came in.

The Islamists were to be unleashed, legalized, and encouraged to take over the populist constituency in Algerian politics, by employment of the most hair-raising rhetoric if need be, in order to deny access to this constituency to Chadli's national-populist enemies within the FLN. The latter were not necessarily opponents of sensible measures of reform as such, but were certainly the political enemies of Chadli & Company and of the reformers' faction with which Chadli was now identified.

And so the 1989 pluralist constitution was produced like a rabbit out of a hat and imposed with minimal public discussion, the FIS was formed in an equally precipitate fashion, the law on political associations was amended out of recognition in order to enable the government to legalize the FIS against the spirit of the constitution,[23] and numerous other moves were made and steps taken by Chadli, Mehri, and Hamrouche to play the Islamist card in their own interests, as I have detailed elsewhere.[24] How this audacious maneuver came to grief is another story, which I have also recounted elsewhere.[25]

What remains to be explained is why the Islamists should have allowed themselves to be used in this way. For there is no reason to suppose that they meekly agreed to be manipulated in this fashion. On the contrary, I do not doubt that the Islamists in general, and the leaders of the FIS in particular, considered that they were the autonomous authors of their own, independent, political strategy. This strategy was nonetheless a strategy of political opportunism that exposed them to the most extraordinary manipulation, and it too came, deservedly, to grief.

THE STRATEGY OF THE FIS, OR ALGERIAN ISLAMISM'S "OPTION OPPORTUNISTE"

By "opportunism" in this context, I mean the deliberate choice of a political strategy that involves departing from, or putting into prolonged abeyance, constitutive principles of the political outlook of the actors in question. The world is full of politicians who behave in an opportunist fashion for so much of the time that the term does not really apply to them at all; they are merely unprincipled, or flexible, or representative (depending on the observer's point of view). But, when a political movement based on an elaborate, radical, and exacting doctrine deliberately departs from well-established principles intrinsic to this doctrine that have previously received substantial expression in its activity, one may well describe this as an instance of political opportunism in the full sense of the term. (I should perhaps emphasize that I intend no value judgment here.) The opportunism of the FIS consisted essentially in its populism and its posturing as the lineal successor and rightful heir (son, *fils*, FIS) of the historic FLN of 1954–1962, the heroic FLN of the national liberation war. Its populism involved a compromise *par le bas*, that is, a compromise with the people. Its posturing as the heir to the "true" FLN's mantle involved a compromise *par le haut,* that is, a compromise with the Algerian state and in particular with the Chadli regime, but more generally with the very idea of the FLN in short, a compromise with precisely those forces it claimed to be committed to overthrowing.

A) The Populist Compromise

The compromise with the people can be regarded as opportunist in nature in two distinct but closely related respects.

First, the decision to form the FIS as a political party, instead of simply as a pressure group canvassing its ideas with all and sundry, committed the Islamists to an electoralist strategy for expanding their audience and influence. But the mobilization of electoral support inevitably involved the FIS in articulating popular sentiments that had nothing to do with, or were frankly contrary to, Islamist doctrine, and in party political controversies that had little or nothing to do, or were frankly at odds, with the Islamist movement's primary concerns.

The two most spectacular examples of this were the mobilization over the United Nations' war against Iraq in January 1991, and the mobilization over unfair electoral laws in May-June 1991. In the former, the FIS abandoned the traditional Islamist hostility towards "Godless" Baathism altogether and took a militantly pro-Baghdad position in order to keep a grip on its popular constituency.[26] In the latter, the decision to opt for confrontation with the authorities represented the triumph within the FIS leadership of those *opposed to* proposals for political unity with the other Islamist parties, that is, with the Al-Haraka li-Mujtama' Islami (Hamas) and the Harakat al-Nahda al-Islamiyya (Mouvement de la Nahda Islamique or MNI).[27]

Second, the decision to found a party committed to a populist strategy meant that the mobilization of electoral support on a demagogic basis very largely replaced the original Islamist enterprise of religious conversion. As such, the FIS unquestionably represented a deviation, at least to some extent (there is room for debate here), from the path of the Islamic *da'wa*, the *religious* mission of conversion by means of which the embattled *umma* of true believers might reclaim their wayward fellows from the snares of the new *jahiliyya*.

A question that deserves to be asked is whether the FIS really changed the outlook of any of the hundreds of thousands of young men it briefly precipitated into millenarian political activity. There is no evidence that it did. It mobilized them against external enemies—the "thieves" of the FLN, and so on—but it did not really mobilize them against *themselves*, against their own fascination with Western materialism, their own attachment to dubious (as in unorthodox, essentially because un-Puritan) Algerian traditions (such as *sha'abi* and *ra'i* music), their own lapses from Islamic precepts in matters of morals, and the weakening of their faith. It channeled their frustration and anger against the FLN, but did so by articulating this anger in very much the same ideological terms as those in which it was already being articulated before the FIS entered the picture. These terms were a mixture of entirely traditional Muslim conceptions of good and evil and the equally traditional vocabulary of the code of honor. The main change the FIS effected was not in the terms or content of the outlook of its populist constituency, but in the target of its wrath.

The target of its wrath in October 1988 was Chadli & Company.[28] But from the moment the FIS got a grip on urban youth in mid- to late 1989 onward, the target of its wrath was "the thieves of the FLN" in general, while Chadli's own position no longer came in for sustained attack. Anger previously focused quite precisely on Chadli himself and his closest associates was being deftly deflected onto a much broader and more abstract target, the FLN, and, insofar as it focused on particular elements within the FLN, it focused on Chadli's enemies. In other words, the FIS was delivering what Chadli and the reformers wanted it to deliver, at the expense of the Islamist movement's former priorities and principles.

B) The Frontist Compromise

How many Islamist political parties elsewhere in the Muslim world have called themselves "fronts"? As far as I am aware, only one, the National Islamic Front of Hassan Turabi in the Sudan. Elsewhere, the term "front" has invariably been associated with the Arab nationalist tradition,[29] not the Islamist one (and the name of the Sudanese movement suggests a concern to enlist the former in the service of the latter).

The Algerian Islamists, when they entered the party political arena, could have employed the usual terminology to describe themselves: *haraka* (movement), *jam'iyya* (association), *jama'a* (group), and so on. Two groupings within Algerian Islamism, Sheikh Abdallah Djaballah's Islamic Renaissance Movement (Harakat al-Nahda al-Islamiyya, known in French as the Mouvement de la Nahda Islamique, MNI) and Sheikh Mahfoud Nahnah's Movement for an Islamic Society (Al-Haraka li-Mujtama' Islami, generally known as Hamas) did just that. But the element of Algerian Islamism that was in a hurry to go places described itself as the Islamic Salvation Front (Al-Jabha al-Islamiyya lil-Inqadh). Its French acronym, FIS, is of course pronounced in exactly the same way as the French word for son, *fils*. And in Algeria, where making a play on words between French and Arabic is a permanent part of popular oral culture, this particular play on words was universally understood and appreciated: the FIS was the offspring of the FLN, a real chip off the old block and no mistake, *and it wanted everyone to know this, and to give it credit for the fact*.

This posture, as heir to the FLN's mantle, involved the Islamists who set up the FIS in accepting the historic legitimacy of the original or "true" FLN of 1954–1962 as exceeding or outweighing that of Ben Badis's Association of Algerian Muslim 'Ulama, which as we have noted was founded in 1931. By giving precedence to 1954 over 1931, the FIS was implicitly accepting the moral precedence of the Front over the Association and thus of the *mujahid* over the *'alim*.

This represented a massive deviation from, if not a straightforward negation or inversion of, the Islamist movement's original perspectives and purposes. A major impulse behind the original inception of Islamist criticism of the FLN state had been the *'ulama*'s hostility to the fact that the revolution had catapulted hundreds if not thousands of men they regarded as gun-toting illiterates into positions of power and had thereby turned the world upside-down at the expense of "the men of learning and authority," that is, themselves. In consequence, a major theme of Islamist agitation prior to 1989 had been the playing up of the significance of the Badisiyya, the movement of cultural and religious renaissance of the 1930s and 1940s, as the really profound and decisive phase of Algerian anti-colonialism, and the playing down of the war of national liberation as a superficial and merely political sequel to the reformist *'ulama*'s activity.[30] With the rise of the FIS, Algerian Islamism implicitly but unmistakably abandoned this fundamental premise of its previous criticism of the FLN state.

Moreover, this change deflected the Islamist movement from mobilizing popular electoral support on the basis of its most substantive and well-grounded criticism of the FLN state, namely the extent to which it was characterized by arbitrary government, or *government unbound by law*. There can be little doubt that it was a widespread exasperation with this state of affairs that underlay the popular receptivity to the Islamist message in the 1970s and early 1980s.[31] It is true, of course, that the FIS continued to insist on the importance of the *shari'a* (Islamic law) in its political project. But the regular, indeed ritualistic, invoking of the need for *shari'a* by the FIS was arguably a different affair from that of its predecessors. In reality, the *shari'a* was invoked as the part standing for the whole, as the keystone of the radiant vision of the *dawla islamiyya* conceived and presented in FIS discourse in entirely millenarian terms. And in the process, the reasoned case for the *shari'a* as an intelligible system of law offering a practical and functional answer to the problem of arbitrary government was almost entirely shelved.

These were the main elements of the political opportunism in which the Algerian Islamist movement engaged in the course of its fatal essay in party political activism. It can be seen that they involved a very substantial compromising of the movement's original principles. In view of the eventual outcome, there is a strong case for the view that the FIS adventure has been a catastrophic mistake for Algerian Islamism in the long run, insofar as its original purposes were taken seriously. What disposed the Islamist movement to compromise itself in this fashion, and make this catastrophic mistake?

The answer lies in the fact that the Algerian Islamist movement has been a far more superficial affair than virtually all its Western observers have supposed, and a far more Algerian affair than its own members and even leaders have realized. And its very Algerianness has been the source of its most debilitating weaknesses as well as its superficial dynamism.

ORCHESTRATED MANEUVERS IN THE DARK, OR THE ORIGINS OF A SELF-DEFEATING OPPORTUNISM

The populist compromise in which Algerian Islamism engaged, through the agency of the FIS, was predicated on an axiom and an impulse. The decision to adopt a populist strategy would not have been taken had the founders of the FIS, perceived the urban mass as fundamentally unreceptive to their message. But they did not perceive the urban mass as unreceptive. They perceived it as extremely receptive. "Le peuple est musulman au fond" was the essential premise of the venture, and it was inevitable that they should think this, because this axiom is a necessary article of faith for the movement as a whole.

What this meant is that the Islamist movement was operating with a profoundly unrealistic view of the Algerian people. It was assuming that the people could be won to the Islamist cause very easily, by a bit of well-judged populist demagogy combined with organizational dynamism. The people certainly were won very easily to the FIS, but because the actual content of the FIS's message was hybrid and alloyed in the extreme, this did not mean that the people had been won to the project and worldview of radical Islamism in any substantial and enduring sense. The FIS made at least as many concessions to the people as the people made to the Islamist outlook. And what was won so easily could be lost equally easily.

This unrealistic and above all superficial view of the Algerian people was a natural corollary of the fact that the Algerian Islamist movement throughout the 1980s was essentially relaying the message from the East. It was relaying an ideological import. The message from the East was not Algerianized by the sustained reflections of an Algerian thinker. It is a striking fact about Algerian Islamism that there has been no Algerian Ghannouchi, let alone an Algerian Qutb or an Algerian al-Mawdudi or an Algerian Khomeini. And it is another striking fact about Algerian Islamism that in its most ambitious political enterprise it did not base itself upon the outlook and thinking of the one truly original and impressive Islamic thinker that Algeria has produced since Ben Badis, Malek Bennabi.[32] And because the message brought into the country on the wind from the East was not Algerianized, the frustrated Algerian intellectuals who took up this latest Middle Eastern fashion were thereafter operating with an abstract vision of the people, in which wishful thinking held sway.

So much for the axiom. The impulse cannot be described without giving offense, for which I apologize in advance, but the truth is revolutionary. An Algerian proverb is, "Dès qu'il entend le tambour, l'ancien musicien remue ses épaules."[33]

The founders and leaders of the FIS were functioning in accordance with their own impulses, that is, characteristically Algerian impulses, in merely relaying an ideological import in an almost entirely unreflecting manner and only modifying the content of this import for tactical reasons in the context of engaging in a bit of populist opportunism predicated upon wishful thinking. The reasons for this state of affairs cannot be described here in a way which would do justice to them. But it should be noted that Malek Bennabi himself described, and deplored, the tendency among Algerians to pick up cultural imports in a wholly eclectic manner in which a kind of cultural snobbery played a large motivating part, and what was true of cultural imports from France and more generally the West when he wrote in the 1950s has also been true of cultural and ideological imports from the Middle East in more recent times.

The superficial political successes of Algerian Islamism were never the hard-earned political fruit of an original work of sustained reflection on Algerian society and history, and for this reason alone it has always been unreasonable to suppose that the Algerian Islamists would ever come to power in their own right.

The "frontist" compromise, that is, the compromise both with senior elements of the FLN state (Chadli, Mehri, Hamrouche, and the reformers) and with fundamental elements of the very idea of the FLN, also has its origin in a necessary axiom and an ingrained impulse. The necessary axiom is that the historic FLN of 1954–1962 was the artisan of, above all, a jihad, that the revolution was first and foremost an Islamic affair, and that Islam was not only the basis on which the people were mobilized for the war but fundamental to the FLN's purpose. This axiom is false. It willfully denies that the real purpose of the historic FLN was the entirely modernist purpose of constituting Algeria into a sovereign nation-state and the Algerian people into a nation, and that the attitude toward Islam of the leaders of the FLN was an essentially instrumental one.

The Islamist movement cannot accept the truth of this matter without acknowledging to itself and admitting to the Algerian people that its true project of establishing an Islamic state, assuming that it is in earnest about this, is profoundly at odds with that of the historic FLN and its legacy. They therefore entertain a vision of the revolution which is profoundly mistaken, and it is in virtue of this misconceived interpretation of the revolution that they are inclined to posture as, or mistake themselves for, its rightful heirs.

The Islamists' attitude to the revolution makes it inevitable that, for all the FIS's aggressive rhetoric about "les voleurs," and so on, Algeria's Islamists have been bound to negotiate their political relationship to the FLN state. If the revolution was Islamic, and the historic FLN an affair of good Muslims, then the state that was born, very directly, of this revolution and set up by members of the historic FLN *cannot* be a wholly bad thing. And at no point have Algeria's Islamists actually *behaved* as if they really thought it was.[34]

The fact is that it has been ideologically, sentimentally, but also practically impossible for Algeria's Islamists not to deal with the FLN state, and they have necessarily been doing so ever since 1962. This state of affairs has meant that the Islamist movement has been seriously handicapped in its relationship to the state. Its impatience to exert influence has left it wide open to being manipulated. Only if it had decided to forego its influence over policy in the present for influence over the society in the long term, and adopted a strategy that put the business of sustained historical reflection at the top of its agenda and left lobbying and populism to the other tendencies in Algerian politics, could the Islamists have made themselves intellectually and morally independent of the FLN state as the preliminary to making themselves eventually a power in the society of which the state would have to take durable account.

But they did not have it in them to take the long view. And so they leaped at the offer which was made them by Chadli and the reformers, and were quite naturally implicated in the latter's defeat. It is the incoherence of the post-Chadli High State Committee regimes, rather than the Islamists' own resources, which has accounted for the subsequent recovery in their fortunes through the armed rebellion, but that is another story.

Notes

1. For a discussion of the role of religion in the Algerian state, see my articles: "The Algerian Bureaucracy," in Talal Asad and Roger Owen, eds. *Sociology of "Developing Societies": The Middle East* (London: Macmillan, 1983), pp. 95–114; "Radical Islamism and the Dilemma of Algerian Nationalism," *Third World Quarterly*, vol. 10, no. 2 (April 1988): 556–89; "The Algerian State and the Challenge of Democracy," *Government and Opposition*, vol. 27, no. 4 (Autumn 1992): 433–54; "From Radical Mission to Equivocal Ambition: The Expansion and Manipulation of Algerian Islamism, 1979–1992," in Martin E. Marty and R. Scott Appleby, eds., *Accounting for Fundamentalisms: The Dynamic Character of Fundamentalist Movements,* The Fundamentalism Project, American Academy of Arts and Sciences (Chicago, Ill.: University of Chicago Press, 1993, forthcoming).

2. The FIS published an outline manifesto of demands in a list of fifteen points in April 1990 (published in *El Moudjahid,* April 20-21, 1990). Point 9 refers to the government"s

"ignoring the claims of the workers" but only insofar as the latter are a cause of "the social malaise and disturbances," and the only demand formulated by the FIS in this context was for the dissolution of the national trade union. Point 10 invokes "the urgent necessity to put an end to the growing unemployment . . . " but no practical measure is advocated or called for in this connection. Nowhere in this manifesto did the FIS call for the maintenance of price controls or subsidies for basic commodities, an immediate concern of its mass constituency, while the critical problem of housing is not even mentioned.

3. The first of the FIS's fifteen points calls on the government to identify the domains to be subject to reform and to propose a calendar for the reform process in stages; in other words, the principle of the reforms is taken for granted and accepted without any conditions, the demands raised being such as would cause the government no embarrassment whatever.

4. Abdelhamid Mehri was ambassador to France from 1984 onward until he replaced Mohamed Cherif Messaadia as head of the Permanent Secretariat of the Central Committee of the Party of the FLN in the wake of the riots of October 1988; he was subsequently elevated to the post of General Secretary of the Party (previously held by President Chadli) by a meeting of the Central Committee on December 14, 1988. A long-standing political ally of Chadli, he contracted a marriage alliance with him in the course of 1989 (Libération, September 11, 1989). Mouloud Hamrouche was Head of Protocol at the Presidency of the Republic 1979–84 (whence his ironic popular sobriquet, "Monsieur Parapluie"), Secretary-General of the Government 1984–86, and Secretary-General of the Presidency of the Republic 1986–89.

5. In an interview on French radio, reported in Le Monde, January 23, 1990. This statement caused an immense brouhaha in Algeria.

6. Roberts, "The Algerian Bureaucracy."

7. For a discussion of the reform process in its earlier, less dramatic, stages, see my article, "The Algerian Constitution and the Re-structuring of State-capitalism," IDS Bulletin, vol. 18, no. 4 (October 1987): 51–56.

8. Roberts, "The Algerian Bureaucracy."

9. Ibid., where the evidence of and rationale for this are explained in detail.

10. This in itself is not conclusive evidence of collusion between the two men; it is possible that Brahimi was acting independently of Hamrouche, and pursuing a parallel strategy of investing politically in the FIS's electoral enterprise—in short, that the two men were doing similar (and congruent) things for similar reasons, but not in concert.

11. Further evidence of this alliance appeared following the military clampdown on the FIS in the summer of 1991 with the formation of a National Committee of Support for the imprisoned FIS leaders (Comité Nationale de Soutien aux Dirigeants du FIS) on the initiative of Abdelhamid Brahimi and former Minister of Foreign Affairs Dr. Ahmad Taleb Ibrahimi ("Chronologies: 3e trimestre 1991: Algérie," in Maghreb-Machrek, vol. 134 [October-December 1991]: 56); for the support given to the Islamist movement during the 1980s by the then Minister of Religious Affairs Abderrahmane Chibane, see Ahmad Rouadjia, Les frères et la mosquée: Enquête sur le mouvement islamiste en Algérie (Paris: Karthala, 1990), 144 et seq.

12. The most prominent focus of this conflict was the role and prerogatives of the party, an issue that was first broached in the course of the debates over the "enriching" of the National Charter in 1985, although this was by no means the only, or even the main, point at issue.

13. The French and more generally Western media consistently depicted the events in Algeria in terms of the Soviet analogy after the riots of October 1988; see *Le Monde* and especially *Libération*, passim, but also *The Economist* and *The Financial Times*, passim. For a critique of this analogy, see my articles "The Algerian State and the Challenge of Democracy," op. cit., and "The FLN: French Conceptions, Algerian Realities," in George Joffé, ed., *North Africa: Nation, State and Region* (London: Routledge, 1993), pp. 111–41.

14. In the 1970s, the Boumediene regime invariably described its socialistic program as Algeria's "socialist choice" (*l'option socialiste*)"; it is an interesting and politically significant fact that Boumediene's successors have never felt able to describe their departure from socialism and their commitment to free-market economics as Algeria's "capitalist choice," although this is undoubtedly what it has amounted to.

15. Walter Bagehot, *The English Constitution*, with an introduction by R.H.S. Crossman (London: Fontana/Collins, 1963), eleventh impression 1975, pp. 61 et seq.

16. For a discussion of this universe, see my articles "The Algerian Bureaucracy" in Asad and Owen, eds., op. cit., and "Radical Islamism and the Dilemma of Algerian Nationalism," op. cit. See also Mohammed Harbi, *Le FLN: Mirage et réalité* (Paris: Editions J.A., 1980), pp. 377–85, and Bruno Etienne, "Clientelism in Algeria," in Ernest Gellner and John Waterbury, eds., *Patrons and Clients* (London: Duckworth, 1977), pp. 291–307.

17. That is, the movement of the so-called *évolués* led by Ferhat Abbas and Dr. Mohammed Bendjelloul in the *Fédérations des Élus* in the 1920s and 1930s.

18. Ernest Gellner, "The Unknown Apollo of Biskra: The Social Base of Algerian Puritanism," in his book *Muslim Society* (Cambridge: Cambridge University Press, 1981), p. 156.

19. Jacques Fontaine, "Les élections locales algériennes du 12 juin 1990: Approche statistique et géographique," *Maghreb-Machrek*, vol. 129 (July–September 1990): 124–40; Arun Kapil, "Portrait statistique des élections du 12 juin 1990: Chiffres clés pour une analyse," *Les Cahiers de l'Orient*, vol. 23 (Summer 1991): 41–63.

20. See, for example, *Libération*, November 7, 8, 28, 1988.

21. See my article "The Politics of Algerian Socialism" in Richard Lawless and Allan Findlay, eds., *North Africa: Contemporary Politics and Economic Development* (London: Croom Helm, 1984), pp. 5–49.

22. The unprecedentedly provocative character of this speech was well noted by Jean-François Kahn in his article "Algérie: La deuxième révolution," in *L'Evènement du Jeudi*, October 13–19, 1988.

23. For a fuller discussion of this point, see my article in Marty and Appleby, eds., op.cit.

24. Ibid.

25. Ibid.

26. Ibid., but see also my earlier article "A Trial of Strength: Algerian Islamism," in *Islamic Fundamentalisms and the Gulf Crisis*, James Piscatori, ed., The Fundamentalism Project, American Academy of Arts and Sciences (Chicago, Ill.: University of Chicago Press, 1991, pp. 131–54.

27. For a full discussion of this point, see my article in Marty and Appleby, eds., op.cit.

28. Ibid.; see also Naget Khadda and Monique Gadant, "Mots et gestes de la révolte," in *Peuples Méditerranéens*, 52–53 (July-December 1990): 19–24.

29. For example, the various Palestinian factions (the Popular Front for the Liberation of Palestine, PFLP; the Popular Democratic Front for the Liberation of Palestine, PDFLP); the Popular Front for the Liberation of Oman and the Arab Gulf, PFLOAG, in Dhofar; the Front for the Liberation of Occupied South Yemen, FLOSY, and the National Liberation Front, NLF, in South Yemen, and so on.

30. See Rouadjia, op. cit., 147–49.

31. See my article "Radical Islamism and the Dilemma of Algerian Nationalism."

32. Author of *Les conditions de la renaissance algérienne: Problème d'une civilisation* (Paris: Édi-tions du Seuil, 1949); *Vocation de l'Islam* (Paris: Éditions du Seuil, 1954); and other works. For a discussion of Bennabi's earlier influence, see the testimony of Rachid Benaïssa in François Burgat, *L'Islamisme au Maghreb* (Paris: Karthala, 1988), p. 153.

33. "As soon as he hears the drum, the former musician begins to move his shoulders." This saying is the Algerian equivalent of "blood will out" or "blood always tells," and so on, professional musicians (as distinct from poets who sing their poems) being virtually an endogamous caste and traditionally held in low esteem.

34. It is possible that some of the elements now engaged in armed rebellion in Algeria are animated by a root and branch opposition to the state, but it is certain that such ele-ments are a minority, and that the Islamist guerrilla movement, which began in earnest only after the constitutionalist strategy of the FIS had come to grief with the army's inter-ruption of the electoral process in January 1992, would be prepared to end its armed campaign if political terms acceptable to it were offered. It should not be forgotten that, in the postcolonial Maghrib, armed rebellion has frequently been a conscious tactic in a group's negotiation or renegotiation of its relationship to the state. See Ernest Gellner, "Patterns of Rural Rebellion in Morocco during the Early Years of Independence," in *Arabs and Berbers,* Ernst Gellner and Charles Micaud, eds. (London: Duckworth, 1972), pp. 361–74, and Jeanne Favret, "Traditionalism through Ultra-modernism," in Gellner and Micaud, op. cit., 307–24.

9

The Al-Nahda Movement in Tunisia: From Renaissance to Revolution

Michael Collins Dunn

The Al-Nahda ("renaissance" or "revival") movement in Tunisia, originally called the Islamic Tendency Movement (MTI), provides a case study of an Islamic revival movement with a political agenda that, in its early years, appeared to be one of the most moderate in the Arab world. Today, however, its leadership is in prison or in exile, charged with plotting to overthrow the government and assassinate the president of the republic, and its followers are displaying a very low profile. There has been no near-uprising comparable to that which followed the suppression of the Islamic Salvation Front in neighboring Algeria. (Later in this essay, I will reflect on the differences between the Algerian and Tunisian cases.) To some this is a sign that the Tunisian government, overreacting to the Islamist challenge, has resorted to repressive measures against an essentially benign movement. In this study I intend in no way to defend repression or to excuse imprisonment without due process. But I do believe that the evidence suggests that the Al-Nahda movement has itself evolved or been driven toward a far more radical and revolutionary position than it originally appeared to hold. This has led to a splitting from the party by the more evolutionist, less confrontational wing of the party once led by 'Abd al-Fattah Mourou—the "moderates" as some might call them—while the party leader, Rached Ghannouchi, has moved to a far more radical rhetoric than he displayed in his earlier career.

Although journalistic coverage of the phenomenon usually called "Islamic fundamentalism" tends to group not only various movements together but also the secular regime that are their targets, those who have a greater familiarity with the subject will appreciate that Islamic revivalism is not a homogeneous phenomenon. Nor is its political incarnation: Islamist political movements range from those that are willing to play a role within the system as they do in Jordan and once did in Egypt, to those seeking to topple governments by force. Modern Islamist movements run the gamut from mere expressions of revivalist piety to quasi-messianic movements seeking to bring about apocalyptic confrontation: there are far more of the former than the latter.

A Note on Categories

I believe that there is grave danger in viewing Islamic revivalism as always and everywhere a threat to Western interests. It is not always even a threat to existing regimes, and where it is it may represent a legitimate expression of democratic dissent from authoritarian leadership, or the resentment of the mass of society against the established perquisites of a narrow elite.

On the other hand, there are some Islamist political movements that adopt a revolutionary, confrontational posture that makes it virtually impossible to incorporate them into even the most liberal body politic. These usually have adapted in some form the religious principle first associated with the Egyptian thinker Sayyid Qutb (1906–1966). Originally a relatively mainstream Muslim Brotherhood leader, years of imprisonment helped radicalize his position. Sayyid Qutb originated the concept of identifying the secular state as *jahili,* or comparable to the state of the Arab tribes before Islam. By extension, his followers and other radicals have argued that it is not only justifiable but imperative to wage jihad against such societies or regimes. Many modern radical Islamist movements have also resurrected the old Kharijite argument that jihad in the sense of war for the faith is a pillar of Islam or at any rate a religious duty. The impossibility of waging jihad against fellow Muslims is gotten around by insisting that secularists are not in fact Muslims. This doctrine, by no means held by all Islamists but only by a radical fringe, is often called *takfir,* proclaiming one's enemies, even if they are Muslims themselves, as *kuffar* (unbelievers).

Certainly in its earlier history the movement which became Al-Nahda did not belong to this radical fringe. Rather, it proclaimed itself a liberal, democratic reformist movement seeking to break the monopoly on power of Habib Bourguiba.

AL-NAHDA: ORIGINS

The Tunisian authorities, convinced that Al-Nahda today is a genuine threat to the state, argue that the movement has always been a radical one seeking to topple the government. They point to the fact that an underground parallel movement did exist at the same time as the overt movement, apparently modeled on the "secret apparatus" (*jihaz sirri*) of the original Egyptian Muslim Brotherhood. But there are problems here, since even the Tunisian Interior Ministry's own charges do not indicate a secret organization in existence prior to the mid- to late 1980s.

The origins of the movement, in fact, were very different from those of most radical groups, stemming from moderate groups and magazine staffs and gradually coalescing into a broader political movement. Most of the later leaders of Al-Nahda, at least those who were in Tunisia at the time, held links with the Society for the Preservation of the Qur'an, a religious-cultural group that had its first congress in 1971. In 1973, Rached Ghannouchi founded the journal *Ma'rifa*. Both owed their origins to the collapse of the socialist experiments of the 1960s and to a general reaction to the excessive secularism of Bourguiba, particularly in the early years of his presidency.

During the 1970s the Islamic groups in Tunisia grew more political. In 1979, according to Ghannouchi, the "Islamic Group in Tunisia" (*Al-Jama'a al-Islamiyya fi Tunis*) was created. It in turn formed a part of the Movement for Islamic Renewal, a broader coalition of Islamist groups. As the Iranian Revolution intensified its confrontation with the Shah, those with a political agenda in the Tunisian Islamic movements applauded the Iranian developments while others, the so-called "progressive Islamists" associated with Hamida Enneifer and the magazine *15/21*, moved in other directions.[1] The more politically oriented group around Ghannouchi soon organized under the name Islamic Tendency Movement or MTI in its French acronym. Meanwhile the Bourguiba regime cracked down on Islamic groups in the wake of the Iranian Revolution; *Ma'rifa* was suspended in 1979 and *Al-Mujtama'*, which had been founded in 1978, in 1980.

Ghannouchi and Mourou

The two men who were to emerge as the principal leaders of the MTI were very different, a fact that goes a long way to explain the split between them in recent years. Rached Ghannouchi was born in 1941 in a town in Gabès province in southern Tunisia. He received a religious education in the local schools affiliated with the Zitouna system, but no formal advanced religious training beyond the secondary level. As he told Nikki Keddie, "My father was a small peasant. There were no 'ulama in my family; 'ulama were in *rich* families, and I was from a poor family."[2] After teaching for a while in the primary schools, he went to Cairo to study agronomy, and reportedly considered working in Albania. He then studied philosophy at the University of Damascus.

In his university education Ghannouchi was exposed to Western thinkers, as well as the secular nationalism of Syria's Ba'ath. Returning to Tunisia he taught in the secondary schools and became involved in Islamic movements. He himself has made clear that he became interested not only in strict Islamic orthodoxy but also in many of the modernist thinkers of Islam.

'Abd al-Fattah Mourou, the man who for many years was Ghannouchi's number two and secretary-general of the movement, had a contrasting background. He comes from Tunis, not from the poor, neglected south. He comes from an old Tunis family of Andalusian origins (Mourou stems from *moro*), a family with many generations of 'ulama. In addition to being a practicing lawyer he was a well known mosque preacher.

From the beginning, Mourou has sought to deal with the existing government. His external allies for years were the Saudis, and it was in Saudi Arabia that he spent his years of exile from Tunisia. Ghannouchi, by contrast, had closer ties with the Iranian revolutionaries. The two men appear to have represented different constituencies, and in 1981 Ghannouchi was elected "amir" of the movement and Mourou secretary-general. Ghannouchi's wing of the movement appears to have always been more confrontational than Mourou's. Ghannouchi, the outsider rebelling against a system that excludes him, was less eager to seek cooperation with the authorities than Mourou, the product of a traditional religious system and seeking to moderate the excessive secularism of Bourguiba's state.

The MTI and Bourguiba

The MTI attracted considerable support in the early 1980s, drawing support in provincial cities, in the universities (particularly in the science faculties), and elsewhere, and also drawing extensive support from women.[3] Mohamed Elbaki Hermassi, who did the first major study of the supporters of the movement, concluded that the "typical member of the Islamic movement may be described as a young person of over twenty years, born in one of the provincial towns of the country, of a popular background and having received a high level of education without the upward mobility which might lead him to repudiate his origins."[4] While it is not absolutely clear that Hermassi's study was as statistically representative as we might wish, or that the patterns of the early 1980s remain in force today, it is clear that the basis of support of the MTI was comparable to that of other revivalist movements in countries such as Egypt.

During the 1980s, the movement increasingly found itself at odds with Habib Bourguiba. Bourguiba the secularist, the man who took away the Zitouna University's name and drank orange juice publicly during Ramadan, was a natural antagonist. He appears to have been personally convinced that secularism was his major legacy to Tunisia, and that anything that threatened his secularist policies threatened the country's future. As he grew older, he appears to have become more and more intransigent in his attitudes towards resurgent Islamic politics.

Hermassi has shown that between mid-1980 and the spring of 1981, criticism of government programs and agendas increased in Ghannouchi's writings from seventeen percent of his articles to more than sixty percent.[5] In part this no doubt derived from the growing social tensions after the general strike and violence of 1978, combined with the Libyan backed Gafsa raid in 1980 and student troubles in early 1981. Then Prime Minister Mohamed Mzali embarked upon a liberalization campaign in 1981, one that included an opening to the Islamists.

In this period, MTI sought to emphasize its moderate credentials. An official program adopted in 1981 emphasized cultural and religious revivalism, although it also included references to the struggle of the "disinherited masses" against the "dominant forces." But it rejected violence as a means of change.[6]

At the same time, the first clashes between the MTI and the government were beginning. The student unrest of the spring of 1981 had shown some Islamist aspects, and MTI discussion groups were organized on the campuses. In a June press conference, Ghannouchi and

Mourou proclaimed their movement a political force. To the authoritarian Bourguiba, even such an innocent declaration probably seemed to be a thrown gauntlet.

In July an Islamist group attacked and damaged a Club Méditerranée resort. Elsewhere there was an effort to replace the imam of a local mosque. While these may not have been MTI operations, Bourguiba presumably saw MTI as at least the indirect inspiration; Ghannouchi, Mourou, and more than sixty MTI adherents were rounded up in July.

In 1984, after the bread riots of that year and the firing of Interior Minister Driss Guiga, Prime Minister Mzali, still committed to an opening to the MTI and other political opposition groups, found his hand strengthened. On August 3 Ghannouchi and the other MTI leaders still in jail were freed (Mourou had been released earlier). The MTI reorganized, began to take a more public stance, and sought to take advantage of Mzali's efforts at liberalization. Mzali's fall from power in 1986 led to a reversal of fortune, however. (Mzali, still in exile in Europe, now supports Islamist causes.)

Beginnings of Radicalization

Up to this point, certainly, MTI had presented a basic moderation to the world, as its very title "Islamic Tendency Movement" implies. There is no sign of radical, Sayyid Qutb-style denunciations of Muslims as unbelievers. A December 1986 Basic Program of MTI, however, began to show the seeds of radicalism, perhaps a recognition that with the end of the Mzali efforts at liberalization, there was no hope of achieving a share in power while Bourguiba remained in office. This program, or parts of it, has been called by former MTI supporter Ziyad Kreichane, now an opponent, "one of the most dangerous texts in our modern intellectual history."[7] Although its section six addresses the issue of *takfir* by stating that "we do not declare Muslims to be unbelievers," it then goes on to qualify this statement, "except for those who agree with words of unbelief or publicly reject the faith or clearly oppose the Qur'an or interpret it in a way not supported by the grammatical rules of the Arabic language or basically behave in a way that does not support anything but unbelief."[8]

The statement is ambiguous enough that one can argue it is not really an argument for *takfir*. At the same time it links one's Muslim identity with considerably more than the traditional notion that anyone who proclaims the *shahada* should not be called a non-Muslim. Both interpretation of the Qur'an and personal behavior are mentioned as possible means of excluding oneself from the body of believers.

The importance of the statement lies, of course, in how it relates to the implementation of the radical Islamist doctrine of *takfir*. If one declares one's enemies non-Muslims and unbelievers—*kuffar*—one also makes jihad against them permissible or, in the doctrines of some of the more extreme factions, even a duty. While the statement is extremely ambiguous, it is indicative of a radical tendency—perhaps only one faction—within the movement as early as the end of 1986.

Bourguiba Attacks

President Bourguiba was increasingly obsessed with the MTI in his last year in office, though he continued his assaults against other opponents as well. In February 1987 he cracked down on the General Union of Tunisian Students (UGTE), under Islamist control. In March Ghannouchi and thirty-seven other leaders of MTI were arrested. By June there were demonstrations that were broken up with teargas, and the government press published photos of weapons caches allegedly discovered near Tunis.

On August 2, 1987, four hotels in the Sousse and Monastir regions— within Bourguiba's own beloved Sahel, much developed for tourism— were bombed, injuring twelve tourists and a Tunisian. A movement calling itself Islamic Jihad and with alleged Iranian backing was charged. Those accused denied any links with the MTI, and in fact Tunisia broke relations with Iran but never charged MTI involvement. Nevertheless the attack on tourist targets revived fears originally awakened by the attack on the Club Med several years earlier, and any loss of tourist revenues could severely hurt the economy. The attacks in Monastir were no doubt taken especially personally by Bourguiba.

The government crackdown and MTI demonstrations both picked up speed during August. Both the MTI militants and the hotel bombers were tried by a State Security Court. On September 27, seven men were condemned to death. Five of these were in absentia; the two in custody were the hotel bombers who probably were not directly linked to MTI. Ghannouchi was given a sentence of life imprisonment. Mourou, in exile in Saudi Arabia working with the Islamic World League, was given ten years. The three MTI figures condemned to death in absentia were Hamadi Djebali, Salah Karkar, and Ali La'aridh. All were senior MTI figures.

Ben Ali's "Honeymoon," 1987–1989

The sentences infuriated Bourguiba, who wanted more extensive executions, particularly including Ghannouchi, according to reports at the time. He fired Prime Minister Rached Sfar on October 2 and replaced him with Zine Labidine Ben Ali, formerly Interior Minister and a military security man by background. He presumably expected Ben Ali to enforce a tougher crackdown. Bourguiba continued constantly reshuffling the government and party leadership and on November 5 ordered that the MTI members would be retried beginning November 9. On November 7, Ben Ali deposed Bourguiba on grounds of senility.[9]

Ben Ali immediately gave indications that he intended to liberalize Tunisian political life. But he had barely taken power when, on November 23, the newly convened National Security Council announced the arrest of a "First Security Group" (as it later came to be called), including army officers and enlisted men for an Islamist plot to take over the government. At the time, the links of these men with MTI were played down, though in later years they would be much emphasized to show that MTI was plotting against the state even then. In fact, both Mohamed Chammam and Salah Karkar were said to be involved in this plot, and both were MTI militants.

Ben Ali proceeded to de-emphasize some of Bourguiba's secularist measures. The Zitouna University got its name back, official publications carried the Muslim date, and the call to prayer was again broadcast on the radio and television. Large numbers of MTI rank and file, but not the leadership, were released from prison. It was several more months before Ben Ali was ready to release the senior figures. In May of 1988 he freed Ghannouchi as part of a Ramadan amnesty. That fall Mourou returned from his Saudi exile.

In the meantime, there were some signs of a growing radical tendency among the MTI militants not in prison. The government in its 1991–92 prosecution of MTI charged that in March of 1988 a clandestine meeting at Sfax, while Ghannouchi was still imprisoned, set in train the development of the "Special Apparatus" aimed at infiltrating government and security services.

In any event, on April 8, less than a month before Ghannouchi's release, Islamist demonstrators attacked a meeting of the Tunisian Human Rights League in Bardo and injured a pregnant woman lawyer. This led to new government criticism of the Islamists and considerable editorializing.

With the release of the MTI leadership, Ben Ali set the stage for some limited role for the movement in Tunisian political life. Over the coming months it was given considerable freedom, including the right to start a newspaper, *Al-Fajr*, to distribute its publications freely, and to organize its cells in popular quarters.

Ben Ali had called elections for April 2, 1989. Although the new party's law forbade the participation of parties based on religion, Islamist candidates were allowed to run as independents. MTI changed its name to Al-Nahda, removing the word "Islamic" from the movement's title but still not meeting the government's criteria for approval as a party, despite appeals. By choosing the word *nahda*, with its familiar implications of the Arab cultural and national renaissance of the nineteenth and twentieth centuries, the movement sought to downplay its Islamist character. The change did not persuade the authorities, however.

The independent list for the 1989 elections, which was essentially Al-Nahda's list, fielded candidates in 22 districts, competing for 129 of the 141 parliamentary seats at stake. It was the third-largest list running, after those of the ruling Constitutional Democratic Rally (RCD) and the opposition Movement of Democratic Socialists (MDS). Al-Nahda had its own newspaper but lacked access to the mainstream media, radio, or television, of course. Government publications sought to portray it as a threat to such Tunisian landmarks as the personal status laws and the prominent status of Tunisian women.

Although the electoral system helped guarantee that the RCD won every single seat—which seems to have embarrassed the government somewhat—Al-Nahda did win some 14.6 percent of the vote nationwide and in Tunis close to 30 percent. The real figures may have been higher in each case. The MDS, by contrast, hardly won votes at all, discrediting the secular opposition and giving Al-Nahda a credible claim to being the only real political force capable of challenging the RCD.

A certain amount of perspective is necessary here. Al-Nahda remained technically a social movement, not a legal party, since it was based on religion. But it had been allowed to freely run candidates, and while none won, it did better than any other opposition party. It had its own newspaper and an unprecedented ability to organize its constituency. There were obvious parallels to the case of the Muslim Brotherhood in Egypt, which in 1989 was the major opposition force in the Egyptian People's Assembly, even though Egypt, too, banned parties based on religion. The Brotherhood had run on the Socialist

Labor ticket, while Al-Nahda ran as independents, but both had been given a means of expressing their political voice.

Of course, the RCD retained its monopoly, and still does so. Clearly by purely democratic standards Al-Nahda was not given a full participatory chance. But whereas the Egyptian Muslim Brotherhood used its political power to move itself into Parliament, Al-Nahda soon abandoned the electoral game entirely.

Ghannouchi's Self-Exile

What precisely went on in the inner councils of Al-Nahda after the electoral experiment is not clear. But on May 13, 1989, Rached Ghannouchi left Tunisia for Europe, and while it was not immediately obvious, this was to become a deliberate self-exile. (At least until late 1990, there was no legal reason Ghannouchi could not have returned home.)

It has been argued that after Ghannouchi's release from prison in 1988 he held an awkward position: the historic founder and leader had been replaced during his imprisonment by Sadok Chourou as amir. To avoid a duplication of leadership claims, Ghannouchi went abroad. This may be a valid explanation, but others are possible. What remains clear is that Ghannouchi's self-exile marked the real end of cooperation and negotiation between Al-Nahda and the government.

The rhetoric and political activity of Al-Nahda within Tunisia became more extreme, and Ghannouchi's sermons abroad also began to openly challenge the regime more dramatically. There would seem to be two possible readings of this. One might hypothesize that the movement within Tunisia had moved to a more radical position while Ghannouchi was in prison, and that while the moderates like Mourou and perhaps still Ghannouchi himself were able to persuade the leadership to try the electoral experiment, the failure to win seats gave the extreme wing the argument it needed. By this argument, Ghannouchi's subsequent increasing radicalism represented simply following the changing opinions of his own constituency.

The other possible argument is closer to what the Tunisian authorities like to claim, namely that Al-Nahda has always been a radical movement and that the decision of Ghannouchi to go abroad merely marked the beginning of open confrontation. The government claims that in 1989, after the release of the First Security Group prisoners, the full-blown "Secret Apparatus" of Al-Nahda was set up under Mohamed Chammam. More on the Secret Apparatus follows below.

In any event, the tactical decision was one that was to prove a strategic mistake, for the increasing radicalization of the movement, the lack of a leader left in Tunisia with the charismatic force of Ghannouchi, and the growing confrontation with the state ultimately led to what appears at this stage to be the destruction of the movement as an above-ground organization.

During the rest of 1989, during the period the government claims the Secret Apparatus was being organized and starting its efforts to infiltrate the military and security forces, Al-Nahda's more traditional leaders continued their political activities, Mourou, for example, issuing a critique of the government's educational reforms.

The year 1990 brought Iraq's invasion of Kuwait and the U.S.-sponsored coalition buildup in Saudi Arabia. The Tunisian street clearly opposed the U.S. intervention, even if it did not fully support Saddam Hussein. Ben Ali did not seek to move Tunisia in directions opposed by the street, however, and may thus have blocked Al-Nahda's efforts to use the Gulf crisis as a means of enhancing its strength. Though it sought to organize some of the demonstrations, the fact that the government did not oppose these made it difficult to use the confrontation effectively.

There were other problems. Mourou and some others in the movement had long had close ties to Saudi Arabia, and the Saudis were believed to be a major source of funding. Despite the popularity in some radical circles of the occupation of Kuwait, Mourou was careful not to criticize Saudi Arabia.

Not so Ghannouchi. In a widely circulated letter, characterized by some as an official message but by Al-Nahda spokesmen as a private communication, Ghannouchi denounced the Western intervention and essentially argued that any regime which invites non-Muslims to Muslim soil, and particularly to the holy places of Arabia, forfeits the right to be considered Muslim.[10] This seems to be an extension of the idea of *takfir* to the national level: the Saudis have invited the Americans in, and are thus unworthy of the name of Muslim; Ghannouchi specifically calls on Muslims to rise up and struggle against the Western presence on Islamic soil. Spokesmen claimed that Ghannouchi's message was a private one and his own opinion; Mourou argued that since he was out of the country, Ghannouchi was no longer leader of Al-Nahda, though the movement's own newspaper continued to refer to him as such.[11]

While the Gulf crisis was deepening, and perhaps as a result of the intensified feelings, Al-Nahda involvement in violence appears to have been stepped up, although perhaps only by the clandestine wing. In November 1990 a group was charged with stealing explosives. Two weeks later a "Second Security Group" was rounded up, including some military men. In late December a number of Al-Nahda leaders were arrested, and at the end of the year *Al-Fajr* was suspended. Then, in February 1991, the RCD Party Coordinating Committee office in Bab Souika, in central Tunis, was attacked. Two guards were covered with gasoline and set alight. One died; the other remained in a coma.

Mourou's Departure

The effect of the brutality was not only to shock public opinion. Three weeks later, on March 7, 1991, 'Abd al-Fattah Mourou issued a statement to the effect that he, Fadhel Beldi (a former acting leader of the movement) and Benaissa Demni were "freezing" their membership in Al-Nahda because of the use of violence in the Bab Souika attack. Mourou announced that he still sought dialogue with the government and denounced Ghannouchi and the in-country leadership for having chosen the path of violence. It is true that the toll of the Bab Souika attack was small compared to some Islamist-related attacks in other countries, but in Tunisia's generally nonviolent political culture, it marked a turning point. Mourou's split strongly suggested that the movement had decided on violent confrontation. The government was soon to try to make a case proving just that.

The Plot Charge

On May 22, 1991, Interior Minister Abdallah Kallel announced a major roundup of Al-Nahda supporters. He also charged that Al-Nahda had created a Secret Apparatus aimed at infiltrating the Armed Forces, National Guard, police, and other institutions. According to the government's claims, the Secret Apparatus was headed by Mohamed Chammam. An elaborate organizational chart was published.

There have been many observers who doubt some or all the details of the plot as charged by the government, and certainly one may raise questions about the interrogations that resulted in some of the testimony and confessions. However, I believe that there is enough external evidence of a new commitment to confrontation on the part of Al-Nahda in 1989–91 (much of it outlined in general earlier) to lead to a conclusion that at least the general outlines of the "plot" are credible.

In a press conference, Interior Minister Kallel outlined the government's basic case: the decision to use force to seize power was adopted in 1988, when Sadok Chourou became amir during the Sfax meeting while Ghannouchi was still in prison. The actual setting up of the Special Apparatus—*jihaz khass*, clearly echoing the *jihaz sirri* of the original Muslim Brotherhood—took place under Mohamed Chammam in 1989. A five-phase plan to seize power was set in motion as follows:

Phase I: Distribution of brochures, extensive use of Islamic graffiti.

Phase II: Intensification of marches and demonstrations.

Phase III: Attacks against individuals and the security forces and party headquarters.

Phase IV: Demonstrations in the universities and secondary schools, aimed at provoking the regime to open fire or to jail large numbers of demonstrators.

Phase V: Had two steps, a civilian and a military one: The civilian step included agitation of the populace, organized civil disobedience, and use of suicide operations against key objectives, preparing for the military step, in which the regime would turn to the army to end the disorders, at which point Al-Nahda cells within the army would use it to seize power.[12]

Government-provided evidence included the testimony of an army major and other documentation.

Subsequently on September 28, the government announced yet another major development: a charge that Al-Nahda elements had arranged to acquire a Stinger missile from Afghanistan via Algeria, and intended to use it to shoot down President Ben Ali's aircraft. Other attacks on key government and party figures were aimed at creating a leadership vacuum.

The trials on these charges took place in 1992. Although the government's case was derided by some, and there were questions about how some of the confessions were obtained, the trials were public. In contrast with the public tension that surrounded the trials of the FIS leadership in Algeria, Tunisians went about their daily business and foreign observers were invited to the trials.

This is not meant to deny that there were irregularities or that the state security trials were fair or fully respectful of the defendants' rights. They were not. The case may have been exaggerated and the degree to which the Al-Nahda leadership were personally involved in some of the plots was not always proven thoroughly. But the government did seem to demonstrate, at least to the satisfaction of this writer, that the plots existed. They may have been, in part, the revolutionary romantic fantasies of true believers, but there was an organized effort to carry them out.

In the wake of the trials, Al-Nahda has lost much of its visibility. Unlike Algeria, there is no evidence of continuing violence; in fact, virtually no sign of even low-grade resistance. Economic prosperity and a general disgust with Al-Nahda's use of violence in Bab Souika may explain the apparent lack of continuing confrontation. Mourou's efforts to create a moderate Islamist party have come to nothing so far.

None of this is meant to suggest that the Tunisian government has eliminated its Islamist challenge forever. President Ben Ali won the support of most of the other political parties in his crackdown, and there will be an electoral reform in place by the 1994 elections, one that should bring opposition members into Parliament. Whether a moderate Islamist party (such as Mourou wants) is to be allowed to emerge is uncertain, but seems unlikely at this writing.

TUNISIA AND THE ALGERIAN CASE: SOME REFLECTIONS

This analysis is not intended to forecast the future, but rather to analyze the past. At least the superficial situation appears to suggest that the results of Tunisia's crackdown on Al-Nahda are far different from the results of Algeria's intervention to prevent the election of the Islamic Salvation Front (FIS).

Al-Nahda is frequently bracketed with FIS. Indeed the two movements have many characteristics in common, including close cooperation between their leaders at various times in the past. Since Algeria and Tunisia also share some societal characteristics in common (both have been among the most avowedly secularist Arab countries, and both were deeply influenced by French culture and values), there has been a tendency to see the movements as essentially equivalent and therefore to assume that the developments in one country may be somehow extrapolated to the developments of the other.

This tendency has been most pronounced among journalists, who often write paragraphs along the lines that "Islamic fundamentalism is challenging the secular governments of Algeria, Tunisia, and Egypt," sometimes adding Jordan for good measure, though political Islam in Jordan is very much part of the system. Academic analysts generally discount such overgeneralization. But there is still a tendency to somehow equate FIS and Al-Nahda and, by extrapolation, to equate the situation in Algeria with that in Tunisia. This often takes the form of presuming that the present situation in Algeria, which at this writing might well be described as a prerevolutionary one if not an outright civil war, could spread to Tunisia in the short term.

I believe that Al-Nahda provides a useful case study of a political Islamist movement that began with a relatively moderate agenda and has, over time and for various reasons, moved to a radical, revolutionary position. At least some elements aligned with FIS have done so as well. Both have been subjected to harsh government crackdowns, FIS in the wake of its apparent victory in the 1991 elections, Al-Nahda after being charged with plotting to overthrow the government and assassinate the President of Tunisia. Both movements have been officially silenced at home.

It is worth emphasizing several differences between the two cases, however. The first may seem obvious to Maghrib specialists, but deserves to be repeated: Tunisia and Algeria, despite some superficial resemblances, are very different countries.

Algeria is three times as populous as Tunisia, and its economic situation has been disastrous for years. By contrast, after a period of severe economic strains in the late 1980s—drought, locusts, and low oil prices being among the causes—Tunisia has enjoyed some success at restructuring its economic system to encourage investment, and at sustaining a growth rate of 3 percent or so, sometimes much higher. The better economic situation certainly has relieved some stresses.

Tunisian society has long been more open than Algeria's was before 1988, despite the lack of an effective opposition in Parliament. The sudden opening up of Algerian society without restraint—dozens of political parties and newspapers were suddenly legalized after years of tight party control—had no parallel in Tunisia.

In addition, Ben Ali has to some extent successfully rebuilt the RCD in his own image, maintaining it as major source of patronage. The Algerian FLN had splintered and virtually collapsed upon itself before the 1991 elections. In Tunisia, Ben Ali removed a senile president; in Algeria, it was a senile party that was the problem.

The wrong lessons may also be learned. Some in Tunisia (and Egypt, and elsewhere) consider that the lesson to be learned from Algeria was never allow the Islamists the right to form a party in the first place since they might win. If that is the lesson drawn, the results may be unfortunate.

Al-Nahda's radicalization in recent years cannot be fully explained from the evidence at hand. Perhaps the radical wing of the party always had greater strength than the Mourou wing, or perhaps the jailing of the leadership by Bourguiba led to the emergence of more radical leaders, such as Sadok Chourou, while Ghannouchi was in jail. Certainly Ghannouchi now, in his frequent visits to Khartoum and Tehran, preaches a rather radical form of Islamism. His sermons to his followers are, I believe, a better means of judging his real thinking than his interviews with Western academics. A man who once claimed that he was a strong supporter of democracy now denounces Western democracies on a regular basis.

One may blame Bourguiba's repression, or the crackdown of the government if one chooses. But to claim that Al-Nahda is still basically a movement that seeks to work within the system ignores the evidence of its own actions and statements.

Notes

1. On the early history, see my *Renaissance or Radicalism: Political Islam: The Case of Tunisia's al-Nahda* (Washington, D.C.: The International Estimate, 1992); 'Abd al-Rahim Lamchichi, *Islam et contestation au Maghreb* (Paris: L'Harmattan, 1989); Nikki Keddie, "The Islamist Movement in Tunisia," *The Maghreb Review*, vol. 11, no. 1 (1986), which has useful interviews; and an account by Ghannouchi in "Ghannouchi: Ce qu'il a dit à la police," *Jeune Afrique*, no. 1396, October 7, 1987.
2. Keddie, op. cit., 33–34.
3. The standard study of membership is Mohamed Elbaki Hermassi, "La société tunisienne au miroir islamiste," *Maghreb-Machrek*, no. 103 (1984): 339–46. On women, see Sohayr Belhassen, "Femmes tunisiennes islamistes," in *Annuaire de l'Afrique du Nord*, 1979; Nikki Keddie, op.cit.; Susan Waltz, "Islamist Appeal in Tunisia," *The Middle East Journal*, vol. XL, no. 4 (Autumn 1986), 651–70
4. Hermassi, op. cit., 46–47.
5. Ibid., 48 ff.
6. For the text, see Dunn, op. cit., 31–33.
7. Ziyad Kreichane, "*Min al-izdiwajiyya al-mawdu'iyya ila al-izdiwajiiya al-taktikiyya*," *Al-Maghrib* (Tunis), no. 150 (May 5, 1989): 16.
8. The text quoted here is based on a Xeroxed text of a typewritten Arabic copy carrying the title *Al-Riwayya al-fikriyya wal-manhaj al-usuli li-harakat al-ittijah al-islami*, dated 1987 but apparently written in December 1986.
9. See Dunn, op. cit., 38 ff for a fuller account.
10. "*Wathiqa: Ayy hawl akbar min hadha?*" in *Al-Maghrib* (Tunis), no. 217 (September 21, 1990).

11. See for example, *"Azmat al-khalij tufarriq qiyadat al-haraka," Haqa'iq (Realités)*, Tunis, September 28–October 4, 1990; Mourou's interview in *Al-Maghrib/Le Maghreb*, October 19, 1990 (the Arabic interview is fuller than the French).

12. The account here is based upon the official texts in Arabic and French of Kallel's May 22, 1991, press conference.

Secularism and Nationalism:
The Political Discourse of
'Abd al-Salam Yassin

Emad Eldin Shahin

nalyzing the role of secularism and Islamism in the process of political and social change in today's Morocco is a far more complex issue than contemporary development theory suggests. The theory assumes that religion is a traditional or, at best, a transitional, force that will wither in the process of modernization and growth of rationalism in society. In fact, the experience of the Middle East since the 1970s reveals that religion is becoming an ideological vehicle in the struggle for power. Traditional reassertions are increasingly playing a role in political and social mobilization that is inexplicable in terms of modernization theory and political change. This suggests that the phenomenon of Islamic revival may not be adequately understood or easily analyzed through a secular conceptual framework.

Post-independence Morocco has not publicly declared a secular state model for itself. The monarch, while having traditional, religious, and historical status, is equally comfortable with modern concepts. Religious symbols are invoked by a rationally manipulative monarchy for the purpose of legitimizing the social and political order. They are further used to give political meaning to the process of change to the apolitical and traditional masses, who have not yet assimilated the secular political values. Morocco's model of statebuilding unmistakably reflects the elements of a secular state: liberal orientation, a constitution, parliament, political pluralism, professional organizations, and a modern educational system.

The modernizing model in Morocco has affected civil society by challenging the issues of identity, nation- and state-building, and the relation between traditional and modern society.[1] As will be seen, the confrontation of Islamism and secularism transpires in religious rather than secular terms. Since the Islamic principles are at odds with the secular norms (Islamic *shari'a* not being implemented), religious symbols are used as an ideological articulation to achieve modernizing ends. In this case, a competition of loyalty to the traditional value system occurs between the modernizing polity and the lay leadership of the Islamic movements, which perceive the elites to be divorced in orientation from the rest of the society. These movements are committed to attempting to establish alternative Islamic social and political systems.

In addition to the dilemma of modernity versus authenticity, the issue of effective political participation poses a serious challenge to the current regime. The limited circulation of the political elites, the centrality of the decision-making process and the nature of the political alliances dominating the Moroccan state have all contributed to widespread cynicism and apathy among the population and to the alienation of the elites from the rest of the society.[2] Despite its attempts to expand the levels of political participation, the regime has not effectively renewed or enlarged the circle of political elites or its base of support. A small network of political elites continues to control the dynamics of the political process notwithstanding the emergence of new counter-elites.[3] As a result, there are emerging forces that do not accept the rules of the political game as dictated and practiced by the monarchy.

LEGITIMACY AND THE ISLAMIC REVIVAL IN MOROCCO

Islamic revivalist groups are challenging the policies of the state and its modernization model. Despite differences in orientation and objectives, many of these groups are highly politicized and aim at the reconstruction of the Moroccan polity and society according to Islamic ideals.[4] These activist Islamic groups are critical of the monarchy and its monopolization of religious legitimacy, which it uses to control the official religious institutions and to bolster its status in society.

They consider the hereditary nature of the monarchy as un-Islamic and therefore do not accept the constitutional stature of the king as the Commander of the Faithful nor as the pinnacle of political authority. Similarly, the Islamic groups in Morocco strongly oppose the use of a "superficial" or "ceremonial" Islam by King Hassan. They accuse the Western-educated elites of steering the country toward secular values and Westernization that distance it from Arab and Islamic roots. The Islamists disapprove of the elite orientation that has led to the introduction of a model for social and political change that in essence contradicts the time-honored beliefs and practices of the majority of the Moroccan society. The Islamic groups also identify these elites with political and social corruption. They charge them with the disintegration of the moral values of the society and the spread of secular ideals in the collective consciousness of the Moroccan people.

Though still in no position to pose a direct threat to the stability of the regime, the Islamic groups attract supporters from the different social segments of the traditional and official religious structures, the Sufi orders, and unemployed and young graduates of state-sponsored religious institutions. These groups have also gained a following among the recently urbanized population, students, and educated professionals. Support for the Islamic opposition continues to grow as a consequence of rapid urbanization, which is eroding the traditional base of support of the monarchy.[5]

YASSIN'S APPROACH[6]

One voice that effectively articulates the Islamic discontent is that of 'Abd al-Salam Yassin. Yassin is an Islamic thinker whose writing addresses Morocco and the rest of the Islamic world. His Berber origins have confirmed his commitment to an Islamic framework of reference and religious basis of identity, thus exacerbating his criticism of the modernization model implemented in Morocco since independence. An original intellectual in his own right, Yassin's thought reflects his broad understanding of the various Islamic trends, such as Sufism, Al-Tabligh wal-Da'wa, the Muslim Brotherhood, and the *salafiyya*. In exploring these practices and movements, he combines their most salient elements.

From the Sufis and Al-Tabligh, Yassin emphasizes the issues of socialization, moral education and spiritual preparation. From the Muslim Brotherhood's experience, he stresses the importance of organization, activism, and the sociopolitical dimension of change. Yassin incorporates the *salafi* trend by basing his ideological discussions on the fundamental sources of Islam, the Qur'an and the Sunna.

Yassin adopted terms used by some leading thinkers of the active Islamic movements, particularly Abul Ala' al-Mawdudi and Sayyid Qutb, to describe the contemporary Muslim societies. He employs the concept of "*jahili*" (un-Islamic) in characterizing the present condition of the Moroccan society. This perception has evident political overtones understood in religious terms. It reflects Yassin's activist thought and his idealist commitment to Islamic values. His ideological position also exhibits his deep realization of the crises and conflicts that confront Moroccan society, and the Muslim countries in general.

From the viewpoint of Yassin, "the nation is torn between two worlds, which do not meet in its conscience. However, it wants to reconcile them to preserve its cultural and national values as well as those of human perfection."[7] The discussion of 'Abd al-Salam Yassin's ideas will focus on four main issues: nationalism, secularism, the ruling elites and ideology of development, and the social structure (the role of Berbers and women, in particular). The objectives behind raising these issues are to understand their impact on the legitimacy and stability of the current political regime and to analyze Yassin's conception of sociopolitical change in Moroccan society.

NATIONALISM: AN IMPORTED IDEOLOGY FOR THE STATE

Firmly rooted in Islamic faith, Yassin does not accept the secular forms, linguistic or ethnic, of national identity. He views the evolution of the ideas of secular nationalism in the Arab world as part of a grand Western imperial project that began with Napoleon's invasion of Egypt and ended with the occupation of Palestine. For Yassin, the secular era introduced new ideas into Arab and Muslim culture and worked for the development of a secular national consciousness. Dual identities have emerged within the Arab social order: secular national and Arab-Islamic. The relationship between the two has been characterized by mistrust and confrontation, particularly since the establishment of the Arab system of nation-states and the control of the secular elites over the political and cultural institutions of these countries.[8]

Yassin abhors the marginalization of Islam in contemporary Arab nationalist thought, which considers Islam a product of the Arab heritage and not its basic component. He blames the Christian Arabs for the spread of secular nationalism and their attempt to secularize the Arabic language in the nationalist discourse by stripping it of its Qur'anic content. He also takes umbrage with the secular nationalist thesis that recognizes the Arabic language as the inspiring force behind Islam and the Qur'an rather than acknowledging that it was the faith that raised Arabic to its highest form.

Here, Yassin refers to the intellectual orientation of the Ba'ath Party, which, influenced by the German school of nationalism, glorifies language and race as the major components for national identity.[9] He delineates this vision by analyzing the decadent conditions of pre-Islamic Arab history that were characterized by severe tribal conflicts, unjust practices, and a lack of cultural progress. Islam rather than Arabism instilled human and moral values, eliminated the tribal basis of solidarity and provided the Arabs with a universal message. Yassin warns the secular Arab nationalists that, if Islam is marginalized, the Arabs will not be able to restore their lost power and their culture will continue to decline.[10]

While lodging harsh criticism against the secular Arab nationalists, Yassin sees the possibility of bridging the gap between the Islamic and secular views. He urges them to acknowledge Islamic Arabism as a common ground for mutual understanding and recognition. As Yassin explains, "the loyalty of the Arab nationalists to the Arabic language, in which the Qur'an was revealed, is similar to our [Islamist] loyalty to the Qur'an itself. We both admire this language and consider it a glorious and honorable one. Here we have found a solid ground for dialogue, reconciliation and understanding."[11]

Yassin sees the transplantation of Western concepts and the adoption of Western-inspired "material language" as a real threat to the future of Islam. This process precludes the evolution of an independent Muslim mind. He cautions against learning modern concepts and methodologies without understanding their embedded contents and epistemological basis because they are a furtive means for cultural domination. In his view, this process leads to submission to Western values, philosophies, paradigms, and languages.[12]

Yassin proposes the need to learn the language of the Qur'an as a religious and cultural armor against the taint associated with Western languages of knowledge. He points out the dangers of attempts to secularize the Arabic language under the pretext of its incompatibility with universal rationalism. He emphasizes the significance of Arabic as a tool in the cultural conflict between a Westernizing secular orientation and the Islamic perspective. For Yassin, language is an expression of sovereignty and a means for achieving independence, free will, and technological progress.[13]

To substantiate his views, Yassin juxtaposes the modern concept of nationalism with the Islamic historical experience. The collapse, under foreign and nationalistic pressure, of the Ottoman caliphate, a symbol of the political unity of the Muslim *umma,* ushered in a new phase in Islamic history. For centuries, Islam managed through its universal and humanistic values to preserve the identity and coherence of the Muslim *umma* despite social and ethnic diversity. Modern nationalism, on the other hand, has enhanced the state of fragmentation and disunity among the Arabs and Muslims by emphasizing ethnic, cultural, and linguistic differences.[14]

Acutely aware of the intellectual dilemma of secular nationalism and its inability to provide an indigenous model of development, Yassin harshly criticizes the eclectic nature of the ideologies of the secular Arab nationalists. During the 1950s and 1960s, Yassin recalls, they attempted to synthesize Arabism and secularism as Arab or Islamic socialism. However, at times of crisis, they had to resort to Islam to mobilize their people —as Nasser did during the 1956 crisis. For Yassin, the 1967 defeat marked the collapse of the Arab nationalist project and its intellectual currents, which had regarded Islam only as an "emotional reservoir." A progressive, socialist, and nationalist Islam was required to confront the old image of a feudal, sectarian, and regressive Islamic state.[15]

Islam for Yassin stands against ethnic and territorial identification. It preserves the unity of the various social segments in Arab society and transcends the issues of race, ethnic origin, tribal identification, and geographic boundaries. He therefore rejects nationalism based on race and language as an alternative to the Islamic state and introduces a new definition in conformity with Qur'anic concepts. He proposes a humanistic religious perspective that views the evolution of a human being into a family, tribe, society, and nation, as a natural process that should promote cooperation and not distinctions, discrimination, or conflicts among different peoples and nations. The only criterion for distinction among nations is the commitment to, and achievement of, the positive values that religion demands.[16]

In brief, Yassin links the idea of nationalism with the modern process of state-building. He strongly opposes it because it enhances divisions among the Arab and Muslim peoples. It also runs counter to the universal characteristics of Islam that considers the *umma* as the umbrella of the social and political Islamic order and the bond of faith as the force for cohesion and social integration. Therefore, for Yassin, modern nationalism and secularism are intertwined.[17]

SECULARISM: FAITH OR MODERNIZATION

Yassin regards secularism as a consequence of the "state of poisoning," characterized by cultural domination of the Muslim world, the spread of a sketchy understanding of Islam in the Arab and Muslim mind, and the use of a modernizing orientation to restrict the role of religion in society. He links secularism to the historical development of the Western Christian societies. In Europe, the Christian church opposed political freedom and resisted intellectual progress.[18] Christianity was also associated with feudalism, religious sectarianism, and intolerance. Hence, secularism gathered momentum and was associated with the reform and renewal of Western thought and society.

Based on this argument, Yassin shares Ali Shariati's belief in the "geography of concepts," which holds that concepts may be applicable in their original locale, but not necessarily so in other cultural contexts. Yassin admits that secularism, for instance, has liberated the Western mind from the shackles of religious dominance and the authority of the clergy, but he contends that Islam was the cause of freedom and progress in Muslim societies.[19]

Yassin views secularism as one aspect of the cultural conflict between Islam and the West. Secularism penetrated the Muslim societies through the forces of imperialism and worked to separate religious values and politics, and to promote new models for society under the names of enlightenment, reform, nationalism, and rationalism.[20]

According to Yassin, sectarianism also played a role in the spread of secular concepts in Arab society. He presented a historical review of the role of non-Muslim Arabs in promoting secular ideas in the region (Western liberalism, Darwinism, socialism, and communism). Yassin attributed this development to their early exposure to Western intellectual currents through missionary schools and to their longing for a guarantee of equal status and complete freedom. Therefore, they embraced equality to replace such concepts as *mili* (belonging to a sect or religion) or *dhimmi* (non-Muslim), espoused liberalism to achieve economic success, and adopted rationalism to liberate themselves from the hegemony of religion. In this process, they efficiently utilized the press, modern schools, and the administration to propagate the new ideas of secularism and couple them with progress.

He marks the spread of this current among Muslim intellectuals by the writings of Ali 'Abd al-Raziq and his book *Al-Islam wa usul al-hukm* (Islam and the Fundamentals of Governance), which appeared around the time of the collapse of the Islamic caliphate and denied the presence of a political system in Islam. Such views received the support of the advocates of Western secular liberalism.

Yassin criticizes the Muslim secular intellectuals for their infatuation with Western civilization, citing Taha Hussein and his book, *Mustaqbal al-thaqafah fi misr* (The Future of Culture in Egypt) as an example. Yassin considers him and liberal intellectuals, such as Lutfi al-Sayyid, Salama Musa (a Copt), Mahmoud Azmi, and Ismail Mazhar, as the proponents of this secular trend. He condemns their attempt to undermine the role of religion by devising a modern cultural current that pieces together the elements of Darwinism, nationalism, pharaonism, Arabism, constitutionalism, and democracy.[21]

In reviewing the theses of the secular Arab intellectuals on religion, Yassin maintains that they view Islam as a source of revisionism, which limits the human will and progress because it does not organize society on a democratic basis or promote equality among the different elements in society. The secularists also blame Islam for not generating a rationalism deemed necessary for advancing societies and building a modern state that possessed a scientific outlook and technological expertise. To these thinkers, religion is a metaphysical power that contradicts and undermines rationalism.[22]

In Yassin's view, the secularists make selective use of Islamic history by focusing on the Ottoman caliphate to generalize the entirety of the Islamic experience. They do this to thwart the implementation of Islamic principles and to minimize the impact of religion on the Muslim majority in society, and cast doubt on the applicability of Islamic principles to the contemporary Muslim order.

Yassin dismisses outright the analogy between the historical evolution of Christianity and that of Islam as inaccurate and misleading. He refutes the secular depiction of Islam as an authoritarian or a clerical religion in which the *'ulama* (knowledgeable persons) constitute a clergy monopolizing the interpretation of the scriptures. He does not see religion as the reason behind Muslim weakness and backwardness; instead, he attributes this condition to the implementation of the Western-inspired models of development, which aggravated the political fragmentation of the Muslim peoples, overlooked their indigenous political culture, and used force and violence to impose and perpetuate these models.[23]

In line with this argument, Yassin articulates his perceptions of the role and extent of secularism in Moroccan society. Historically, Islam has constituted an integral component of Moroccan political and social culture as well as a source of legitimacy for the state. The political system and its official discourse must declare a commitment to Islam and its principles if only at a symbolic level. For Yassin, the post-independence Moroccan state is secular in content, even though it does not explicitly adopt a secular path.[24] As we will see in the following sections, he believes that secularism is the real model of the state and the driving force behind its institutions and modernization programs. He considers the Western-educated elite the pawns for implementing these modern projects.

THE RULING ELITES AND THE IDEOLOGY OF DEVELOPMENT: INTELLECTUAL AND CULTURAL DEPENDENCE

Yassin laments the current state of underdevelopment of Moroccan society, and of the Arab world in general. In his opinion, the secular elites in control of the political regimes in the Arab countries and their hegemony over the "means and wills," through a strategy of cultural domination, play a central role in the shaping of current Arab conditions. He considers these elites to have been produced and socialized by the colonial experience and Western schools of thought. In addition, the educational policy of the colonial power aimed at the creation of a parallel school system, which led to the cultural bifurcation of the society and to the spread of a Western mentality and behavior among the educated elites.

An education inspector by profession, Yassin considers the present system of Francophile education as alien, backward, and designed in part to disorient and dislocate the future generations of the country.[25] It is a system designed by an alienated elite and administered by a group of educators—"with an employees' mentality"—who have been seduced by the consumerist values of a conquering culture. They transfer these values to their students and turn them into job-seekers, competing to join the service of the state apparatus. In a society in which the unemployment rate is very high, this process increases the frustration of university graduates and generally exacerbates social problems.

Yassin proposes an alternative educational orientation, geared toward change and aimed at the mobilization of wills, the development of human intellect, and freedom of the mind. He recommends the reorganization of the school system, its administration, and curricula.

These recommendations involve the resocialization of school administrators and teachers, changing the relationship between teacher and
student, and designing indigenous educational programs that combine
belief with reason and a scientific outlook, while avoiding emulation
of Western models.[26]

Yassin denounces the ideologies of political and economic development embraced by the modernizing elites. He considers them to be
eclectic in orientation and a medium for imposing foreign models: "In
order to acquire the instruments of confrontation, the leadership of the
national movement had to improvise an intellectual blend of Qarawiyin
[Islamic] culture and the liberal, and later socialist culture. Future
practices were based on this cumulative thought. The result is what we
see now: factionalism, division and a bitter class struggle."[27]

For that reason, Yassin believes that the colonial period has not
ended. It has been sustained by the native elites who implemented
inappropriate development schemes and policies of change in the
Arab and Muslim societies. In this regard, Morocco is no exception.

> After independence, we expected Morocco to assume the correct
> path, restore its Islamic life and return to Islamic principles. What
> happened was the opposite. The colonial powers left our country only
> after it had entrusted those it had raised with power and authority.
> More than a quarter of a century has now passed since independence.
> Yet our dependence on the infidels (former colonial powers) is
> increasing because the policies and systems controlling every aspect
> of our lives are those of the infidels.[28]

Yassin is convinced that these imported values and concepts have
built a *jahili* society in Muslim Morocco. "The *jahili* systems which are
equipped with technology and material resources intent upon eliminating Islam cannot hide behind different colors, names and ideologies."[29]
Yassin asserts that the culture of Moroccan society is inherently an
Islamic one that rejects Western concepts. "The Moroccan people of
this Muslim nation do not accept a Qur'an-based constitution or a
prophetic approach that has been molded by a political class and
intellectuals produced in the factories of Westernization."[30] He criticizes the development models adopted in Morocco for overemphasiz-
ing economic aspects while neglecting the cultural and social
dimensions of development. He attributes this shortcoming to the
materialistic philosophy behind these frameworks and the Western
view of the human being as merely an instrument, rather than an

objective, of development. In Yassin's judgment, these models have failed to solve chronic economic and social crises of Moroccan society, such as those of social justice, fair distribution, and productivity. Yassin believes that Islam offers a solution for economic crises. Anticipating that such a solution will be very difficult, he points to the need for an economic transformation and restructuring as prerequisites for the foundation of a sound economic system. In rejecting the liberal and socialist models of economic development, he presents a model that is based on the following moral and practical principles: (1) a fair distribution of rights and duties in order to prevent the disproportionate accumulation of wealth; (2) the reallocation of national resources to achieve the general prosperity and welfare of the nation; (3) the elimination of social injustice and poverty; and (4) the full mobilization of the nation's resources and potential.

Yassin considers the elimination of class differences as the most important barrier to a solution. He expects the concept of Islamic moderation (rifq) to replace class struggle.[31] It is a pivotal task to replace the socioeconomic conditions inherited from fitna (disorder and weakness) with a sound Islamic order, without destroying the economic institutions of the country or resorting to radical measures. Yassin holds that "the Islamic solution for the problem of distribution is the achievement of justice; for the problem of productivity, it is reliance on individual initiative; for the contradiction between just distribution and sufficiency, it is nationalization, not as a rule but as a possible means."[32] Thus he recommends that the members of the Islamic movement align themselves with the mustad'afin (the oppressed).

According to Yassin, the pressing need to overcome the problems of underdeveloped economies can be met by fulfilling the following requirements:

1. The full mobilization of national resources, while respecting private property, in order to reach the level of self-sufficiency.
2. The liberation of the labor force of the country from capitalist exploitation.
3. The encouragement of private initiative, which should be well integrated within the general framework and objectives of the national economy.
4. The establishment of Islamic industrial cooperatives to divert capital from nonproductive investments and fixed assets.
5. The nationalization of banks and their gradual transformation into interest-free institutions in order to stimulate productivity.

6. The nationalization of the major industrial means of production that are related to public interest.
7. The formulation of a development plan to enable the state to direct, encourage, and organize the production process of the country without impeding private initiatives by state bureaucracy.
8. The implementation of labor-intensive techniques to provide benefits to the workers, while realizing the need for capital-intensive techniques for heavy industry and the armed forces.
9. The training of the necessary technical cadres and the initiation of prompt educational reforms to rectify the problem of brain drain.
10. The creation of a domestic market for Islamic products by enhancing the purchasing power of the impoverished masses and curbing the wealthy from squandering the surplus of domestic investment returns in foreign markets.
11. The implementation of land reform.
12. The expansion of a market for Islamic products by establishing an economic coalition among the Islamic countries, regardless of their types of regimes.
13. The provision of patterns of technology, planning, production and consumption appropriate to Islamic values in order to liberate Muslims from the *jahili* model.[33]

During the transformation period, the national resources of the Muslim community should be directed towards achieving development, self-sufficiency, food security, and economic and military power. In this phase, it may be necessary to rely on the available patterns of technology, planning, production, and consumption until alternatives are developed.

More important, he argues that the Islamic economy cannot be established in a non-Islamic society. The process of production and distribution of wealth cannot work in isolation.[34] Yassin calls for the renewal of the ideology of Islam to resolve the crises facing Moroccan society, to break the cycle of underdevelopment, divisiveness, and cultural dependence, and to achieve unity and prominence.

The renewal of Islam aims at ending the state of *fitna* of the Muslim nation, shifting the Muslim people away from the practice of individualistic Islam, engaging them in the practical and scientific level of the faith. It also aims at transforming the underdeveloped, fragmented Muslim societies to a level of self-sufficiency, independence and strength. Then it seeks to unite these societies and sever their dependence on the *jahili* systems to assume a leadership role and carry the message of Islam.[35]

SOCIAL STRUCTURE

A) The Berbers

Berbers and the status of women are two topics that are directly related to the model of nation-building and the modernization process in Morocco. Yassin recounts the French colonial experience and its Berber policy. During the early 1930s, the French introduced the Berber *zahir*, which allowed the Berbers to implement their customary laws in lieu of the Islamic *shari'a*, while simultaneously expanding the implementation of the French legal code in the country's civil courts. The French authorities also tried to separate the Berbers from the Arabs through the administrative and educational systems. They issued a decree forbidding the use of classical and colloquial Arabic in the areas inhabited by the Berber tribes, and encouraged the use of Berber dialects and French. Missionary schools and activities were expanded in these areas and Berbers were enticed to reject the "Arab" dominance.

Referring to the French role in dividing Moroccan society, Yassin cites Junnier Labonne, a prominent French intellectual in North Africa.

North Africa should be divided. The question was how? I realized that, historically, half of the population was of Arab origins and the other half was of Berber origins. However, it was hard to distinguish between them. After extensive research, I noticed that the Berbers had strong ethnic identifications, while the Arabs had strong religious affiliations. I, therefore, recommended the spread of national ideas and scientific values among the Arabs in order to undermine their religious affiliations, and the spread of religious influences among the Berbers so that they could be separated from the Arabs after they had been assimilated through Islamic bonds. The way to achieve that was through nationalism.[36]

Although Yassin does not view the issue of the Berbers from an ethnic or minority-majority perspective, he does acknowledge that the French Berber policy rallied interest in ethnic identification.[37] He views the Berber issue against the background of Islam and history. Islam has infiltrated the social fabric and popular culture of Morocco's Arabs and Berbers. Issues of ethnic diversity did not pose the same problems in the Maghrib as did the presence of non-Muslim minorities in the Arab East. This is attributable to the fact that the relation between religion and politics contributed to the integration of these two ethnic groups in Moroccan society. Culturally speaking, there has been no distinction between the Arab and the Islamic identity. The integration of the two groups was also reinforced by the sharing of the same Maliki legal doctrine that has been in place in Morocco throughout its Islamic history. The unity of the legal doctrine resulted in a positive religious, social, and political relationship between the Arabs and the Berbers.

The historical experience indicates the coexistence of the Berbers and the Arabs and their preservation of their original characteristics without the occurrence of political rifts similar to those in other societies that have religious or ethnic minorities. The Arabs and Berbers share a common history of collaboration against internal and external challenges. Throughout history, the two groups have been intermingled through social ties, economic interests, and political conditions either in support of or in opposition to the regime. Yassin views the relation as characterized by coexistence and not by conflict.

B) Women

Yassin associates the call for women's emancipation with the modernizing model being implemented in Morocco. He believes that Western perspectives have dominated the treatment of this issue and infiltrated Moroccan society, among the modern educated elites in particular. He bases his arguments on purely Islamic and functional perspectives. According to Yassin, under the pretext of modernizing society along Western models, women have been misled and burdened by slogans calling for their equality and emancipation. He deplores the current condition of women in Morocco, which he attributes to cultural deterioration and not to the teachings of Islam.

Today, the role and status of woman are determined by foreign influences derived from Western culture, and by the burdens of underdevelopment. Yassin makes a clear distinction between the social condition of rich and poor women. Wealth enables the rich woman to experience emancipation as it may have been intended in the West, while only further increasing the deprivation of the poor woman, who falls victim to need and hard labor. The secular outlook lowers rather than raises the standard of the majority of Muslim women and is detrimental to their dignity and psychological makeup.[38] He describes the typical poor woman as "a victim of the fields and urban life. In the city, she is more encumbered."[39] In addition, wealth has affected

Moroccan men. In an implicit reference to many members of the Moroccan elites, Yassin is critical of the marriage of Muslim men to non-Muslim women; he considers it an avenue for undermining Islamic values in the Muslim household, as the children are raised under Western influences.

He sees family relations as based on justice and the concept of *qawama*, the duty of men to sustain and protect women. The authority granted to men is understood and determined only by this concept, and not by any inherent privilege of gender. It is the responsibility of men to work and preserve the integrity of their families, while it is women's duty to maintain the moral and social integrity of the family. Yassin is not opposed to women working outside the home, in conformity with Islamic principles, especially in the case of need.[40]

Yassin sees Western values regarding gender as a direct threat to the social balance in society. They produce new patterns of social relationships that eventually undermine the values of the Islamic society, particularly in areas pertaining to the family, work, and production. They also result in a state of conflict and competition between the sexes. In the end, women in an underdeveloped society can only be further exploited and their families are negatively affected by the confusion in social functions.

Yassin notes that, regarding marriage, divorce, and inheritance, the Islamic legal system grants women complete emotional and financial independence and guarantees them full rights in a manner unparalleled by Western positivistic laws. He also takes issue with secular trends that deplore the status of Muslim women, pointing to the issues of veiling, divorce, and inheritance. He considers that such views lack substance, and fail to understand the Islamic social system and the basis for social stability.[41]

SOCIAL AND POLITICAL CHANGE

Yassin's evaluation of modernization in Moroccan society reveals his dissatisfaction with the process. He counters by proposing his own ideas of change. In Yassin's perception, the human being is the objective of change. Education and awareness are the means to change and develop that human being. In order to play its central role in the process of social change, the Muslim family must become capable of maintaining social functions and ties in the face of perversion. In this regard, the Muslim mother assumes a leading role in the moral and religious education of future generations. Yassin considers young people the focus and objective of programs for change.[42]

He views progress as a complete process in which the material and spiritual needs of the human being are met. Progress is a revolution against oppression and inequality, redeeming the dispossessed and preserving the social and moral dignity of the individual. Progress also means freedom from cultural and economic control. He explains, "Progress and liberation require the mobilization of the people and efforts to achieve economic independence and development. Our independence should be from *jahiliyya,* East and West."[43]

Although Yassin levies strong criticism against the submissiveness of the religious scholars and their co-optation by the Westernized elite, he perceives a central role for the *'ulama* and the Muslim intellectuals in the process of social and political change. He bases his criticism on the ground that these Muslim scholars, who were traditionally models of veneration, are no longer fulfilling their duty of defending the moral integrity of the Muslim community. The corruption of the Westernized elites has transformed them into nothing more than pawns, employed by the state to legitimize the right of these elites to run the affairs of the country. This policy has in part been achieved through a process of coercion and the dismantling and bureaucratization of religious institutions. Scholars are not free to speak out against or prevent un-Islamic practices in society. They must serve, moreover, in the capacity of state employees, thus isolating themselves further from the masses and leaving themselves no alternative but to defend the regime or to lose their job.

Yassin also condemns the manipulation of the *'ulama,* whom the king uses to defend his legitimacy. He harshly describes them as "*'ulama al-qusur*" (court scholars); custodians of traitors, who corrupted Islam.[44] As Yassin perceives the situation, "The scholar has no choice but to comply, and this type of corruption is based on the fear and intimidation that runs through every Moroccan."[45] He therefore calls upon the scholars to "look to the example set by their counterparts in Iran—who have restored the turban with its integrity and glory—in order to liberate the Muslim mind from the domination of imported values and invading cultures, free the people from *fitna,* and rid them from hunger and poverty."[46]

He urges them to assume their moral and religious responsibility by: representing a true model for the Muslim scholar; relinquishing their official posts and privileges; liberating Muslim minds from alien cultures;

standing against the political tyranny of the rulers and their authority; mobilizing the people against the current conditions; and reviving the concept and the duty of jihad among the Moroccan people.[47]

To effect change and achieve mobilization, Yassin calls for the revival of Islamic institutions, particularly the mosques. He presses for the renewal of the cultural and social role of the mosques, which must become the organizational base for Moroccan society. He declares:

> We will make the mosque our barrack for combating the state of *fitna* which is shrouded in *jahiliyya* and inspireds by its slogans. From the mosques we will start. We want to make it our *ribat*, as had been the case in early Islam. We learn our religion in it, settle our disputes, contemplate the revival of Islam, and organize our activities to accommodate the rush of young people towards Islam.[48]

Yassin's criticism of the Western models of change inherited from the colonial experience stems from a profound belief that they have deepened the differences among the social classes in Morocco and widened the gap and social stratification between the urban and rural areas. The economic, political, cultural, and social control of the urban aristocracy has disturbed the social balance of Moroccan society and perpetuated the privileges of a tiny elite at the expense of the deprived majority of the society.[49] Yassin complains:

> Despite the presence of a constitution declaring Islam as the religion of the state, the systems and policies that control our life are those of the non-Muslims. Where are the signs [principles] of Islam in our life? Are they revealed through the oppressive laws that rule us through our economic system which impoverishes the poor and enriches the wealthy or in our democratic political system which produced crises in our society?[50]

In Yassin's view, the reconstruction of a new Islamic society in Morocco requires confronting several problems and providing workable answers. Chief among these problems are: the issue of rule and law, the role of the Qur'an as the source of the legitimacy of the regime, submission and cooperation with the forces of imperialism, the economy and dependence on foreign powers, the dichotomy between urban and rural areas, Westernization and cultural submission, and social and moral perversion caused by media, tourism, and administrative and economic policies.[51]

Yassin does not advocate violence as a means for changing society. He considers the formation of clandestine organizations and the use of violence in politics as illegal acts that would lead to political suicide. Instead, he calls upon the Islamic movements to formulate clear and detailed Islamic programs.[52] He urges them to participate in the political process in the systems that have adopted democracy and he views this as a sign of the intellectual and political maturation of the Islamic movements.[53]

CONCLUSION

Yassin epitomizes the concerns of an Islamic modernist. He operates out of an intense sense of the need for change at the individual and community levels: at the individual level, through a comprehensive process of socialization and mobilization; and at the community level, through the integration of Islamic values into the political, economic, and administrative structure of society.

As noted, the main themes of Yassin's ideas bear resemblance to those of other Islamic thinkers. This is evident in his critical view of the West; his call for renewal and reform along Islamic lines; and his rejection of the secular forms of nationalism and Western-inspired development models.

Yassin adopts a gradualist stance with regard to social change and economic reform. His activism and discourse take place at a purely intellectual or theoretical level. However, the significance of his views lies in his vision of an activist Islam as an alternative to the current ideology of the state and the society. This clearly distinguishes him and his followers from secular-oriented political parties in Morocco that are easily co-opted by the regime.

At the present, the Islamists in Morocco do not represent an imminent threat to the stability of the system. However, the continuation of this situation is not guaranteed, especially in light of possible crises associated with the issue of transition of power in the near future or the success of their efforts to move from the margins to the center of the political process through organized political action.

Notes

*I am grateful to my wife for her patience and support,
and would like to express my profound thanks to Khaled Awamleh and Rachelle Naab
for their insightful comments on an earlier version of this article.*

1. For the secular aspects of Moroccan society, see, Rémy Leveau, "Islam et contrôle politique au Maroc," *The Maghreb Review*, no. 1-2 (January–April 1981): 13–14.
2. William Zartman, "Political Dynamics in the Maghrib: The Cultural Dialectic," in Halim Barakat, ed., *Contemporary North Africa* (Washington, D.C.: The Center for Contemporary Arab Studies, Georgetown University, 1985), pp. 28–30.
3. See John Entelis, *Culture and Counterculture in Moroccan Politics* (Boulder, Colo.: Westview Press, 1989), pp. 77–100.
4. For a detailed discussion of the Islamic movements in Morocco, see Mohamed Tozy, "Champ et contre champ politico-religieux au Maroc," Thèse Pour le Doctorat d'État en Science Politique, Marseille Faculté de Droit et de Science Politique d'Aix, 1984; Emad Shahin, "The Restitution of Islam: A Comparative Study of the Islamic Movements in Contemporary Tunisia and Morocco," unpublished Ph.D. diss., The Johns Hopkins University, School of International Studies, 1989; and Henry Munson, "Morocco," in *The Politics of Islamic Revivalism: Diversity and Unity*, Shireen T. Hunter, ed. (Bloomington and Indianapolis, Ind.: Indiana University Press, 1988).
5. Dale Eickelman, "Religion and Power in Polity and Society," in *The Political Economy of Morocco*, I.W. Zartman, ed. (New York: Praeger Publications, 1987), pp. 89 and 92.
6. 'Abd al-Salam Yassin is the leader of the 'Adl wal-Ihsan (Justice and Benevolence) group, and is considered an influential ideologue among the current Islamic revival movements in Morocco. He was born in 1928 to a poor Berber peasant family. Yassin received a traditional education, but educated himself in foreign cultures. After independence, he became inspector, then an inspector-general, in the Ministry of Education. He joined the Boutchichiyya Sufi order for several years, but later parted company with them to begin an activist career on his own. He wrote several books on Islam and activism in Morocco and was imprisoned for three years in 1974, after writing a critical letter to the king. In 1979, he began publishing his periodical *Al-Jama'a*, which was banned four years later. Yassin was again imprisoned in 1984 for two years. Since 1989 he has been under house arrest and his repeated requests to form an Islamic political party have been denied. See 'Abd al-Salam Yassin, *Al-Islam aw al-tufan* (Islam or the Deluge) (Marrakesh: n.p., 1974), pp. 4–6.
7. 'Abd al-Salam Yassin, *Al-Islam ghadan* (Islam Tomorrow) (Casablanca: Matba'at al-Najah, 1973), p. 693.
8. 'Abd al-Salam Yassin. *Al-Islam wal-qawmiyya al-'ilmaniyya* (Islam and Secular Nationalism) (Casablanca: Dar al-Khattabi lil-Tiba'a wal-Nashr, 1989), pp. 28–29.
9. Ibid., 10–11.
10. Ibid., 12.
11. Ibid., 9.
12. Ibid., 14–5.
13. Ibid., 17–23.
14. Ibid., 88–90.
15. Ibid., 119–22.
16. Ibid., 133–37.

17. Ibid., 144–70.
18. Ibid., 45–6.
19. Ibid., 48–63.
20. Ibid., 85–8.
21. Ibid., 116–8.
22. Ibid., 124–5.
23. Ibid., 121–3.
24. See Muhammad 'Adid al-Jabri, *Al-Maghrib al-mu'asir: Al-Khususiyyah wal-huwiyyah, al-hadathah wal-tanmiyyah* (Contemporary Morocco: Uniqueness and Identity, Modernity and Development) (Casablanca: Mu'assat Binshira lil-Tiba'a wal-Nashr, 1988), p. 73.
25. Yassin, *Al-Islam ghadan,* 722 and 727.
26. Ibid., 685–95, 707–28, and 739–68. See Shahin, op. cit., 251.
27. *Al-Jama'a,* no. 1 (March–April–May, 1979): 66.
28. A letter to the editor, published in ibid., no. 4 (1980): 70.
29. Ibid., 103.
30. Ibid., 101.
31. Yassin, *Al-Islam aw al-tufan,* 109–10.
32. *Al-Jama'a,* no. 2 (1979): 66.
33. 'Abd al-Salam Yassin, "*Al-Minhaj al-nabawi,*" *Al-Jama'a,* no. 10 (1982): 98–101.
34. Ibid., 101–5.
35. Ibid., no. 5 (Rabi' al-Awwal and Rabi' al-Thani, 1980): 45–46. See also, Shahin, op. cit., 268–71.
36. Yassin, *Al-Islam wal-qawmiyyah,* 39.
37. Ibid.
38. Yassin, *Al-Islam ghadan,* 652 and 654.
39. Ibid., 654.
40. Ibid., 659.
41. Ibid., 657–58.
42. *Al-Jama'a,* no. 10 (July 1982): 23.
43. Ibid., no. 1 (March–May 1979): 10–11.
44. 'Abd al-Salam Yassin, "*Al-Jihad tanziman wa zahfan*" (Jihad: Organization and March), *Al-Jama'a,* no. 11 (May 1983): 51.
45. Ibid., 54-5.
46. 'Abd al-Salam Yassin, "*Iftitahiya wa istiftah*" (Prologue), *Al-Jama'a,* no. 1 (March–April–May 1979): 12. See also Shahin, op. cit., 248
47. Ibid., 12.
48. Ibid., 62–63.
49. Al-Jabri, op. cit., 51–53.
50. *Al-Jama'a,* no. 4 (1980): 71.
51. Ibid., no. 10 (July 1980): 21–22.
52. Ibid., no. 1 (March–April–May 1979): 54.
53. Ibid., 55–6.

Militant Islam and Its Critics: The Case of Libya

Marius K. Deeb

The main thrust of this study is to explain why Libya has not witnessed a militant Islamic opposition movement like, for instance, Al-Nahda in Tunisia, Al-Jabha al-Islamiyya lil-Inqadh (FIS) in Algeria or, on a somewhat lower scale, Al-Jama'a al-Islamiyya in Egypt, and Al-Ikhwan al-Muslimun in Syria. I maintain there are five major determinants that are dialectically interrelated and that could shed light on this phenomenon. The first two determinants are the "given" on the eve of the revolution, or the Hegelian thesis. The first of these is the Islamic legacy of the Sanusiyya in prerevolutionary Libya, that is, the relationship between religion and the state under the monarchy; the second consists of the salient characteristics of Libyan society that have inhibited the rise of a dominant militant Islamic movement. The third and fourth determinants constitute the antithesis: what Qadhafi has imposed on Libya as a political and a socioeconomic system that is at once nonmonolithic and egalitarian; and the way Qadhafi has interpreted the relationship between Islam and politics in two more or less distinct periods, 1969 to 1974 and 1975 to 1981. Both of these determinants have made the emergence of a militant Islamic movement more difficult. The fifth determinant is a synthesis that is still in the making, namely the Libyan opposition and its vision of the post-Qadhafi era.

THE SANUSIYYA AND ITS LEGACY

Although the Sanusiyya began as a Sufi order with a universal mission, Italy's invasion of 1911 and its successful campaign to conquer and subdue Libya during the Italo-Sanusi War of 1923-32 transformed the Sanusiyya from "a religious movement into a primarily political and national movement."[1] Sayyid Idris as the head of the Sanusiyya order had a religious-tribal 'asabiyya but also acquired, during the struggle against the Italians, the status of a national leader that was basically mundane and secular. When the Cyrenaica Constitution was promulgated in October 1949, Sayyid Idris, the undisputed leader of that region, did not refer to the Sanusiyya movement in the constitution for he did not want to impose the Sanusi beliefs on the whole population of Cyrenaica. This was partly due to the fact that he wanted Libyans to regard him as the national leader, but was also due to the tolerant and moderate beliefs of the Sanusiyya itself.

The Sanusiyya movement contained both fundamentalist and reformist elements. On the one hand, the founder of the Sanusiyya was influenced by Ibn Taymiya; he believed that the Qur'an and the Sunna constituted the basis of Islam, and rejected qiyas and ijma'. The Sanusis played down the role of the various schools of jurisprudence rather than follow the dominant school in Libya, namely the Malikite school. On the other hand, the Sanusiyya was the epitome of the Khaldunian synthesis of the religious 'asabiyya with the tribal 'asabiyya. The head of the Sanusiyya had the dual role of the 'alim-Sufi, which did not lend it to a fundamentalist frame of mind. To the vast majority of the followers of the Sanusiyya the head of the Sanusiyya "was a murabit who possessed various miraculous powers and superhuman abilities."[2] Unlike the Wahhabiyya and the Mahdiyya the Sanusiyya was not interested in spreading its mission by force. The Sanusiyya fought only when attacked. Thus the Sanusiyya left a legacy that was uncongenial to the rise of militant movements because even at its heyday it was more of a peaceful reformist rather than a fundamentalist movement.

THE SOCIOECONOMIC FEATURES OF PREREVOLUTIONARY LIBYAN SOCIETY

In a previous work I have analyzed the fragmented character of the urban socioeconomic structure in Libya on the eve of the revolution.

This was coupled with the dispersed spatial distribution of the population of a great number of villages.[3] This dispersion still persists in spite of the concentration of a large proportion of the population in the two main regions of Tripolitania and Cyrenaica. The rural and pastoral structure was equally fragmented. For instance, the Sanusiyya movement emerged in a tribally based society, and the symbiosis between the Sa'adi tribes of Cyrenaica and the Sanusiyya movement was almost complete. Evans-Pritchard in his classic *The Sanusi of Cyrenaica* has conclusively shown that the Libyan tribal structure is highly segmented at all levels. "The tribal system . . . is a system of balanced opposition between tribes and tribal sections from the largest to the smallest divisions, and there cannot therefore be any single authority in a tribe. Authority is distributed at every point of the tribal structure and political leadership is limited to situations in which a tribe or a segment of it acts corporately."[4]

QADHAFI'S SOCIOECONOMIC AND POLITICAL SYSTEM

Qadhafi's economic policies of encouraging only small-size family enterprises, implementing his slogan "Partners not Wage Laborers," and the principle of the self-sufficiency of the economic producer, further enhanced the socioeconomic fragmentation of the urban population. Qadhafi's egalitarian drive culminated in the Law of May 6, 1978, concerning the ownership of property that deprived the urban landlords of their wealth. As I have pointed out in an earlier study, Qadhafi attempted to transform, in a radical manner, property relations in Libya. He tried to abolish capitalist private property, which he characterized as exploitative in nature as it led to the accumulation of wealth by some individuals and families at the expense of others. Qadhafi regards private property as being at loggerheads with "natural principles," which governed the precapitalist golden age of "natural socialism" (*ishtirakiyya tabi'iyya*). Capitalist private property should be replaced, according to Qadhafi, by personal property (*milkiyya khassa*), which is the property needed to satisfy one's basic needs without employing others, and by socialist property (*milkiyya ishtirakiyya*), which is owned by society as a whole. In the latter category, workers are partners (*shuraka'*) in contrast to capitalist property where they have no control over what they produce.[5] All these measures in property relations virtually eliminated social mobility because those who sought to move upward, based on what they owned in real property or in commercial and industrial enterprises, ceased to have the means to do so.

The political system Qadhafi devised, which culminated in the declaration of Libya as the Republic of the Masses (*al-jamahiriyya*) in March 1977, was not a monolithic one-party system but rather a fragmented system of political authority with the population divided into basic local popular congresses and popular committees. He tried to undermine traditional leadership by dividing localities to cut across tribal boundaries. The only semi-monolithic structure one can discern in Libya is the phenomenon of the Revolutionary Committees, which are not unlike a political party.[6] Qadhafi's socioeconomic and political reforms resulted in bridging the gap between social classes by eliminating economic differences but paradoxically reaffirmed the differences in social status. In other words Qadhafi to a large extent froze the classes based on social status (as in urban notables and tribal leaders) rather than replacing them by other social groups and classes. Thus the nonexistence of abject poverty, the absence of social mobility, the systematic effort to obliterate economic class differences, and the nonmonolithic political system have tended to hamper the rise of a dominant militant Muslim opposition in Libya.

FROM QUASI-FUNDAMENTALIST TO DE FACTO SECULARIST

Qadhafi's ideas on the relationship between religion and the state have gone through two phases. In the first phase from 1969 until 1974, Qadhafi seemed to be a quasi-Muslim fundamentalist. When Qadhafi came to power in 1969, he wanted all legislation to be examined in the light of *shari'a* and he held the view then that positive law in Libya should be replaced by laws based on *shari'a*. He also issued a decree stipulating that the dates of the Hijra calendar should precede those of the Gregorian calendar on official documents, and that sign boards of shops, enterprises, and companies should be written in Arabic only.[7] It is significant to note that Qadhafi's attempt to merge Libya and Egypt in 1972–73 failed inter alia because of Qadhafi's insistence on adhering to *shari'a* as the source of all legislation in the projected new state.[8] It was also during this phase that Qadhafi put forward his Third Universal Theory as an alternative philosophy to both capitalism and communism. He maintained that this theory was rooted in Islam and was therefore, like Islam, universal in its appeal.[9] All these instances were clear indications of Qadhafi's quasi-Muslim fundamentalist stand during this first phase. Despite this quasi-fundamentalist position Qadhafi had ideas that were either at logger-heads with Muslim fundamentalism or presaged the de facto functional secularism of the second phase. For instance, he took the Muslim Brotherhood to task when it denied the existence of Arab nationalism and accused it of distorting both Islam and the Qur'an.[10]

Qadhafi's legitimacy during the period 1969 to 1974 rested on his pan-Arab nationalist credentials, especially his close relationship with Egypt and with Nasser, in particular, during his first year in power. Qadhafi removed the foreign (American and British) military bases from Libyan soil and expropriated and expelled the Italian community, which was a remnant of Italian colonial rule in Libya. Furthermore, Qadhafi's Libyanization of the economy and the eradication of what he viewed as alien and non-Islamic laws, customs, and symbols enhanced his legitimacy. In April 1971, Libya joined the Federation of Arab Republics (FAR) with Egypt and Syria and in 1972–73 Qadhafi pushed hard to merge with Egypt as Sadat had sought close relations with Saudi Arabia and other oil-rich Arab states of the Persian Gulf.[11] Egypt acted as Libya's protector during the first phase and for all intents and pur-poses a Libyan opposition to Qadhafi was virtually nonexistent.

During the second phase of the Qadhafi regime in Libya between 1975 and 1981, Qadhafi's conception of the relationship between Islam and politics had changed, as political opposition to Qadhafi began to challenge him by 1975. As a reaction to the rise of this domestic opposition, Qadhafi started advocating a functional secu-larism. He maintained that mundane matters should be separated from spiritual or otherworldly matters. Fearing opposition from the imams he addressed the latter in May 1975 urging them not to deal with mundane problems (political, economic, and social matters) and stating "Sermons on Fridays must deal with matters which man has come to the mosque to seek, which are prayer and God's remem-brance only."[12] By then Qadhafi seemed to have exhausted his use-fulness according to a large segment of Libyan society, which prompted 'Umar al-Muhayshi, a fellow member of the Revolutionary Command Council, to attempt a coup in August 1975 that failed but was definitely a watershed in terms of what followed it.

Qadhafi's reaction to the coup was to embark on a program of rev-olutionary transformation of Libyan society to undermine both polit-ically and socioeconomically the growing opposition and all potential challengers. It was in this process of drastic changes in the political, economic, and social spheres that Qadhafi moved from the quasi-fundamentalist Muslim to the de facto functional secularist in this second phase of his rule. The changes that Qadhafi introduced in the political system were not based on Islamic doctrines. He envisaged a Lockean state of nature that he called "natural socialism" (al-ishti-rakiyya al-tabi'iyya) as the precapitalist golden age rather than finding it in the reign of the first four caliphs. Unlike fundamentalists who would argue that sovereignty belongs to God, Qadhafi, who has been influenced by Western political thought, has maintained that "sovereignty in the people is indivisible."[13] Qadhafi maintained that his ideas expounded in the Green Book are not rooted in Islam, unlike his earlier assertions that his Third Universal Theory was based on Islam. "The Green Book does not state that Islam should be the religion, or the Qur'an the shari'a, of any particular society."[14] By the end of the 1970s, Qadhafi had put forward the view that man does not need intermediaries between him and God. "The Qur'an is in the Arabic language and we can therefore comprehend it ourselves without the need for an imam to interpret it for us."[15] He regarded Islamic jurisprudence as not unlike positive law. Qadhafi, during this second phase, became consistently anticlerical and projected himself as a protestant reformer of Islam, the Luther or the Calvin of Islam advocating a kind of Protestantism that bypasses all intermediaries between man and God.[16] In 1979, Qadhafi decided to change the starting date of the Muslim calendar from the Hijra to the death of the Prophet in 632 A.D. on the grounds that the death of the last Prophet was more significant than his Hijra.[17] Thus Qadhafi's radical socioeconomic policies, especially with respect to private property, and his separation of religion from the state and the undermining of the power of the 'ulama, who were mostly members of the leading urban notable families, paved the way for the rise of a formidable opposition that in reaction to Qadhafi's policies would constitute the new Hegelian synthesis in the post-Qadhafi era.

THE LIBYAN OPPOSITION: THE SYNTHESIS

The mid-1970s witnessed the rise of a significant opposition against Qadhafi's regime in Libya. First, there was the unsuccessful coup led by 'Umar al-Muhayshi in August 1975. The external dimension was apparent: "This military coup coincided with the deterioration of Libya's relation with Egypt in the wake of the October War of 1973 and the signing of the first disengagement agreement between Egypt and Israel."[18] Secondly, and more significantly, was the publication of Qadhafi's Green Book, *Al-Kitab al-Akhdar* (the three parts of the Green Book were issued between early 1976 and 1978), and its implementation during the period 1977 to 1980, which changed drastically the political and socioeconomic character of Qadhafi's regime. The most formidable challenge to Qadhafi has been the formation of the National Front for the Salvation of Libya (Al-Jabha al-Wataniyya li-Inkadh Libya) on October 7, 1981. The NFSL was founded, one should note, on the thirtieth anniversary of the promulgation of the first Libyan constitution under the monarchy on October 7, 1951. The emphasis on the constitutional nature of the political system that the NFSL wants to establish after the overthrow of Qadhafi's regime is unmistakable.

In the post-Qadhafi era, the NFSL would work for the establishment of a transitional government and a supreme or presidential council (*majlis ri'asa*), which would rule for a maximum of one year and which would "make all the necessary preparations which will ensure and guarantee the honest and speedy formation of a constitutional national government."[19] Within six months of setting up the transitional government and the presidential council, general elections would be held to choose a national founding body, whose major task would be the drafting of a permanent constitution that would be adopted through a national referendum. The NFSL is clear in its objectives after the toppling of Qadhafi: "the holding of a general election to select a head of state and legislative body according to the newly adopted Constitution . . . [and] the transfer of power to the duly formed institutions according to the new Constitution."[20]

In 1992 the NFSL circulated to its members at various levels a draft of what it called a "Platform for the Future" in which it outlined its vision of the post-Qadhafi era in quite specific terms. The first section of this platform deals with the rights of individuals that would be guaranteed, such as freedom of thought, freedom of assembly, and freedom of travel, the right to private ownership, and the right to equal protection under the law. In a society such as Libya, where clans and tribes are important traditional institutions, it is not surprising that the second section deals with the revitalization of the family. "Respect and support of the family is conducive to the inculcation of strong moral values."[21] The NFSL outlines a political system that separates the legislative, executive, and judicial branches of government.

The new constitution would promote the principle of checks and balances and the establishment of a pluralistic democracy "in keeping with the democratic heritage of our nation as found in the Libyan Constitution of 1951, which was suspended by Qaddafi in 1969."[22] The NFSL believes in the formation of political parties, interest groups, and pressure groups as part and parcel of the democratic process. The role of these groups and the independent free press would be vital in the formation of public opinion. The legislative branch, which would be composed of elected representatives, would enact legislation in accordance with the constitution. The legislature would appropriate the national budget and oversee the various government agencies. The executive branch of the government would be decentralized, as was the case prior to Qadhafi's coup d'état. Administrative districts would be granted more power, for this "gives the individual greater control over decisions affecting his or her daily life."[23] The head of the executive branch would be elected in a popular vote and serve for a limited term of office. The judicial branch would be separate from both the executive and the legislative branches. Its functions would be to examine the constitutionality of the actions of the other two branches, as well as to guarantee the rights and freedoms of individuals.

The NFSL believes in the free enterprise system and upholds the right of individuals "to pursue their desires for achievements as far as their inventiveness and initiative will take them within the lawful pursuits of business."[24] The NFSL advocates the creation of corporations in a free market and of a viable stock exchange, and believes in the promotion of the private sector in non-oil-related industries and in agriculture. Finally, the NFSL maintains that the state in the post-Qadhafi era "must compensate those who have had their businesses and properties confiscated or ruined through Gaddafi's nationalizations programs."[25]

The NFSL's program gives an inkling of what to expect in the post-Qadhafi era. Although the NFSL is *not* the whole opposition, it is the most important and most active opposition organization. It is remarkable that the NFSL espouses a liberal democratic political and economic ideology despite the fact that it has within its ranks different groups of various political currents and ideologies extending from the liberal democrats through traditional supporters of the Sanusiyya to former sympathizers with the Muslim Brotherhood.

One can discern a certain development in the NFSL's program. In the early and mid-1980s, the NFSL was more reserved in its liberal and democratic ideology than it has been since the late 1980s. In the earlier phase the NFSL tended to couch its program more in traditional terms. For instance, free elections and plebiscites were regarded as the most appropriate methods of determining "the legitimate *bay'a*."[26] Nevertheless, the vision of the NFSL is still a synthesis of the religious and cultural legacy of the Libyan people prior to the revolution, and of constitutional democratic rule, basic freedoms, and the sanctity of private property, which are lacking in Libya under Qadhafi.[27] In an interview in 1990 with the leader of the NFSL, Muhammad Yusuf al-Mughayrif,[28] the NFSL was accused of having "a religious tendency." Al-Mughayrif gave an answer that shows that the traditional legacy is still of paramount importance. "As for the 'religious tendency,' we do not regard it as a slur, we regard it as a genuine manifestation of our belonging to Libyan society. The Libyan people are 100 percent Muslim, by tradition and practice. Are we supposed to depart from our society's traditions and faith?"[29]

As Qadhafi's regime is not monolithic—the *mukhabarat* character of the regime notwithstanding—the opposition has not produced a monolithic movement. The secular character of the opposition was further enhanced when Libyan military officers and soldiers, taken prisoner by the victorious Chadian regime of Hussein Hibri in the aftermath of the Libyan defeat in Chad in 1987, decided to form on June 21, 1988, what they called the Libyan National Army and join the opposition as the military arm of the NFSL. The decision to become part of the NFSL was made by Colonel Khalifa Haftar, who comes from the Farjani tribe and was the commander of the army in March 1988.[30] When the Hibri regime in Chad was overthrown by Idriss Deby in December 1990, the Libyan National Army had to move on to other African countries until it ended up in the United States. The NFSL has always been supported by the United States and whenever it managed to get support from Arab countries, these countries were invariably pro-Western, such as Sudan under al-Numayri, Egypt, Tunisia, and Morocco.

Furthermore, Qadhafi's de facto secularism, anticlericalism and anti-Sufism have forced the Libyan opposition to defend the traditional *'ulama* of the urban centers, the Sufi orders and the saints, who have tended to steal the thunder from the militant Islamic groups, such as Islamic Jihad and even the mainstream Muslim Brotherhood. The latter criticized Qadhafi in 1981 on the grounds that his conception of jihad is erroneous, that he has not regarded the Sunna and the *hadith* as binding, and that he has put "Shari'a or Islamic Law on par with Roman Law or Napoleonic Code."[31] Qadhafi declared in a speech on July 19, 1990, that any person who belongs to the Muslim Brotherhood or to the militant Takfir wal-Hijra or Tabligh "is doomed and must be executed because his existence harms other[s]."[32] The NFSL retorted that "Gaddafi's attack on Islam stems from his strategy to weaken Libyans, and maintain his rule. Libya's population . . . is traditionally devout without being extreme and radical."[33] The NFSL regards Qadhafi as secular and even anti-Islamic. He

> is not a practicing Muslim. His private lifestyle and conduct are regarded as offensive and anti-Islamic. Every Libyan, by instinct and through his simple understanding of his faith, considers Gaddafi's policies to contradict and subvert Islam. Gaddafi has challenged the Libyan people's faith, by re-interpreting Muslim doctrines, values, traditions and customs. All these factors led the Libyan people to seek shelter in their faith.[34]

Therefore, the more secular the discourse the regime in power is conducting, the less the chances are for the rise of a dominant militant Islamic movement. This phenomenon is part and parcel of the dialectic between Libya's religious and socioeconomic legacy prior to the revolution on the one hand and, on the other, the radical reforms imposed by Qadhafi, which in a way have kept Libyan society frozen in terms of social class based on status and tribal and regional fragmentation. The synthesis that could emerge after Qadhafi would not be a dominant militant Islamic regime. The Libyan opposition itself has already given us a clear notion of what to expect in the post-Qadhafi era, namely, a free democratic polity that guarantees the rule of law and respect for the various tribal customs and mores of the Libyan people.

Notes

1. Marius Deeb and Mary-Jane Deeb, *Libya Since the Revolution: Aspects of Social and Political Development* (New York: Praeger Publishers, 1982), p. 95.
2. Salaheddin Hasan, "The Genesis of the Political Leadership of Libya 1952–1969: Historical Origins and Development of its Component Elements," Ph.D. diss., George Washington University, 1973, p. 60.
3. Deeb and Deeb, *Libya Since the Revolution,* 110.

4. E.E. Evans-Pritchard, *The Sanusi of Cyrenaica* (Oxford: Clarendon Press, 1949), p. 59.

5. Marius Deeb, "Radical Political Ideologies and Concepts of Property in Libya and South Yemen," *Middle East Journal*, vol. 40, no. 3 (Summer 1986): 448–50.

6. Deeb and Deeb, *Libya Since the Revolution*, p. 121.

7. Ibid., 98–99.

8. Ibid., 132.

9. Marius Deeb, "Islam and Arab Nationalism in Al-Qadhafi's Ideology," *Journal of South Asian and Middle Eastern Studies*, vol. 2, no. 2 (Winter 1978): 14.

10. Ibid., 21.

11. Mary-Jane Deeb, *Libya's Foreign Policy in North Africa* (Boulder, Colo.: Westview Press, 1991), pp. 76–81.

12. Mu'ammar al-Qadhafi, *Al-Sijil al-qawmi, bayanat, wa khutab wa ahadith, 1974–1975*, vol. 6 (Tripoli: Al-Thawra al-'Arabiyya, n.d.), p. 469.

13. Mu'ammar al-Qadhafi, *Al-Kitab al-akhdar, al-fasl al-awwal*, p. 12.

14. Deeb and Deeb, *Libya Since the Revolution*, 103.

15. *Al-Fajr al-Jadid*, February 21, 1978, p. 4.

16. *Al-Mustaqbil* (July 22, 1978): 17–18.

17. *Al-Mustaqbil* (March 10, 1979): 21.

18. Marius Deeb and Mary-Jane Deeb, "Libya: Internal Developments and Regional Politics," in *The Middle East Annual: Issues and Events*, vol. 4 (Boston, Mass.: G.K. Hall & Co., 1985), p. 138.

19. *Libya Under Gaddafi and the NFSL Challenge* (Chicago, Ill.: The National Front for the Salvation of Libya, 1992), p. 291.

20. Ibid., 306.

21. Ibid.

22. Ibid., 307.

23. Ibid.

24. Ibid., 310.

25. Ibid., 314.

26. *Al-Inqadh*, no. 8 (April 1984): 52–53.

27. Deeb and Deeb, "Libya: Internal Developments and Regional Politics," 140.

28. Born in the city of Benghazi, he hails from one of the largest Libyan tribes, al-Maghariba, which inhabits the coast between Sirte and Ijdabya.

29. *Libya Under Qaddafi and the NFSL Challenge*, 277.

30. *Al-Hayat* (March 23, 1993): 10.

31. Mary-Jane Deeb, "Militant Islam and the Politics of Redemption," *The Annals*, vol. 524 (November 1992): 61.

32. *Libya Under Qaddafi and the NFSL Challenge*, 213.

33. Ibid.

34. Ibid.

III.

Reform or Repression:
State Responses to the Islamic Revival

12

The Challenge of Democratic Alternatives in the Maghrib

I. William Zartman

The thesis of this chapter is that the most important obstacle to democratization in North Africa is not Islamic fundamentalism nor single-party authoritarianism, but the inability of the political systems to produce credible opposition parties capable of attracting voters, representing broad interests, and presenting alternative programs. Instead, established single parties find themselves facing either small, narrow, inexperienced groups with no claim on the allegiance of large sectors of the population, or utopianist religious movements with no sense of the practical needs of government.[1] The result is the perpetuation of authoritarian rule and the alienation of the electorate, as evidenced by the massive abstention and nonregistration rates. Thus, opening the political systems to competitive pluralism is no answer when, in reality, structural barriers obstruct the legal possibilities. This chapter cannot change that reality. It can only analyze the situation to show its contours and use that analysis to raise questions about ways of meeting the challenge.

Unlike many similar situations, the availability of laws and practices is ahead of the potential users. The laws in all three North African countries are relatively liberal and permit the organization and activity of political parties with few restrictions. Only parties with a religious, regional, or ethnic focus are forbidden, and the numerical or other legal requirements for registration are not restrictive. (It should be remembered that the Islamic Salvation Front [FIS] in Algeria was legalized but unconstitutional.) In electoral competitions, voting is relatively free and fair. Complaints have been issued by opposition parties with regularity but government control of the results (such as occurred in Tunisia in the first multiparty elections in 1981) are not characteristic. Administrative interference in campaigning is typical throughout the region but it does not explain the poor performance of the opposition. Nothing, in fact, explains the poor performance of opposition parties except their own inability to make a credible appeal to the electorate. They are beaten fair and square (more or less) by the single party and by the abstentions.

One electoral law problem with serious implications is that of the choice of electoral systems. Tunisia's law, held over from the Bourguibist period, provides for large multimember districts with seats allocated on a winner-take-all basis, a real hindrance to any opposition party. The law was changed in 1993 to add to the number of seats filled through the old system a number elected from among the losers by a proportional representation list system, which will ensure some opposition party representation in the National Assembly. The Algerian law provided for family voting (by the head of the family) and included such inept gerrymandering that the party that made the law had to "spend" 100,800 votes for a seat whereas the first and third parties "spent" only 16,800 and 20,426 votes for each seat, respectively. But in both cases, the law does not alter the picture already presented of weak oppositions and large abstentions.

From the outset, a number of objections may be addressed to this thesis. It may be objected that the argument focuses on the camel's horns rather than on the camel—on a phenomenon that does not exist rather than one that does—and therefore ignores the real problem: an authoritarian single party facing an Islamic movement. As noted, this constitutes part of a larger problem, and would be less significant if small parties and large abstentions were not characteristic as well.

Another objection might be that abstention is a universal phenomenon and a sign of the times. After all, the Rome and Mecca of democracy, the United States, has a president elected by a minority of the voters and has a long record of low participation. But the United States and other countries following a democratic system do not have the associated problem of authoritarian single parties and utopian religious opposition, or an absence of democratic alternance. The existence of these associated problems in North Africa leaves the problem of democratization on the agenda.

A third objection is that abstention is a way of voting. Unfortunately, abstention can clearly indicate one of two opposite attitudes—either contented indifference between the choices, or alienated rejection of all the alternatives. In North Africa, the first can hardly be the case, and it is the second that is indeed the problem. Abstention is voting "none of the above," weakening the support and legitimacy of the state.

It may also be objected that the discussion is really only an account of two countries—Algeria and Tunisia—each with its own problems, and is therefore merely an idiosyncratic exercise. But Algeria's and Tunisia's problems are the same—small parties and abstentions— even though the forms of the single-party and Islamist factors are partially different. And Morocco shares the problem as well, with its many parties in search of a clientele and its high abstention rate, even though its single-party and Islamist problems have been solved (for the moment) by the king and the constitution.

Finally, it is often claimed that electoral participation is contrary to the historic political traditions of the Arab Maghrib, and hence abstentions should be of no concern, since they never have been an indicator of state illegitimacy. But if that is the case, the new element of mass participation introduced by the nationalist movements and the partially fulfilled demand for self-determination is historically insignificant, as is the current wave of demands for democratization. Yet that wave is at the very heart of current concern over authoritarianism, utopianism, and abstentionism.

This chapter will review the party system in each of the three North African countries and then examine more closely the status and weakness of the small parties, particularly in regard to their clientele, and the basis of nonparticipation. It will then draw conclusions about the requirements for the better development of democratic alternatives for voters.[2]

POLITICAL PLURALISM IN THE MAGHRIB

Each of the North African countries has had a different experience with political pluralism. None of them has attained a full democratic system as yet. This fact should not be taken as a denial of the importance of the steps that each has taken, including the lessons that those steps have provided. But neither should those steps be confused with arrival at the presumed—and indeed, announced—goal or with any assurance that arrival will occur. On the way to that goal, all three countries share the same problem of nonparticipation of half their populations in political life and weak democratic alternatives for voters.[2]

Morocco

Morocco began its independent life with a dominant nationalist movement, led by the Independence (Istiqlal) Party, although it was not the only organization in the independence struggle.[3] Partly because of Morocco's bizonal status as both a French and a Spanish protectorate, it had a number of lesser parties; more importantly, as a monarchy, it had a number of independent nationalists attached to the palace rather than to a party. All of these took part in the first independent governments, from 1955 to 1958. Morocco's first elections, for local assemblies in 1960, were not only a nonpartisan but in reality also a multiparty affair, and took place only after a law on political associations had been passed, allowing for both the breakup of the Istiqlal and the legalization of non-Istiqlali competitors. The first was done to break the monolithic nature of the party of the nationalist movement; the second was to provide parties for unrepresented segments of the body politic, notably in the first case for the Berbers of the Army of Liberation. These two purposes were to govern party formation over the next three decades.

The first general elections for a parliament, taking place in 1963 under Morocco's first (1962) constitution, were multiparty elections, giving 52 percent of the vote to the two parties created in the split of the independence movement and 34 percent to an electoral alliance of the other parties and independent "King's Men." The new parliament was dissolved and the constitution suspended two years later. After the creation of a new political system ending the state of emergency,[4] under Morocco's third (1972) constitution, local elections beginning in 1976 and general elections in 1977, 1984, and 1993 have been contested by an array of parties, generally categorized as the parties of the independence movement and the parties of the *makhzan*. About 60 percent of the eligible (voting-age) population cast valid votes in 1963, 64 percent in 1977, 47 percent in 1984, and 44 percent in 1993.

Elections in Morocco tend to be free and fair, but their results only approximate the actual strength of parties as indicated by votes. Results are the outcome of the voting strength of the parties as corrected by negotiations with the palace, with no absolute assurance that the candidate with the highest number of votes will always be elected. Not all the distinctions among parties are significant. Some of the *makhzan* parties are Tweedledee and Tweedledum, but most parties attract different clienteles and even in the *makhzan* category new parties—notably the Constitutional Union in 1984—have been created precisely for the purpose of attracting groups who do not have a political home in the current party array. Cogent criticisms of government programs are leveled in parliament and by the press, particularly by the Socialist Union of Popular Forces (USFP) and the Party of Progress and Socialism (PPS-Communist). Since 1959, Morocco has also had a Berber party (and since 1967, two of them), reflecting ethnic as well as socioeconomic differences.

Morocco has never faced a demand for an Islamic party, in part because it had an Islamic party ahead of the times in the Istiqlal under the leadership of its *salafi 'alim,* 'Allal al-Fasi, and in part because the king is the imam and *khalifa* of the west, the patron of Islam in Morocco. Perhaps more importantly, Moroccan history has been peppered with rural preachers who rose to work wonders and to call rulers and commoners to repentance; while in earlier centuries, these figures occasionally succeeded in establishing new dynasties, in recent centuries they were rapidly brought under control when they threatened to be too great a nuisance and this response continues to be practiced and accepted to this day.

Political pluralism arose in Morocco above all because of the natural tendency of nationalist unity to break down into component interest and leadership groups once the unifying demand for independence had been achieved. Morocco was therefore a leader in the evolution of single-party regimes.[5] But the underlying political fact that made that evolution possible so early in Morocco was the presence of a strong unitary authority, which, during the reign of Muhammad V, favored the breakup of the single party and, during the reign of Hassan II, continues to orchestrate further party divisions and creations in order to implement the unusual constitutional provision against the existence of a single party. Unity at the top has meant pluralism in the middle, in order for the king not to find himself faced with a single organized force speaking for his people.

The same force that made organizational pluralism possible in Morocco also limits its effectiveness. Parties are not the governing agencies in Morocco; the king is. The decade since the general elections of 1984 has seen a declining faith and interest in the pluralist political process and a growing awareness of the king's responsibility. A referendum on December 1, 1989, unsurprisingly ratified a royal decision to put off elections for two years to await a decision on the fate of the Western Sahara. Already in 1980, a constitutional referendum had extended the four-year term of parliament to six years because the Saharan affair was turning out badly and the scheduled date, 1981, was no time for elections. When 1983 came, electoral preparations could not be made in time and Morocco was governed for a year without a parliament. The 1989 referendum gave Morocco a parliamentary term of eight years (subsequently extended by yet another year in order to organize the elections), one of the longest terms in the world and a sign of the ineffectiveness of pluralism as a reflection of societal interests and political power. A third constitutional referendum on September 4, 1992, made the government responsible before the parliament to be elected and increased the government's powers. The subsequent direct elections on June 26, 1993, were generally viewed as the freest and fairest since 1963, with the greatest promise for responsible participation in governing. But participation was still below 50 percent of eligible voters, around 15 percent less than the more than 60 percent participation in 1963 and 1977.

Tunisia

Tunisia also represents a predicted case of democratic pluralism.[6] The nationalist movement, which after independence became the Socialist Constitutional (Dusturian) Party (PSD), had long provided a textbook case of single-party rule, with all its strengths and weaknesses, that could break up into a multiparty system as a normal stage of its evolution. Indeed, when the nationalist movement came to power at independence in 1956, it had to establish its monopoly of power over competing factions and especially to undo an attempt by the General Union of Tunisian Workers (UGTT) to set up a separate Socialist Party. But the single-party system grew rigid along with its formerly charismatic leader, Habib Bourguiba, who had frozen its evolution in the mid-1970s at the same time as he had himself made president for life.

In the early 1980s, Bourguiba's prime minister Mohamed Mzali tried both to revive the PSD and to hold competitive multiparty elections. The Tunisian Communist Party (PCT) and two splinters from the PSD—the liberal Democratic Socialist Movement (MDS) and the socialist People's Unity Movement (MUP)—participated in multiparty elections in 1981. But Bourguiba and Mzali could not bring themselves to announce the real results and usher in the multiparty era; so the figures were falsified. The bread-price riots of January 1984 showed the incapacity both of the party to mobilize popular support for policy and of the president to steer a firm course. As he became more and more sharply engaged in a battle over the social and political program for Tunisian society with the Movement of the Islamic Way (MTI), which benefited from the rising current of Islamic values and also from the absence of any other means of expressing disillusionment with the sclerotic regime, Bourguiba led his country toward a collapse of civil order. On November 7, 1987, he was replaced in a "constitutional coup" by his prime minister, General Zine Labidine Ben Ali.

Ben Ali was personally committed to free and fair elections among competing parties and felt, correctly, that the preservation of his initial legitimacy depended on deeper change than merely in the presidency. But he was inexperienced as a party politician (although skilled as a palace politician) and he had to rely on party officials to help him change their own system. As a result, he decided to revive the party, renamed the Democratic Constitutional Rally (RCD), before he installed competing pluralist formations. Some competing bodies were the three old parties that had run in 1981. Others were personal creations of well-meaning individuals, friends of the president, who had no real following or appeal. The troublesome challenge was the fundamentalist movement, which renamed itself the Renaissance Party (Hizb al-Nahda) in order to shed any specifically religious reference. Its leaders' statements of moderation and legality were not enough to win it authorization as a party, and so when election time came, it presented broad slates of candidates as independents. Even the drafting of a National Pact among all the parties (including an Islamist representative) in the fall of 1988 did not provide enough convincing assurance to the leaders to enable them to legalize the fundamentalist party.

The presidential and parliamentary elections of April 2, 1989, were Tunisia's first free and fair, nonviolent, competitive multiparty elections. They gave Tunisia a de facto two-party system without a formally constituted second party and with an opposition of uncertain loyalty. The reinvigorated dominant party, the RCD, won all the seats by the winner-take-all electoral system retained from the old regime. The largest opposition force was the independents, who stood for the still unauthorized MTI or Renaissance Party. The election was characterized by normal and inevitable pressures and practices by both the RCD and MTI such as are often found in machine politics, but it was also criticized by the MDS and MTI for outright falsification of results. As a result of these complications, Tunisia hobbled into the democratic era with less clarity than would have been desirable. Of the four million potential voters, only 2.7 million registered and 2.1 million voted. The president was voted by plebiscite, the RCD won, but participation fell to its lowest point (51 percent of the eligible voters), after having risen from 51.3 percent in 1979 to 58 percent in the multiparty elections of 1981 and 56.5 percent in 1986.

Tunisia had another go at pluralism a year later, in June 1990, when municipal elections were held. Once again, the Ben Ali regime tried to involve all parties in the preparations so as to improve the chances for a pluralistic outcome. In January, the Council of the National Pact discussed the opposition's major objection to participation—the electoral system. In place of the winner-take-all lists, a new system gave half the seats to the leading party of the district and allocated the rest by proportional representation, with a 5 percent floor. But the opposition parties still felt so weak that they boycotted the elections; the Nahda, still unrecognized and possibly past its peak of attraction, fielded independent lists in only a few municipalities; and the RCD, strengthened by a presidential decision to limit representatives' terms and to prohibit holding multiple positions, brought in new candidates for 83 percent of the seats and ran a campaign as if there were an opposition. As a result, the RCD made a clean sweep of all the municipalities, except for al-Chebba in the south, which fell to a breakaway slate of independents.

Preparations for the 1994 elections began with a revision of the electoral law to provide for opposition representation in the legislature (opposition candidacies for the presidency being excluded). The new law voted in December 1993 was sometimes criticized as contrived and still did not provide for single-member representation of the constituencies. However, it made the best of the situation by insuring minority party representation in the National Assembly in a more independent way than did the previous proposal for a single national list of RCD and opposition candidates, which was offered and rejected in 1989. In addition to the 144 seats won outright by the RCD in the March 1994 elections, 19 seats added to the parliament were filled by a proportional distribution of opposition candidates, some of whom were the most outspoken members of their party (ten from the MDS and the rest from three other parties). Equally significantly, 66 percent of the 4.3 million eligible voters cast valid ballots and the spoilage rate was insignificant (0.3 percent). After having twice lost its chance for significant pluralism, in 1981 and 1987, Tunisia has been trying to enter the democratic era in a way that does not challenge the dominant party but still retains voter participation.

Algeria

Algeria at the beginning of the 1990s presents an astounding case of a sudden transition from single-party rule to pluralism and back.[7] Unlike Tunisia and, earlier, Morocco, nothing in Algeria pointed to a multiparty future. The National Liberation Front (FLN) was a historically famous case of a revolutionary nationalist movement that triumphed in a seven and a half year war of independence, evicting the colonial ruler but also destroying those of its nationalist competitors that it could not absorb. Both during the war and afterward, under President Ahmed Ben Bella, other parties existed but were either crushed or pulled into the fold of the Front. The General Union of Algerian Workers (UGTA) never had the autonomy of the UGTT and it was soon brought to heel as a party auxiliary.

There was never any question of either a multiparty evolution or a multiparty experiment; after 1967, 1969, and 1977, local, provincial, and national Peoples' Assembly elections, respectively, were held with two or more candidates per seat, but the candidates were all carefully selected from the FLN, even if they sometimes represented different factions within it. No observers ever foresaw a pluralistic evolution to the FLN. A number of parties claimed existence, but all were banned and all but one lived in exile. All were proclaimed illegitimate, as well as illegal, not just because they opposed the single party but because they challenged the heir of the victorious nationalist movement. All political activity was to take place within the nationalist Front, the legitimizing Algerian political culture being one of democratic centralism and collective leadership.

On the other hand, because the FLN was everything and the only thing, it was nearly nothing. The real operative force for independence was the National Liberation Army (ALN), and the party was merely a symbol. It had less life than the PSD at any time, and periodic attempts to give it some were all failures. Unlike Bourguiba, Colonel Houari Boumediene came to power in 1965 in a military coup without, and even against, the FLN. The only parts of the party that functioned were its top organs—Political Bureau, Secretariat, committees, to name the most important—and these bodies were clubs of cronies and factions that surrounded and often hemmed in the president. When, upon Boumediene's death, Colonel Chadli Benjedid was nominated by the party caucus for president in 1979, he too sought to revive the party while seeking to apply a policy of liberalization.

But Benjedid's policies, much like the problems of Mikhail Gorbachev in the Soviet Union, promised consumer benefits at a time when the Algerian economy was in decline. Near the end of his second term, in October 1988, a series of strikes led to calls for a general strike (probably by Benjedid's opponents within the party and the labor union), which, in turn, led to massive riots. Benjedid's answer was to promise even greater political liberalization, while holding the line on economic austerity, and the constitution was amended in February 1989 to allow multiple parties. Suddenly fifty-six parties of all types sprang into existence. Some were old parties revived, such as the Vanguard Socialist (Communist) Party (PAGS); others were personal vehicles of old leaders from the early days of the republic (two of which—the unlicensed Algerian Democratic Movement (MDA) of Ben Bella and the licensed Socialist Forces' Front (FFS) of Hocine Ait Ahmed—boycotted the elections); still others were liberal clubs without a following, and some were ethnic representatives, such as the Kabyle (Berber) Rally for Culture and Democracy (RCD). At least three—the Islamic Salvation Front (FIS), the Islamic Society Movement (Hamas), and the Islamic Renaissance (Al-Nahda) Movement (MNI)—were Islamist fundamentalist parties.

Algeria's first free and fair competitive elections were held without violence or intimidation two days after the Tunisian elections of June 1990; they resulted in a major upset. Over two-thirds of the votes were won by the FIS, giving it control of two-thirds of the forty-eight regional assemblies (APWs) and over more than half of the 1,541 communal assemblies (APCs), including all thirty-four municipal assemblies in Algiers. Only fourteen APWs and a third of the APCs were won by the FLN; the Berber RCD came in third with one APW in the Kabylia region, and independents beat out eight other parties for the remaining APW. Claiming a popular mandate, the FIS immediately called for new national elections and then for the resignation of Benjedid's government. While, as in Tunisia the previous year, the vote may be seen above all as a protest against the former single party and may not represent the real strength of the opposition, the FLN also benefited from the boycotts since some voters opposed to the ruling party were more opposed to the Islamist challenge and ended up voting FLN. On the other hand, whatever the motives behind the actual distribution, pluralism came to Algeria in the form of a polarized two-party system structured roughly on the potent socioeconomic dichotomy between modernization and neotraditionalism.

Under the hammering pressure of the new majority party, Benjedid called parliamentary elections for June 1991 and proceeded to redistrict in such a way as to strengthen FLN chances. The redistricting, but even more so the lackluster performance of the local FIS governments and rising popular fear of the effects of FIS leadership at the national level, led observers to see a decline in FIS appeal and predicted a vote of 30 percent. As in Tunisia in different conditions, declining prospects led to escalating ends and means. The FIS called for presidential elections at the same time as legislative elections, protested the redistricting, and opened a general strike in early June. The army, already divided over the acceptability of a FIS victory at the polls, could not accept the breakdown of law and order, and imposed on Benjedid a state of emergency and a limited military takeover.[8]

When the first round of the elections was finally held on December 26, 1991, it appeared that Algeria was on the way to having a new single party. FLN support had fallen to 23.4 percent of the vote, 12 percent of the registered voters, and 7 percent of the elected candidates. The FIS won 188 of the 430 seats, nearly a majority of the total and 81 percent of the seats won in the first round; 198 seats remained to be decided in the second round, where the FIS was in a good position for an equally conclusive showing. But while the FIS received 47 percent of the valid votes, it only received 24.6 percent of the registered voters. The valid votes had dropped to a striking level of 52 percent of the registered voters, significantly down from the earlier single-party parliamentary elections of 1977 (78 percent), 1982 (67 percent), and 1987 (87 percent). The second round was canceled two weeks later and an army-backed government installed.

THE DEMOCRATIC ALTERNATIVE PARTIES

Alongside the phenomena of single parties and high abstentions, the smaller parties—the democratic alternatives—present a more elusive subject of analysis. They fall roughly into three categories: ethnic (Berber) parties, salon parties, and potential mass parties. Most third parties in North Africa are in the second category and not all of these will be analyzed. In Algeria alone, fifty-six parties were recognized for the 1991 elections and forty-nine presented candidates; half a dozen deserve some attention. The point of the following analysis is to identify characteristic obstacles to third-party success in presenting a credible democratic alternative.

The Berber parties present potentially credible alternatives in Algeria and Morocco; each has its own political appeal in addition to its Berber aspect. The Popular Movement (MP) of Mahjoubi Aherdane in Morocco is a party of rural interests (nearly a third of its candidates in 1984 were farmers), and it won 15.5 percent of the directly elected seats with 15.5 percent of the vote. (By 1993, Aherdane's party had become the National Popular Movement, winning fourteen seats, whereas the faction of Mohand Lansar that kept the party name won thirty-three seats, the two together winning 23 percent of the vote.) The Rally for Culture and Democracy (RCD) headed by Said Saadi in Algeria is a liberal, middle-road party that aspires to a wider non-ethnic appeal, whereas the Socialist Forces Front (FFS) of Hocine Ait Ahmed is a social democratic party. The RCD received 2.9 percent of the 1991 vote and the FFS 7.4 percent, the latter winning twenty-five seats to become the second largest party in the National Assembly.

But all of these parties are limited by the very element that assures them of their current degree of support—their Berber appeal. Despite their interest or programmatic orientation, they are unable to attract Arab voters. There are other two-sided characteristics common to some other parties. Both the MP and the FFS are creations of a charismatic leader who incarnates the personalized appeal of the party but who also repels voters who see him as an authoritarian *za'im*. The breakup of the MP in 1989 and 1990 was in part a reaction to the dominance of the party's founder.

The largest number of third parties are salon parties, gathering together a living room full of the friends and family of the founder but unable to reach further. For example, the Social Democratic Party (PSD) of Abderrahmane Adjerid in Algeria, the first party to be recognized under the new constitution, is a centrist party drawing on middle-class professionals and businessmen, notably but not exclusively from Oran. Its interest focus gives it little appeal outside of the modernized middle class and, partly as a result, its leadership has spent more time and energy in interpersonal rivalries than in expanding the party's support base throughout society.

Although the Tunisian salon party par excellence is the Beja coterie of liberal lawyer Mounir Beji, called the Social Party for Progress (PSP), which gathered 0.2 percent of the votes in 1989, others also qualify. Two leftist pan-Arabist parties, the Socialist Rally for Progressive Unity (RSP) of Nejib Chebbi and the Unionist Democratic Union (UDU) of Abderrahmane Tlili, received only 0.4 percent and 0.3 percent of the vote, respectively. Both were localized parties with few candidates, the former in Tunis and the center, the latter largely in Gafsa where the Tlili family has historic roots. The parties both launched vast ideological appeals that had no resonance with voters' interests.

In Morocco, the Organization of Democratic and Popular Action (OADP), a party of schoolteachers (who made up nearly three-quarters of its candidates), fielded few candidates, held few meetings, and elected only its leader, Mohamed Bensaid, in 1984 and an additional member in 1993. Its appeal came more from the fact that a number of its top members had been among the jailed opposition until a month before the election than from its vague platform.

Many of the salon parties were made of *progressistes* and were more of a symbol of the regime's liberalism than of a leftist trend in the electorate. The communist parties in all three countries can be mentioned in the same category. In Morocco, the Party of Progress and Socialism (PPS) is a group of intellectuals with a trenchant analysis of government policies. It placed candidates throughout the country, nearly half of them schoolteachers, and the 2 percent of the vote it received elected it two deputies. The Socialist Vanguard Party (PAGS) of Algeria and the Tunisian Communist Party (PCT) group together small numbers of workers and professionals and presented no candidates of their own in their countries' parliamentary elections.

The list could be extended greatly, but it would only reiterate the fact that the liberal and leftist analyses presented by the parties do not address voters' interests. Even pooling these parties' efforts on a common slate, as was done in Monastir and in Gafsa in Tunisia in 1989, will not increase their audience.

The third group of parties is more problematic, since they have the potential for constituting a democratic alternative to the single party and for overcoming the massive abstentions. Yet each party has a disability that removes it from serious contention.

The Movement for a Democratic Algeria (MDA) of former President Ahmed Ben Bella might be considered such a party. Its leader is known and experienced, and was once considered highly charismatic. His program has moved from the *progressiste* left to the populist Islamic, but it only attracted 2 percent of the voters in 1991, making it the seventh party on the ballot. The problem is obvious and typical of many figures trying for a political comeback: Ben Bella is passé, a has-been, his personal appeals jaded, and his programmatic shifts viewed as opportunistic.

In Tunisia, the search for a potential democratic alternative is of a different nature, since no options yet exist. Nonetheless, a move is under foot for the upcoming parliamentary elections of 1994 to create a socialist labor party based on the General Union of Tunisian Workers (UGTT), in the image of its earlier ambitions in the mid-1950s. Such a development was not possible under the Socialist Dusturian Party (PSD) of Habib Bourguiba, and while the mutation of the PSD into a Democratic Constitutional Rally (RCD) under Zine Labidine Ben Ali left the way open for a new socialist labor party, the UGTT was in too much disarray and too busy reestablishing itself in the late 1980s to be able to mount a challenge to the RCD. As the mid-1990s approach, conditions for a new party that would complete the triangular constellation of Tunisian political organizations—liberal, Islamic, and socialist—are coming into place.

There is not a Moroccan equivalent to this frustrated potential, in part because the time of challenging the single party occurred thirty years ago, beginning with the first general elections, and in part because the challenger came together from among king's men, not the opposition. A temporary electoral alliance, the Front for the Defense of the Democratic Institutions (FDID), was constituted with the benevolent attention of the king. When he put the political system back together again on a new footing in the mid-1970s, Hassan II encouraged his brother-in-law and prime minister, Ahmad Osman, to give a permanent organization to the independents and create the National Independents' Rally (RNI) in 1977, and then encouraged the next prime minister, Maati Bouabid, to organize yet another party, the Constitutional Union, to capture the unaffiliated voters in the next election, in 1984. In this case, the parties had no trouble attracting voters; known as the *makhzan* parties, they won an almost identical number of votes in 1977 (2.254 million), 1984 (2.271 million), and 1993 (2.123 million). But part of the same problem remains for Morocco as for its neighbors: between 1977 and 1984 the voting-age population rose by 1.5 million, but apparently none of them voted, as the total number of voters remained about the same from one election to the other. In 1993, the number of voters rose by two million (out of four million potentially newly eligible) but the number of cast but invalid—mainly blank—ballots doubled to almost a million. The participation percentage in Morocco in 1984 was the lowest ever of any North African country. It fell to 47 percent in 1993, including only a quarter of the newly eligible voters figure.[9]

PARTIES: THE OBSTACLES

It is difficult to analyze what it would take for small third parties to offer a credible alternative, since the task is not only one of identifying necessary attributes but also of providing them in the face of continued serious obstacles. A party needs at least four things in order to get what it needs most—votes. These are financial support, patronage, an interest clientele, and state neutrality. For various reasons, the current single parties have these and the small do not.

Originally, single parties, notably in Tunisia and Algeria, received money from the state budget. When they were cut loose from state financing at the end of the 1980s, they turned to private sources for funds, in addition to membership fees; businesses, eager to keep their own bread buttered, buttered the parties' bread in turn. Private sources have no interest, other than for charity, in financing a party that has yet to show its ability to accede to power, and corporate charity is not well developed in North Africa. In Morocco, the nationalist parties—both Istiqlal and Socialist—possess business ties from their government days that assure them of funding despite their opposition status. The *makhzan* parties' business ties do the same. In Algeria, the FIS is able to rely not only on members' contributions, presented as *zakat* (religious obligation), but also on massive funding from the Gulf; a similar situation exists for Al-Nahda in Tunisia. Secular opposition parties do not have this advantage. On the other hand, when small parties receive state subsidies to help them overcome the lack of private support, they become dependent on the state and vulnerable to its pressures, as the small parties and political press have learned in Tunisia.[10]

Patronage comes with power but it is also the key to coming to power. Small parties have no patronage to dispense to their members, and even if they achieve a few symbolic seats in the National Assembly, as is likely in Tunisia and has occurred in Morocco, parliament offers little in the way of jobs for members' followers. This is why the local elections of 1990 were so important to the FIS, for it gave them access to many local jobs when it took over local governments. However, importantly, the FIS was able to overcome this handicap even before coming to power by offering social services and serving as a public intervenor on behalf of the needy. By providing soup kitchens, clothes closets, emergency assistance, and pressure on bureaucracies, it created benefits to distribute in the absence of direct access to state jobs. Its inventiveness paid off.

Third, parties need to be able to claim representation of a defined sector of interests as well as a specific program. Claims to do the same thing better may be attractive when the government is doing it badly, but they are still not credible when the claimant has no experience to present and no specifics to propose. Moreover, the programmatic appeal is unlikely to take hold if the party cannot lay claim on an identifiable sector of society with definable interests. Such a claim is particularly difficult in an era characterized by single parties, which claimed to represent the general will and be all things to all voters and which delegitimized sectoral interests as being divisive. The potential for a Tunisian socialist labor party is a notable exception, but the small parties of Tunisia and Algeria have a hard time finding someone for whom to speak.

Finally, and perhaps the most difficult catch of all, is the need for state neutrality. As long as control of patronage, finances, and the administration of the rules is in the hands of an institution that sees itself as an arm of the dominant party, the chances for a fair electoral contest are slim. The state cannot be candidate and arbitrator among candidates at the same time, and the training in thinking and acting that it has received over decades of single-party rule make it difficult to see the distinction between party and state. External pressure for, and teaching about, the rules of democracy, coupled with internal pressure for neutrality by opposition parties (often at great cost and risk), are an important part of the answer.

These elements represent specific requirements and formidable obstacles. Training in running a campaign and experience in running government (available to breakaways from the current dominant parties) are important to presenting a credible appeal, but they are no substitute for money, patronage, and interests. Perhaps the only answer is a longer agenda for the hopes of democratization, leading first to the admission of small parties to symbolic representation—democracy *à la Sénégalaise*—without actually challenging the monopoly of the government party, followed later by agenda realignment, defections from the monolith, and an opportunity for real democratic alternatives.

CONCLUSION

The centralized monolithic political systems of North Africa have all been challenged, but nowhere is the result a credible alternative that can attract a major segment of the voters. In Morocco, the parties of the independence movement and the parties of the *makhzan* have established a rough balance. In Algeria, the FLN has been reduced to a quarter of the vote, replaced by the FIS with nearly half. In Tunisia, the RCD (ex-PSD) received four-fifths of the vote, with little room for anyone else. But in all three cases, only about half of the voting-age population participated. Thus it takes three *makhzan* parties in Morocco to amass only a quarter of the eligible population, and the potential new single party of Algeria, the FIS, is only able to mobilize a quarter of the voting-age population, even in a crucial election that would determine its chances of staying in the political system. The challenge of achieving the conditions for a credible and attractive alternative remains daunting.

Notes

1. The utopianist characterization is clearly discussed by Addi Lahouari in *The Annals of the American Academy of Political and Social Sciences*, vol. 522 (November 1992), special issue on *Political Islam*.

2. For an analysis of North African political parties and past performance, see the excellent article by Clement Henry Moore in *Polity and Society in Contemporary North Africa*, I. William Zartman and Mark Habeeb, eds. (Boulder, Colo.: Westview Press, 1993).

3. For a recent study of Morocco see I. William Zartman, ed., *The Political Economy of Morocco* (London: Praeger, 1986). For earlier studies, see John Waterbury, *The Commander of the Faithful* (New York: Columbia University Press, 1970); Rémy Leveau, *Le fellah marocain: défenseur du trône*, 2d. ed. (Paris: PUF, 1985); I. William Zartman, *Morocco: Problems of New Power* (New York: Atherton, 1964).

4. I. William Zartman, "King Hassan's New Morocco," in I. William Zartman, ed., *The Political Economy of Morocco* (New York: Praeger, 1987).

5. I. William Zartman, "Political Pluralism in Morocco," *Government and Opposition*, vol. II, no. 4 (Fall 1967): 568–83.

6. For the most recent study of the new Tunisian regime, see I. William Zartman, ed., *Tunisia: The Political Economy of Reform* (Boulder, Colo.: Lynne Rienner Publishers, 1990). On the Bourguiba regime, see Michel Camau, ed., *Tunisie au present* (Paris: CNRS, 1987); Clement Henry Moore, *Tunisia Since Independence* (Berkeley, Calif.: University of California Press, 1965); Charles Micaud, L. Carl Brown, and Clement Henry Moore, *Tunisia: The Politics of Modernization* (New York: Praeger, 1964).

7. On Algeria since the October 1988 riots, see John Entelis and Philip Naylor, eds., *State and Society in Algeria* (Boulder, Colo.: Westview Press, 1992); on the previous period of Benjedid's regime, see John Entelis, *Algeria: The Revolution Institutionalized* (Boulder, Colo.: Westview Press, 1986); and on the Boumediene regime, see Jean Leca and Jean-Claude Vatin, *L'Algérie politique* (Paris: CNRS, 1975).

8. See Jean Leca, Rémy Leveau, Abdelkader Djeghloul and Arun Kapil, "Algérie: Politique et societé," *Maghreb-Machrek* vol. 133 (July 1991): 89–138, with particular attention to the section by Leveau on the army.

9. Phrased this way since there is no way of knowing whether the 5.5 million registered voters who did not cast valid ballots came from the new or old registrants, although indications are that new registrants are less likely to vote than old registrants.
10. Ben Jaafer, one of the leaders of the Democratic Socialist Movement (MDS), quit in 1993 in protest against the docility of the party following its annual subsidy and its lease of a luxurious government building.

Islam, Democracy, and the State: The Reemergence of Authoritarian Politics in Algeria

John P. Entelis

PREFACE

On January 11, 1992, senior military officers forced President Chadli Benjedid to resign, canceled the second round of legislative elections, and annulled the results of the first round, which saw the opposition Islamic Salvation Front (FIS) achieve a major electoral victory, and imposed a year-long state of siege. Constitutional government was replaced by an army-dominated so-called High Council of State responsive to no one but itself. In the weeks and months that followed further draconian measures were undertaken intended to subvert the incipient democratic process that Algeria had been experiencing in the several years following the deadly riots of October 1988. As part of the army's effort to regain control of state and society, it reined in the freewheeling press, abolished the country's most popular political party (FIS), dissolved the National Assembly, and reimposed on civil society the apparatus of the omnipresent state security system (*mukhabarat*).

Subsequent military trials of Islamists led to prison sentences and violent retaliation by radical forces. The junta's figurehead president, brought back from nearly thirty years of self-imposed exile in Morocco, was himself assassinated in June 1992.

What had gone wrong? Algeria's transformation from a socialist one-party authoritarian state to a liberal multiparty democratic polity seemed to be advancing with almost inexorable certainty. Almost all the major attributes associated with democratic politics seemed in evidence in the Algeria of the late 1980s and early 1990s. With the scheduling of the first-ever multiparty national legislative elections in December 1991 and January 1992, it appeared that Algeria was on the verge of becoming the Arab world's first true democracy. In some ways, the experience of Mikhail Gorbachev in the Soviet Union was about to be duplicated in North Africa's largest and most powerful nation. Yet, where the Soviet coup of August 1991 ultimately collapsed in the face of widespread popular opposition, the army in Algeria was able to impose its authoritarian will upon a fractured society.

But the military takeover did not eliminate the fundamental structural problems that first led to the massive uprising against the Algerian state in late 1988 and that forced Chadli's reformers to push for ever greater political and economic reforms. For nearly thirty years the Algerian state imposed its authoritarian will on civil society. Although an impressive state-dominated, technologically advanced infrastructure was created, it was achieved at enormous social, economic, and political cost. As oil prices and revenues plummeted in the mid-1980s, the regime's ability to satisfy the ravenous appetite of the gargantuan bureaucratic state declined as well. As a consequence, long-suppressed sociopolitical tensions boiled over, resulting in the radicalization of society, the rise of an alternative Islamist discourse, and the delegitimization of the incumbent ruling party (FLN). Despite the revival of authoritarian politics, the Algerian state will inevitably have to be decentralized, deconcentrated, and democratized if it is to overcome its myriad socioeconomic problems.

POLITICAL ISLAM AS CONCEPT

Algeria's short-lived experiment with democracy provides analysts with several important theoretical and public policy observations regarding the interaction of Islam, democracy, and the state in modern North Africa. The socioeconomic and political preconditions that undermined the Algerian *mukhabarat* (secret police) state are well understood, paralleling similar authoritarian breakdowns in the Soviet Union, Eastern Europe, Asia, Africa, and Latin America in the late 1980s. A bloated, mismanaged bureaucracy—overextended and notoriously inefficient—suffered irreparable damage when the state's economic lifeline—hydrocarbon-generated revenues—collapsed precipitously in the middle 1980s. Concurrently, uninspired political leadership, rampant corruption, and loss of ideological vigor left Algerian state and society open to the kind of popular unrest that occurred in October 1988, usually associated with the last phase of authoritarian breakdown and the first phase of political pluralism, which witnesses the emergence of protodemocratic groups, tendencies, and discourses.

The innovative element in Algeria's democratic "passage" occurred with the rise of so-called traditionalistic groups in the forefront of democratic representation, organization, mobilization, and participation. To the surprise of many and the disappointment of some, Islamist political movements outdistanced all other groups in power and out in their ability to inspire support, generate confidence, and demonstrate skills of governance in confronting, if not resolving, some of the multidimensional problems facing Algerian state and society. The dismay and puzzlement of so many observers on this score revolve around the misinterpretation of "political Islam" in the Algerian context and the relationship of Islamic discourse to democracy and democratization.

Whatever Islamic revivalism may represent elsewhere in the Arab and Islamic worlds, in Algeria the phenomenon, especially as expressed in the discourse, leadership, and public policies of the Islamic Salvation Front, assumes a distinctive if not unique form. The principal characteristics of this distinctive political Islam (PI) are as follows: (1) In virtually all of its major configurations, PI is fundamentally "modern"; that is, it seeks to resolve contemporary problems in polity, economy, and society through modern ways utilizing the instrumentalities of modern education, modern technology, modern science, modern management, and modern governance. It embraces all of the advances of science and technology in its ability to provide solutions to backwardness, underdevelopment, unemployment, inadequate production, and generalized material failure. (2) It is deeply tied to, and inextricably intertwined with, Algerian popular and political culture, including its nationalistic component, revolutionary heritage, Islamic identity, and ethnic diversity. (3) It is committed to, and a product of, democracy and democratization. Given its deep expression of nativistic culture and respect for Algeria's diverse past, political pluralism is the sine qua non of political and economic development. Anything less reproduces the nonrepresentative elitist project for containing and controlling the mass public. In other words, FIS

opted for functional and procedural democracy for a simple reason—
it works, providing the greatest good to the greatest number in the
most efficient way possible. (4) It is essentially nonviolent, with goals
and principles articulated through rhetoric and discourse, not through
"the barrel of a gun." Public performance and political persuasion substitute for solidarism and unitary ideology imposed from above. This
political approach does not exclude the use of force, however, when
society is confronted by the oppression and violence of an illegitimate
(as in, nonelected, nonrepresentative) state power. All appropriate
actions are then justified, including the use of counterviolence. In this
regard, such actions are similar to the bloody yet populist revolts of
eighteenth-century Europe and America. (5) Questions of societal
morality, ethics, norms, and values are conceived within an Islamic
construct consistent with the "reality" of Algerian experience and
practice. (6) Finally, PI is not fundamentally anti-Western in any
broad conceptual or philosophical sense. To be sure, differences over
specific domestic, regional, and/or foreign policies with select Western
states will always arise. Yet, this results from valid differences in perspectives, priorities, and national purpose and not from some intrinsic antipathy or animosity toward all things Western.

The second innovation in the Algerian experience is that Islamic
democracy, permitted to operate, albeit in a limited and local way,
passed the crucial performance test demonstrating the accommoda-
tionist and problem-solving orientation of FIS. Through scores of different examples and situations, PI was able to establish its capacity to
deal with concrete political, socioeconomic, and administrative problems in effective and culturally sensitive ways, gaining it further support among a broad cross-section of Algerian society. Using its
well-developed network of mosques and civic assemblies, FIS representatives established, inter alia, soup kitchens for the poor, social welfare services for the needy, health clinics for the sick, and tutoring
services for the illiterate.

Possibly as a consequence of the above, a third innovative albeit disturbing feature of the Algerian PI/democracy experiment has been the
reemergence of the delegitimized authoritarian project with its ability
to reimpose its hegemony over state and society. No convincing explanation has yet been put forth as to why Algerian society failed to rally
against the state in the manner of the populist response to the attempted
coup against Gorbachev in Russia in August 1991. The absence of an
Algerian Yeltsin? The persistence of an authoritarian political culture?

Foreign support for the coup-makers? Mass-based political apathy following decades of central domination under colonialism and the post-colonial state? Exaggerated assessments about the intensity, if not the scope of, Islamist support among ordinary men and women? While I will not be attempting to respond to such concerns in this study, the societal "breakdown" in the Algerian democratic-Islamist experiment continues to require careful and thorough investigation.

ASSUMPTIONS AND CONTEXT

Several assumptions and contextual presuppositions inform my arguments. The first concerns the Arab world's oppressive authoritarianism. In the last fifty years or so, not a single Arab state has permitted the legal and peaceful transfer of national authority by an opposition political party elected to power by free, open, and contested elections. For more than five decades, power in the Arab world has been concentrated in the hands of the state security apparatus and its bureaucratic/administrative appendages headed by the military. It is this reality more than any other facet of Arab state, society, and culture that explains the region's pervasive political underdevelopment, and not political Islam, Arab personality or culture, patrimonialism, or economic dependency.

A second assumption is that any study of political change, development, or democracy in the Arab world demands the same standards of analytical rigor, methodological precision, and objective interpretation as that which would be applied to the study of political systems elsewhere. Thus, any notion of authoritarianism as a culturally determined condition of Arab society, one inbred within the Arab personality, is simply unacceptable. Unacceptable as well is the widely held notion that an electoral turnout of 50 percent or less fails to meet the test of political legitimacy when applied to Arabs but not to anyone else. It is curious, indeed, that prior ridicule of 99.9 percent electoral turnouts in former Communist states has become the new standard of democratic performance in instances where Islamist parties achieve majority victories in contests with low voter turnout—contests not too dissimilar, one may add, from American national elections, which barely reach 50 percent participation.

A third assumption concerns the clear theoretical and empirical correlation among mass political culture, political sovereignty, and political legitimacy. No political system can claim to be legitimate if it lacks political sovereignty and no political sovereignty can be achieved without a congruent mass political culture. In the Arab world that political culture is rooted in Islam.

A fourth assumption flows from the third. Any notion of democracy in the Arab world that does not incorporate Islam into its analysis is simply a nonstarter. Nothing in Islamic history, culture, or theology contradicts the key democratic dyads of political participation and public contestation.

Finally, my primary concern is with the nature of political change and political development in the western Arab world of which democracy, not Islam as religion or belief-system, is the operative component. Only the men and women of Algeria, Morocco, and Tunisia can decide for themselves the nature of their societies, their cultural identities, and their political purposes. What I seek to explain by looking at Algeria's brief experiment with democracy is how a closed political system is transformed into an open one. That Islam should be the ideology of choice for great numbers of Muslim peoples of the Maghrib as they seek to establish a democratic political order is a statement of fact, not a normative assertion.

BACKGROUND

In the early 1970s, Algeria began to harness the new wealth derived from its oil reserves and vast deposits of natural gas.[1] The country concentrated on large industrialization projects consistent with the strategy of "industrializing industries"[2] advanced by former president Houari Boumediene (1965–1978). Many of these initiatives soon proved to be less sources of economic gain than symbols of national pride. Most heavy-industry plants either overproduced or underproduced. Factories were built on some of the richest agricultural land, weakening this critical sector of the economy. The agricultural sector was collectivized along socialist principles, but the government neglected the sector, focusing instead on the more glamorous heavy industries that, in theory, were intended to create a locomotive effect that would eventually pull along the agricultural domain. Instead, agricultural production stagnated and suffered from poor organization and motivation and from counterproductive pricing policies. Imports of food skyrocketed because agriculture was being neglected and because of the country's relentlessly increasing population, which had more than doubled in the quarter century since independence (in 1992 the population was 26 million).

These shortcomings were part of a broader condition of generalized failure. Algeria had long been plagued by serious problems of inadequate housing, overurbanization, unreliable food production and supplies, a decrepit transportation system, chronic water shortages, overcrowded schools, poor quality medical facilities and health services, an uncontrollable birth rate with one of the world's youngest populations, and consistently high rates of unemployment and underemployment. For the better part of the 1960s and 1970s, however, vast revenues generated from oil and natural gas sales managed to contain many of these problems. Indeed, buoyed by high oil and natural gas prices, Algeria was for many years a high-flying model for most of the world's developing nations. It spent billions of dollars on rapid industrialization and at the same time heavily subsidized food prices so that it won a reputation as one of the Third World's few welfare states.

However, the plummeting of oil prices in the 1980s combined with the mismanagement of Algeria's highly centralized economy brought about the nation's most serious social and economic crisis since the early days of independence. Serious shortfalls in oil-generated revenues aggravated already existing problems within the Algerian economy. Even moves to liberalize the economy initiated by Benjedid in the mid-1980s tended to favor those with money:[3] Unskilled workers, the unemployed, and those without access to foreign currency or the means to obtain goods on the flourishing black market lost out. Government policies intended to restructure the economy along market-oriented lines at the same time the government was trying to service an increasing external debt resulted in food shortages, rising prices, and rampant corruption. Increased social tensions were reflected in waves of labor strikes, street disturbances, and public demonstrations.

The sense of desperation was vast. It tied into deeper grievances associated with political disillusionment, cultural disaffection, and spiritual alienation. The dominating role of the state, buttressed by its tripartite bases of power located in the FLN, army, and government bureaucracy, effectively destroyed autonomous political life for the better part of Algeria's postindependence history. Centralized authority suffocated choice and extinguished opportunity, leading to a generalized sense of political purposelessness.[4]

In the cultural realm, an ambiguous mix of Arab, Berber, and French cultural strains created a confused national identity confounded further by uncertain government policies regarding language use,

Westernization practices, schooling, and the treatment of women. To this was added a profound sense of spiritual aridity felt by many of the country's young. The revolutionary rhetoric of the past along with a commitment to domestic and global socialism failed to capture the hearts and minds of most Algerians. State-directed secular ideology proved little more than political rationalization for maintaining the power of the few at the expense of the disaffected many. By the late 1970s a revived sense of spiritual purpose ensconced in Islam's universal truths aroused the nation's moral consciousness. It would be only a matter of time before this revivalist spirit was transformed into a powerful political message.

Finally, the world itself began to change in dramatic and fundamental ways coinciding with the elections of Margaret Thatcher in Britain, Ronald Reagan in the United States, and, most dramatically, the selection of Mikhail Gorbachev as secretary-general of the Communist Party of the Soviet Union in March 1985. The 1980s witnessed the revival of democratic principles, the validation of privatization policies and initiatives embedded in reinvigorated market-oriented economies, the disintegration of left-wing authoritarian regimes in the Third World and the concomitant collapse of communism in Eastern Europe, and the plunge in the price of oil and other basic raw materials. These and other related developments created a global environment generally hostile to Algeria's domestic agenda and foreign policy orientation.

Algeria's multiple crises at home and abroad generated a continuous series of domestic conflicts and disorders culminating in the bloodbath of October 1988.[5] It is indeed ironic that Algeria's mobilizing themes, which it had long articulated in urging the Third World front to struggle against an oppressive global political economic order—"the misappropriation of wealth, the constitution of privilege, and the stubborn defense of an inequitable order"[6]—were the very same forces extant at home against which ordinary Algerian men and women rebelled. By the end of the 1980s there was an enormous gap between revolutionary rhetoric and the oppressive nature of Algeria's domestic political economic order. Fundamental change was required in both national and foreign policy spheres to reestablish a congruence that most people would find credible.

RESTRUCTURING AND REFORM

The government of Chadli Benjedid initiated a series of cautious domestic reforms within a year of assuming power in February 1979.[7] These accelerated significantly in the mid-1980s, affecting the country's economic, bureaucratic, political, and foreign policy orientations. Both polity and economy were liberalized through a calculated program of decentralization, deconcentration, and limited democratization intended to redress many of the socioeconomic and political failures previously identified.

Three reform phases could be identified. From 1980 to 1987 the government directed most of its attention to overcoming structural problems in the economy. Specifically, reform measures revolved around four basic axes: shifting domestic investments away from heavy industry and toward agriculture, light industry, and consumer goods; breaking up large state enterprises into smaller and more manageable units; privatizing portions of state-owned farmlands and their commercial networks; and encouraging private investment in industry.

On balance these measures proved too timid, too schematic, and too underfunded to challenge significantly the enormity of the state bureaucracy with its ensconced cadres jealously protecting their power, privileges, and patronage. The world price of oil fell from almost $40 a barrel in 1979 to under $10 in 1986, immediately impacting Algeria's balance of payments, which had received more than 95 percent of its foreign currency earnings from hydrocarbon sales. The combination of poor domestic planning, political timidity, and the collapse of the price of oil aggravated further the many problems in the economy.

Responding to the country's aborted perestroika or economic reform,[8] Chadli's government confronted the challenges more directly. Starting in 1987 with the second phase of reforms, measures were undertaken to further liberalize polity and economy. An Algerian human-rights league was legalized; the right of associations to organize, recruit, and propagate was officially recognized by the National Assembly in its law of July 21, 1987; laws were passed to accelerate the privatization and exploitation of state-owned lands; and new legislation granted considerable managerial autonomy to the many newly created reduced-sized enterprises that were now being asked to operate by the laws of supply and demand rather than by the dictates of central planning.

In many ways Chadli's initiatives to address the fiscal deficit mirrored recommendations made by the World Bank and the International Monetary Fund for overcoming structural problems extant in many Third World countries.[9] Specifically, to stimulate production, subsidies on basic consumer staples were reduced and price controls lifted from state industrial and agricultural sectors, thereby allowing market forces to regulate resource distribution. These measures constituted only part of an overall austerity initiative that proved capable of meeting its designed purpose. By the late 1980s, tax increases and reductions in credit, imports, and government spending served in tandem to reverse the trends in GDP growth.[10]

The social costs for such reform measures were high. Unemployment went from 11 percent in 1984 to 25 percent in 1988, and family purchasing power declined drastically. Attempting to reform state and society simultaneously proved beyond the capacity of an increasingly besieged regime. The explosion of October 1988[11] was the consequence of this conjunction of crises.[12]

Following the bloodbath and destruction, Chadli took the opportunity to implement another wave of reforms, which went beyond anything Algeria had experienced since independence. In short, a veritable democratic revolution was initiated that was intended to unleash the country's productive human and material forces. This third reform period witnessed an explosion of institutional changes intended to create a "nation of laws." Major constitutional reforms were undertaken along with fundamental revisions in the organization, power, and position of the FLN in state and society. For example, the FLN was officially separated from the state, and its monopoly of political power was eliminated. The military as well was removed from playing any direct role in party and politics. All these and other related measures were intended as a prelude to the institutionalization of democratic life.

Following his reelection as Algeria's president for a third consecutive term in December 1988, Chadli carried through with his version of glasnost or political openness. On February 23, 1989, a new Algerian constitution was voted in by national referendum. Among its more significant features was the elimination of all references to socialism or socialist principles as necessary to Algerian political identity or development. Not only was this a dramatic turnaround in the country's official political ideology, which had long defined its revolutionary and populist identity, but it also signaled a formal break with the ideological foundation of its foreign policy orientation, based as it was on militant collective self-reliance among Third World states organized along socialist principles of redistributive justice, collectivization, nationalization, global cartelization, and Western "paybacks" for past practices of colonialist exploitation and pauperization.

Other noteworthy constitutional changes included unrestricted freedoms of expression, association, and organization (Article 39), the right to unionize and strike (Articles 53 and 54), and the right to form "associations of a political nature" (Article 40). This latter constitutional provision formalized an authentic multiparty system whose status was codified in the enabling law of July 5, 1989 (Law 89-11).

In only nine months, from October 1988 to July 1989, the Algerian regime was fundamentally transformed from a single-party authoritarian state to a multiparty, pluralistic nation of laws.[13] Nearly thirty political parties representing ideological tendencies ranging from the Marxist left (PAGS-Parti de l'Avant-Garde Socialiste) to the Islamist right (FIS) were officially recognized and registered. Within a year this revolutionary system was given its first electoral test.

The June 1990 municipal and provincial elections resulted in a major defeat for the ruling FLN and a massive victory for the Islamic Salvation Front.[14] It was also a victory for democracy, as both the electoral process and the voting results were allowed to stand.[15] Responding to the defeat, Chadli announced that elections for the National Popular Assembly (APN) would be held in the first quarter of 1991 (postponed to June 1991 and then again to December 1991). If these elections had been permitted to proceed according to established constitutional procedures, it seems unlikely that the democratic process could have been reversed regardless of who came to power.

In sum, after nearly three decades of authoritarian rule by a Leninist-type party (FLN), it seemed that democratic forces were gaining ground in Algeria. Since the early 1980s, but accelerating with incredible speed following the nationwide riots of October 1988, political space for electoral competition in Algeria had opened up, the degree of political contest had intensified, and the scope of political discourse in the public domain had widened. Authoritarian political structures were being dismantled—including the much-feared and detested internal security police apparatus (DGDS)—rules for democratic politics had been established, civic organizations were forming, and entry barriers to organized political competition had been removed. Numerous political parties were organized and legally recognized.

Whether institutional changes had been sufficiently deep to overcome an existing political subculture of distrust cannot yet be determined. However, the January 11, 1992 coup d'état against Chadli, the declaration of martial law in the same month, and the dissolution of the FIS on March 4, 1992 once again raise serious doubts about the

depth and durability of democratic politics in Algeria. The reintro-
duction of the military in civilian politics cannot help but put into
question the regime's commitment to expanding societal rights at the
expense of state authority and power.

THE ISLAMIC VICTORY

The FIS emerged during the months leading up to the June 1990 APC
and APW elections as the only serious nationwide competitor to the
FLN. With its some 1,265 communal candidate lists to the FLN's 1,520
and 248 *wilaya* (provinces) lists compared to the FLN's 269, the FIS
revealed its widespread presence throughout the country.[16] Although the
1980s witnessed the renaissance of Islamic discourse in Algeria and
throughout the Arab world, it was only in the aftermath of the riots of
October 1988 that these ideological currents took root and culminated
in the creation of formal organizations with succinct political platforms.

The death of numerous citizens—many supportive of the FIS—at
the hands of government troops created disillusionment and revulsion
on a large scale. For many, Islam offered both continuity and security
at a chaotic time and also held promise for the future. At Friday
prayer services throughout the country, religious leaders argued for
traditional Islamic views with respect to such issues as the status of
women and personal morality and at the same time inveighed against
government waste, corruption, and complicity with the West.[17] In
approaching Islam as the overarching framework for the social order,
traditionalists saw the use of mosques for political purposes as entirely
natural; the approach also proved to be highly useful. The religious
network provided an excellent organizational base for the FIS to promote its particular ideology and actively recruit supporters.

It proved capable of gaining the confidence of Algerians and successfully mobilizing mass support. The electoral law enacted in July
1989 allowed the FIS, under the joint direction of Abbassi Madani and
Ali Belhaj, to declare its existence officially and to campaign openly.
The moderate views of Madani,[18] a philosophy professor, stood in
stark contrast to the militancy of Belhaj, a high-school teacher and
religious leader. In his capacity as official spokesman for the party,
Madani, with his subdued erudition, served as a source of reassurance
in the maelstrom of Algerian politics. The message that Islamic political discourse may well complement social development—a message
delivered through the vehicle of an effectively led, well-organized,

and well-financed party network—proved a powerful political call to action for many young Algerians.

In breaking the monopoly of power held by the FLN for nearly three decades, the FIS took control of every APW in the heavily populated north and every APC in Algiers, Oran, and Constantine. By taking more than 55 percent of all municipalities, the FIS became one of the first opposition groups to be voted into a position of power in an Arab or African country.

The Islamist victory also constituted a crushing rejection of rule by the FLN establishment.[19] It showed that the Islamists were strong not only in the urban areas, where they had recruited strongly among the ranks of disaffected youth, but also throughout much of the country, where it had been expected that FLN officials would mobilize their traditional bloc votes to win at least a thin majority for the FLN. Only in Berber-speaking Kabylie, with its own distinctive political configuration, and in the south (where independents were strong and the FLN well-entrenched) did the Islamic Salvation Front not win convincingly.[20]

Like observers everywhere, most Algerians were surprised by the voting results. Yet many Algerians, including non-FIS voters, took comfort from the fact that an opposition party could overturn the FLN, in which public confidence had reached new lows. This latter factor may have been important in the voting and may have led to the subdued response within the country since. In this milieu of lost confidence and political disillusionment, the FIS (outside Kabylie) benefited most, capitalizing on the work of its militants, now numbering in the tens of thousands, and on its image as the most genuine opposition party. The FIS win was a vote for a less corrupt, more equal Algeria; it was a vote against those authorities closely associated with the violent suppression of the October 1988 riots.

This analysis implies that the FIS victory signaled opposition to the FLN rather than popular support for the introduction of *shari'a* or religious law, and other elements of radical Islam. This may have been the case for some voters given the high rate of abstention and the fact that these were "only" local elections.[21] However, the popular urban base of radical Islam should not be underestimated. And, away from the coast, negative elements of FIS policies, which range from discouraging the use of the French language and other European practices to closing bars and dividing the sexes at social events, are much less apparent in the deeply religious Arabized communities of the interior. Students from the south and mountain regions, as well as the urban poor, have provided ideal FIS recruits.[22]

Many of Algeria's Islamists and in particular those supporting the FIS are middle class, urbane, educated and, in some ways, moderate in their political views. As such, the broad-based support of traditional religious values may be seen in part as a reflection of a profound concern for a troubled social order, a society largely based on inequities in the distribution of both material and political resources.[23]

The local elections confirmed the view that the FIS had created a well-oiled political machine organized around a network of mosques.[24] On polling day it proved its potency in a number of ways: by posting militants as observers at every ballot box; through acts such as praying in polling stations and stationing members outside to persuade voters to choose the FIS list; and by exploiting proxy voting procedures. No other party, not even the FLN, could compete. The FIS acted as a ruling party is usually allowed to act in North African elections, supervising the ballot counting on polling day and being subject to complaints of electoral malpractice from its rivals. These same electoral practices were put to advantage by the FIS in its aborted victory in the December 1991 legislative elections.[25]

The style and substance of Islamist governance at the local and regional levels produced mixed results. In the immediate weeks following the FIS victory, for example, there were many newspaper accounts of incidents involving crackdowns by FIS-run municipal councils. It was also reported that Islamic radicals had moved to segregate beaches and ban swimwear and shorts from seaside towns (but not beaches or pools), and prohibit alcohol sales. However, when in August 1990 I spent a day at the beach in Chenoua in the Tipasa commune controlled by the FIS, I saw no evidence of any restrictions. Bikini-clad Algerian women sunbathed freely, and men ordered bottles of beer at nearby cafés without incident. To be sure, examples of Islamic zealousness existed and may have led many Algerians to rethink their vote in the first round of parliamentary elections. Yet extremist municipal rulings were very localized and in some cases overruled by the local *wali* (governor). For his part, Abbassi Madani, in interviews with this writer, expressed a certain frustration with councils that moved "too quickly," taking the law into their own hands and alienating voters. The FIS leader had preferred to move more cautiously in the consolidation of the FIS position through a slow process of winning hearts and minds rather than imposing its values overnight.

This more moderate and civic-minded approach had been in evidence in many areas of public life. Almost at the outset the FIS became involved in demonstrating its good intentions, as when it started cleaning the filthy streets of Algiers in defiance of a garbage strike. Independent reports on the performance of FIS communes in certain coastal towns found new APC presidents to be moderate and well-educated professionals professing not only Islamic values but also a firm conviction that the FIS was the only way to overcome FLN mismanagement.

Had this pattern prevailed, a FIS-dominated government could have created a new, popularly acceptable political configuration that would have continued many of the economic reforms instituted by the previous government while also seeking to inculcate Islamic values and uphold Algeria's deeply rooted traditions of social justice that have been in retreat in recent years. Yet this analysis assumed that Abbassi's moderate wing could control the more radical elements in the party and that all groups would agree to play by the political rules during a period of high tension and uncertainty. Not surprisingly, however, when the electoral process collapsed altogether in January 1992 it was neither Islamist "radicals" nor "moderates" but the state itself that was principally to blame.

THE FLN IN DISARRAY

Chadli Benjedid was elected to the presidency in February 1979, two months after the unexpected death of Houari Boumediene, who had come to power in June 1965 in a military coup d'état staged against the country's first postindependence president, Ahmed Ben Bella.[26] Within two years, Chadli managed to consolidate his position at the expense of opponents on the left and right wings of the ruling FLN. His government then began to reverse the rigorously socialist economic policies pursued by Boumediene in the 1970s. This process continued with the party being brought more firmly under Chadli's control as secretary-general and an increasing number of new faces joining the government. Chadli's reappointment as secretary-general at the FLN's fifth party congress in December 1983 automatically made him the FLN's candidate in the presidential election in January 1984, in which he was reelected for a second five-year term as head of state with 95 percent of the vote. He immediately consolidated his position further with a major reshuffling of both party and government posts.

By the mid-1980s the Chadli government had proved more flexible than any before, employing a number of strategies, including the encouragement of private enterprise and the modernization of administrative procedures, to enliven Algeria's extensive and ponderous bureaucracy. As the Chadli regime became more secure it also felt able to make conciliatory gestures toward dissident members of the FLN establishment, both living and dead. In February 1985 Chadli announced that Boumediene's 1976 National Charter would be "enriched"—that is, revised—to take account of new realities.[27] After an extraordinary party congress the draft charter was submitted to a national referendum. In January 1986 more than 95 percent of the electorate voted for its acceptance, effectively giving President Chadli a public mandate for his policies.

Liberalization of the economy and an overhaul of the cumbersome state machinery gained pace in the period following the 1985-1986 oil price crash. Increasingly, liberal technocrats came to replace old-guard politicians in senior posts—a process mirrored by reforms to the Algerian National Army (ANP) that seemed to reduce the influence of the military even though it remained probably the country's most powerful political institution. However, although many Algerians and overseas bankers welcomed the beneficial effects of Chadli's reforms, the reforms had adverse effects on the vulnerable sectors of the society, as liberalization measures magnified the divisions between wealthy citizens and the majority who were hard-hit by rising prices and cuts in both social benefits and public-sector jobs.[28]

The limits of accelerated liberalism during a period of economic austerity became clear in September 1988, when the country was hit by a wave of paralyzing strikes, in part orchestrated by members of the UGTA (General Union of Algerian Workers), the national trade union affiliated with the FLN. Following a buildup of tensions in early October, especially around the Rouiba vehicle assembly plant, rioting broke out in Algiers and other cities. Unlike earlier incidents, such as violence involving Berber nationalists and Islamic militants in the early 1980s or riots in the Algiers Casbah (1985) and Constantine (1986), the "black October" riots proved very difficult to control.

By the time order was restored, hundreds had been killed and thousands injured in six days, October 6 through 11.[29] The October riots highlighted the gulf between a predominantly youthful population—who made up the vast majority of the rioters—and the older FLN establishment. They also revealed an unexpected vulnerability in the regime. At no time were more than 30,000 people mobilized against the forces of order, yet the police were unable to cope and the brutality of the army's response was such that the ANP finally lost its revolutionary mystique.[30] This was confirmed in early 1989 when the ANP withdrew from the central committee of the FLN, marking the army's effective withdrawal from public life (at least at a formal level) and a major step further in the process of demilitarization and civilianization, moves considered necessary for "true" democratic politics to take place. Subsequent creation of a ministry of defense separate from the presidency and the abolition of the security police force confirmed this trend toward the civilianization of politics.

The most important message of the riots was that after three decades the FLN had lost its way. It was clear that radical action was necessary. Chadli then acted decisively, underlining his commitment to economic liberalism and opening the way for major political reform.[31]

After the excesses of the riot period, more reform was essential to rebuild public confidence. Because reform had previously been opposed mainly by hard-liners within the FLN, Chadli turned the situation to his advantage by dismissing unpopular party leaders and by offering potentially sweeping political reforms. On November 3, 1988, Algerians voted in a referendum to amend fourteen of the constitution's 199 articles, dividing the executive presidency from the government, placing the president above day-to-day politics, and making the government responsible to the legislature—the National Popular Assembly (APN)—which would have considerably more power than in the past. The vote in favor was 92 percent. On the promise of further reforms—and a widespread view that for all the faults of his regime, Chadli should continue as head of state for the time being—the process was consolidated by an 81 percent vote in his favor in the presidential elections of December 1988.

Further constitutional amendments were approved in a plebiscite on February 7, 1989, and rounded off the first phase of the post-riot political reforms. The amendments included one allowing for the emergence of political parties ("associations of a political nature") to compete with the FLN. This was confirmed by a law on political associations, passed after much debate in the APN in July 1989. Although there were significant constraints—for example, the associations may not have overtly religious or regionalist platforms—the new framework opened the way for a controlled multiparty system to develop.

Almost immediately political parties representing virtually all ideological tendencies sprung up to challenge the dominant FLN. In response the FLN convened an extraordinary party congress in November 1989 to put its own house in order. Instead, the convention revealed how deep the divisions were between old-guard hard-liners and liberal reformers. Specifically, four factions emerged at the congress:[32] reformers led by Chadli and his prime minister, Mouloud Hamrouche; hard-line socialists—the old guard—opposing reforms ("neo-Boumedienists"); FLN cadres and bureaucrats fearful of rapid change and opposed to a multiparty system; and Islamists supporting greater Islamization of society. Although intended to set out the FLN's platform for the future in a more liberal, multiparty Algeria, the event was widely seen as a victory for the old guard. Yet what Chadli and his supporters failed to achieve in late 1989, the June 1990 local elections accomplished with a vengeance.

The vote of unemployed and working-class Algerians for the FIS—backed in places like Tlemcen, Constantine, and even some of Algiers's wealthiest areas by elements of the traditional bourgeoisie and by traders—was a rejection of the values of a largely Francophone middle class that had developed around the FLN hierarchy. The debate, launched with accusations made by former prime minister Abdelhamid Brahimi of large-scale corruption, further undermined the FLN, as did divisions between the government and reformists within the party and their old-guard rivals. An overconfident, self-obsessed FLN went into the election campaign irreparably divided after the return in force of old-guard elements at the extraordinary November 1989 congress. With its overwhelming defeat in the June 1990 elections, the FLN was effectively delegitimized. If it was to survive at all, it had to be reconstituted along completely different lines or break up into separate political entities. The usurpation of the democratic process by conservative forces within the military and ruling party in January 1992 in no way altered, and possibly may have even reinforced, this assessment.

POLITICAL OPPOSITION: SECULARIST AND ISLAMIST

The historic victory of the opposition Islamic Salvation Front in the June 12, 1990, local elections answered some crucial questions but left many more unanswered.[33] The FIS win confirmed the potency of Islam as a mobilizing force. More than any other movement, Islamism was able to focus opposition to the FLN establishment. FIS was also able to establish that, in those communes and provinces it controlled, it had a right to hold the moral and political high ground it claimed in the elections.[34] In the immediate period following the 1990 elections many Algerians, including members of the ruling group, believed that once in power, Islamic zealots would undermine the popular base that the FIS had developed and that formed the core of its success in June 1990. However, some of those running the new FIS local communities (sometimes known as Islamic communes) were the sort of young technocrats the FLN's reformists had hoped to recruit to rejuvenate the party. This factor, coupled with the enthusiasm of FIS supporters for getting things done—such as sweeping the streets or distributing housing more fairly—could have been the basis for the consolidation of FIS power at the national level had the democratic process been permitted to continue.

For this reason, divisions within the FIS between moderates led by Abbassi Madani and the party's radical wing, whose most vocal spokesman is Ali Belhaj, had assumed great importance. Prior to the imposition of the June 1991 state of siege, it was assumed that if the moderates had played their cards well, they could have been poised to take advantage of an historic compromise. If the radicals ended up on top, however, political deals would have been much harder to negotiate and the potential for highly dangerous and violent divisions to polarize further a society already undergoing a traumatic process of transition would have been much increased, thus fueling fears of a military coup. As events were to show, the radical politics of hardliners in both the FLN and FIS created the unstable social environment the army used to justify its political intervention, first in June 1991 and then, decisively, in January 1992.

The political situation in Algeria was extremely uncertain before the 1991 legislative elections. In a revealing television interview on October 8, 1990, on the nation's popular news-interview program "Face à la Presse," Chadli Benjedid confirmed his government's determination to permit legislative elections to proceed in the first quarter of 1991 provided that there was not "an electrified or unsuitable atmosphere." This veiled warning followed closely on similar comments made by Defense Minister Khaled Nezzar, who in mid-September 1990 declared that the army was prepared to intervene in next year's general elections if national unity was threatened by "organized excesses." Appointed defense minister by Chadli in July 1990, Nezzar declared that the army was apolitical and would not help or hinder any party taking part in the voting. Yet he added that "the army wants the elections to take place in calm and peace without any harm to the inalienable rights of citizens."[35]

For its part, the FIS made it clear that it would not tolerate army interference in the domestic political process under whatever pretext or circumstances. In April 1991, for example, Madani went so far as to warn the Algerian military not to "descend onto the streets. If one drop of blood should be spilled," the usually mild-mannered educator declared, "I swear to God that we will fight the army to its complete destruction."[36]

These reinforced warnings came at a time of feverish activity in the streets of major Algerian cities. Wildcat strikes, demonstrations, political gatherings, organized assemblies, and unruly street activities were occurring virtually every day. In mid-October 1990, for example, Constantine was the site of a demonstration of approximately 5,000 protesting the lack of jobs, housing, food supplies, public transportation, and inadequate wages for those employed in the public sector. Social and political tensions were evident throughout, and society seemed on the verge of total breakdown.

In his October 8, 1990, interview, Chadli confirmed that he did not intend to step down from the presidency regardless of the outcome of the general elections. The statement was intended to dampen speculations on the subject following Ahmed Ben Bella's return to Algeria on September 27, 1990, and former premier Kasdi Merbah's resignation from the FLN with the intention of creating his own political party. At the time Merbah called for presidential elections following legislative ones.

The divisions and fissures within the FLN turned into complete separation. This process began with Rabah Bitat's resignation on October 3, 1990, as president of the National Assembly, a position he had held continuously since the parliament was officially reactivated under Boumediene in 1977. He said he was leaving in protest of the reform policies of then premier Mouloud Hamrouche. Bitat's stepping down was followed in early October by Kasdi Merbah's resignation from the FLN's Central Committee to form his own party.

Both resignations reflected the deep dissatisfaction of the old guard with Chadli's efforts at dismantling the public sector. These complaints were echoed by other veteran leaders like 'Abd al-'Aziz Bouteflika, Mohamed Salah Yahiaoui, Mohamed Cherif Messaadia, Belaid Abdessalam, and Ahmad Taleb Ibrahimi. All issued statements criticizing reformers like Hamrouche and his allies. These hard-liners were later instrumental in reversing Algeria's fragile democracy and once again promoting the socialist agenda. Those propounding the latter position have been supported by the senior officer corps along with organized labor, which has been deeply concerned about the reforms' effect on jobs. The UGTA has been among the most active of political groups in demonstrating in the streets to protest the economic changes underway since the mid-1980s. It is, therefore, no surprise that Belaid Abdessalam was handpicked by the military-created Higher Council of State to form a government in July 1992, revealing more clearly than ever the hard-liners' determination to reimpose the state-centered authoritarian order despite its massive rejection by ordinary Algerians as expressed in the October 1998 riots, the June 1990 elections, and the first round of national legislative elections in December 1991.

Other resignations and withdrawals followed during the month of October 1990. Former prime minister Abdelhamid Brahimi resigned from the FLN Central Committee in protest of what he called "the absence of real democracy" in the party. Earlier in the year (March 1990), Brahimi—premier from 1984 to 1988 and now an economics professor at the University of Algiers—caused a sensation by claiming party and government officials had pocketed nearly $30 billion in bribes and commissions. These allegations helped undermine the FLN preceding the local elections in June 1990. Brahimi's departure confirmed the ongoing trend of divisions within the FLN. This process was capped when Chadli himself withdrew as head of the FLN, thus technically separating the party from the state.

Despite all the efforts of the military-backed government, including the formal dissolution of the party in March 1992, the FIS remains the dominant opposition party if not the most popular political movement in the country. Even the arrest and imprisonment of both Madani and Belhaj in July 1991 did not significantly diminish the electoral appeal of the FIS. Although there were those who voted for the FIS in June 1990 simply to record their disgust with nearly three decades of FLN rule, many others were inspired by the message of moral rectification that the Islamists communicated with vigor and conviction. The same organizational strength and depth of connection with the populace—through local mosques located in virtually all parts of the country—that existed in the local contests were predictable in future elections should the FIS be allowed to run candidates once again. "In its call for the enactment of *shari'a* law and emphasis on Islamic values, the FIS [has struck] a chord in a society with a declining standard of living and outraged by the corruption of the political class"[37] of the kind publicly revealed by former premier Brahimi in March 1990. The establishment of Islamic restaurants and Islamic vendors selling food at a fraction of the conventional market cost during Ramadan (March) 1991 added to the credibility of the FIS as a party of social action, moral consciousness, and economic justice.

Despite the existence of numerous socioeconomic cleavages, Islam versus secularism is now the major bipolarity in Algerian politics.[38] The debate has largely centered on the designated role of religion in the sociopolitical order. For the FIS, the very legitimacy of the state rests on the integration and implementation of holy law in the furtherance of traditional Islamic views. In contrast, for the ruling elite, the role of *shari'a* and Islamic jurisprudence in Algerian politics must be a small one, confined largely to the realm of personal status issues. The tensions of a political climate divided between two opposing worldviews have proven to be profound, leaving little room for practical reconciliation.

THE RETURN OF THE STATE

By Algeria's own standards as well as by those of other Arab states, its democratic opening was radical, even historic. Still, an underlying subculture of elite political authoritarianism continued to limit the scope of national-level power sharing. This became dramatically visible with the violent events immediately preceding the planned legislative elections of June 27, 1991. The imposition of martial law by the Algerian army on June 5 effectively short-circuited the democratic experiment awaited by many in and out of the country. Elections were postponed for several months, and the Hamrouche government was replaced by a transition cabinet headed by Sid Ahmed Ghozali, an old-line Boumedienist who was being portrayed by the pro-government Algerian media as a pragmatist, technician, and conciliator.[39]

These government actions represented a serious move away from the country's commitment to political pluralism, conciliation, and democracy and toward a policy of militaristic coercion against those who challenged the political status quo. This movement toward authoritarian politics raised serious doubts about the country's commitment to fundamental political and economic change, which everyone agrees is essential if Algeria is to overcome its myriad social, economic, and political problems.

What had gone wrong and why? Were the preliminary efforts toward political liberalization nothing more than tactical steps undertaken by a defensive-minded leadership fearful of losing grip on its political, economic, and social power? Regardless of political intent, was Algerian political culture so ensconced in an authoritarian past, including its socialist phase, that it could not permit a truly democratic opening allowing all political groups, including Islamic ones, to participate freely in the political process? Clearly the bipolarity of Algerian political life between an Islamist discourse and a secular discourse was severely aggravated to the point that by 1992 it provoked chronic civil violence if not civil war.

The strategy and policy of military development was outlined in a new legislative formula covering medium and long-range strategy for defense in 1991-1997. In theory, this involved civilian legislators in the compiling of plans for investment and infrastructure development, previously the domain of the secretive and extremely powerful military establishment. This legislative initiative formed one element of ongoing reforms aimed at bringing the military under the formal control of a civilian government. These included appointing in 1990 a defense minister, Khaled Nezzar, theoretically answerable to the APN and scrapping secret police organizations.

In spite of these changes, there was never much doubt that the military-security establishment (*mukhabarat*) remained an essential element in the political arena—even if the army had officially retired from politics. During the volatile weeks between the presidential press conference on April 3, 1991, announcing the date for legislative elections and June 5, 1991, when a state of siege was declared giving full authority to the military, Chadli consistently hinted of the possible return of the army to the political stage if events got out of hand or civilian authority broke down. Such warnings were intended to keep his political opening under control with opposition politicians, who, for the most part, preferred to contest elections and publish newspapers rather than face tanks.

For its part, the army had found this ambiguous situation to its satisfaction given its disastrous performance in the October 1988 riots. Clearly that experience was deeply disturbing to an institution more used to seeing itself as the defender of the revolution and the guardian of national integrity than as an apparatus mindlessly killing and shooting innocent civilians. Nonetheless, the security services remained a force to be reckoned with as they gradually regained strength and influence. There can be little doubt that the decision in mid-1991 to impose martial law, declare a state of siege, send tanks and troops into Algiers and other Algerian cities, arrest both Madani and Belhaj on charges of armed conspiracy against the security of the state, and imprison nearly three thousand FIS militants as part of an intensified crackdown on all antistate activity was taken by the highest national security command. The fall of the reformist and liberal-minded Hamrouche government in the aftermath of the civil violence and military intervention and its replacement by a transitional cabinet headed by neo-Boumedienist Sid Ahmed Ghozali was further testimony to the renewed strength of the armed forces. The army's latest intervention in January 1992 was less a coup d'état than a coup de grâce, a decisive finishing blow against the democratizing body politic.

ISLAMISTS VERSUS THE ARMY

Under the pretext of restoring law and order, the July 1, 1991, arrest of FIS leaders Madani and Belhaj underlined the military authorities' determination to destroy the power and prestige of Algeria's leading Islamist movement. Coming soon after the roundup of several thousand FIS supporters, the arrest of the FIS leaders led to the possibility of further crises if disaffected groups maintained their challenge on the streets. All this seems to suggest that the military was intent on transforming the political environment in a way certain to limit the extent of the democratic "opening."

To be sure, the arrests occurred after a period of mounting tension that followed the state-of-siege declaration on June 5. Following regular clashes between FIS militants, disaffected youths, and the security forces, threats by Madani and Belhaj to call a holy war if the state of siege was not lifted provided the immediate rationale for the army to act. But the military made full use of the powers vested by the martial law decree, which allowed for administrative internment, house arrest, and other controls. The decree's Article 11, for example, allowed military tribunals to try crimes against state security no matter who the defendant was.

Within five weeks of the nationwide curfew order and with social tensions easing, the army spoke of lifting the state of siege in advance of its declared four-month duration. Yet it left no doubt who was in charge of the affairs of state. In a communiqué issued by the army command, the government appealed to the country's twenty-five million people to "observe the civic duty of everyone to guarantee the achievement of a return to normal life."[40]

The military's actions ended a period of increasing frustration among officers with the government's "laxness" toward the FIS. Initial fears among military commanders that FIS supporters within all ranks of the army might oppose a military crackdown and refuse to participate in it proved unfounded, although few doubt that strong Islamist sympathies prevail within all segments of the security services. The assassination of figurehead president Mohamed Boudiaf in June 1992 by a member of the presidential security guard was viewed by many as clear testimony to the scope of Islamist infiltration into Algeria's highest military command structure.

ABORTED ELECTIONS

Chadli Benjedid lifted the state of siege and announced in mid-October 1991 that previously postponed legislative elections would proceed in two rounds on December 26, 1991, and January 16, 1992. These elections would be conducted under the terms of an electoral law that had been revised for the second time in one year after an acrimonious debate in the FLN-dominated legislature. Even then the new code was finally approved only after a constitutional court nullified sections intended to maintain electoral boundaries advantageous to the FLN.[41]

For its part the FIS remained skeptical of the government's intentions especially since both FIS leaders, Madani and Belhaj, waited in jail for trial by a military court. Even to the last moment it was uncertain that the FIS would participate in parliamentary elections intended to fill the 430-seat National Assembly. In the final analysis, however, the decision to proceed with the democratic process that the FIS had been so instrumental in fostering proved a brilliant strategic decision given the enormous victory it achieved in the first round of votes on December 26, 1991.[42] FIS candidates secured 188 of the 430 seats and were leading in 150 other constituencies, whose seats were to be decided in the next round of voting (for those who failed to achieve a majority). It seemed almost certain that the FIS would, in the January 16 second round of voting, win majority control of the assembly.

What remained uncertain, however, was how the intensely nationalistic officer corps would respond to a possible takeover, albeit democratic, of legislative and presidential power by Islamists. The answer came quickly and brutally in early January 1992 when defense minister Nezzar joined Major General Larbi Belkheir (interior minister) and Major General 'Abd al-Malek Guenaizia (army chief-of-staff) in declaring a state of siege, in forcing Chadli's resignation, and in assuming power through a Higher Council of State (HCS) consisting of non-elected civilian politicians and senior army officers. The HCS's first act was to annul the election results of December 26, 1991, and to cancel the scheduled second-round voting of January 16, 1992. In the weeks and months that followed, the HCS systematically cracked down on the FIS, imprisoned thousands of its members and, on March 4, 1992, officially dissolved the organization as a legal political party. In so doing, the army overturned Algeria's brief experiment in liberal democracy and plunged the nation into an environment of deep anxiety, fear, and disillusionment.

DEMOCRACY DERAILED

"When I saw the tanks rolling through the city streets, I began crying," a twenty-year-old Algerian male declared to a reporter. "Not because I was fearful of the army nor afraid of the Islamic Salvation Front, but because I suddenly saw disappear in a matter of moments the liberty that we had struggled so hard to achieve these last three years."[43] This poignant admission captures in human terms the attitude of many ordinary people toward the reentry of the army into Algerian civilian life. Whatever else may have been happening in the weeks and months prior to the declaration of a state of siege, Algerian politics was bursting with vital energy, political discourse and competition, exchanges of ideas and points of view, and, not surprisingly, strikes, demonstrations, and street rallies. In virtually all democracies, especially emerging ones with little history of legitimate contestation, the first experience with freedom and liberty is volatile if not violent. Clearly most Algerians were willing to accept such consequences on behalf of a larger goal, namely the right to determine the political system and political leadership of their own choosing. That the government, army, and FLN were unwilling to allow that process to evolve naturally speaks volumes to the strong residue of authoritarianism that continues to permeate Algerian political culture, attitudes, and behavior.

In other newly democratizing Third World regions, certain structural properties are associated with the emergence and maintenance of democracy.[44] One is the rise of civic participation, including the willingness of ordinary men and women to sacrifice physical and mental comfort to participate in the civic experience. Second is the increasing commitment to the electoral process. The intensity of electoral campaigns and of voter participation in many areas, often conducted under hazardous conditions, indicates a remarkable willingness on the part of ordinary citizens to utilize ballots to express preferences, settle conflicts, and confer authority on leaders. Third is the withdrawal of military leaders from formal office and, as a result, the emergence of civilian presidents. In Algeria today, all three structural properties of democracy are visibly absent; their future is in doubt so long as the army rules the country.

CIVIL SOCIETY IN THE BALANCE

The liberalization policies of Chadli predated the democratic revolutions in Eastern Europe. Thus the so-called demonstration effect seems incidental to the Algerian experiment with democracy. So too were the influences of liberal democratic principles, which have never been taken seriously even (especially?) by highly Francophone intellectuals. More important had been the breakdown of the "ruling bargain," or "social contract," that the regime struck with its people at the time of independence.

A collapsing economy caused by state mismanagement, corruption, and declining oil prices combined to undermine this social contract. These structural conditions of the domestic and international economies imposed hardships on a civil society that soon began to become restive. Social turmoil, civil disobedience, public demonstrations, wildcat strikes, campus unrest, and Islamic militancy came together to challenge the efficacy of the state's social "contract." Violence and bloodshed soon followed, with the October 1988 riots representing the most serious challenge ever to the regime. A limited degree of political pluralism and democracy was the carrot offered to the populace at large in an effort to temper the effects of strict austerity policies. In making such concessions, it was hoped that momentum created in the political arena would carry over to the economic realm.[45]

Elsewhere, the emergence of a new "democratic" bargain has been aided by the resiliency of civil society, which has enabled vigorous associational groups, especially professional movements and intellectuals, to play crucial roles in revitalizing institutional life so necessary for democratic politics to emerge. In other parts of the Arab world, this process has been either nonexistent or barely visible. The explanations for this vary, but many scholars have expressed the belief that the disorganization of associational structures—structures stratified by patron-client ties—has rendered Arab civil society virtually incapable of coherently articulating collective interests vis-à-vis the state.[46] The "'unincorporated' nature of Arab civil society" has both served and frustrated Arab regimes. It has freed authoritarian leaders from exclusive reliance on coercive measures and hegemonic constructs to retain control. Paradoxically, it has also impeded efforts to mobilize resources to achieve substantive economic change. As a result, the accomplishment of steady progress toward political and economic modernization remains an elusive goal.[47]

In this regard the case of Algeria may stand out as an exception. Unlike Egypt with its "unruly corporatism,"[48] Algerian civil society is more complex, if not more "modern" and "developed." The French colonial legacy; close educational, cultural, and socioeconomic ties with the former metropolitan state; and the "sophisticated" nature of elite politics have all combined to create a subtle institutional system of representation that has effectively withstood the entire authoritarian phase of single-party dominance. Once the ruling "bargain" became unstuck, civil society, institutional life, and associational activity (re)asserted themselves in ways never before imagined. State domination long obscured the development of social forces that state economic and educational policies themselves fostered. Also, continuous travel to and work in France for hundreds of thousands of Algerians afforded direct experience with more modern forms of associational life, whether in the workplace or on university campuses. These experiences formed an inchoate but adaptive civil society that simply needed the opportunity or historic moment to assert its power and presence. Economic failure forced structural changes, and enlightened leadership promoted liberal values.

That associational life and civil society have reacted chaotically if not violently is understandable given the contradictory impulses long forming in society's underbelly during these many years of authoritarian rule. Current organizational manifestations of associational activity appear to have limited popular support, with personality more than program defining a multitude of newly created interest groups. Yet this condition obscures a more enduring reality that finds well-developed attitudes, predispositions, and capabilities of associational activists as they were beginning to operate in a more open environment. If the initial shake-out period had been allowed to proceed, civil society would most likely have been represented by a multitude of institutionalized associational groups. This, of course, assumed that the military authorities would not use short-term social unrest and instability as excuses to reimpose the power of the *mukhabarat* state. In the final analysis, however, it became clear that the expansion of associational life proved an ineffective counterweight to state power in Algeria as civic potential ceded to authoritarian reality. By mid-1993, for example, despair rather than democracy defined the country's political situation as state and society indulged in a virtual civil war involving scores of political assassinations, state-ordered executions, and random killings.

ISLAM AND DEMOCRACY: CONFLUENCE OR CONFLICT

Has the Algerian state exhausted its current democratic phase, moved into a period of temporary stocktaking in preparation for a further democratic advance, or retreated back to its authoritarian past? In 1993 this remained the central question for Algerian political development. Even before the January 1992 coup d'état, there were unmistakable signs of hard-line influences reemerging in the Algerian body politic.

Government reformers seemed to have run into the limits of what they started when Chadli began to liberalize society, economy, and polity in the early 1980s. Trying to unleash the creative energy of a suppressed society, he set loose forces that are now tearing at Algeria's social fabric. A wide array of social forces have been vocalizing their discontent in ways ranging from the massive 500,000-strong demonstration of FIS supporters in December 1990 against government Arabization programs to fundamentalist grievances against secular policies. Trying to break the paralysis of fear, those now in power find themselves afraid of the consequences. Warnings against breakdown, disintegration, and collapse continue to be made by government officials as justification for maintaining the state of siege.

Almost at the onset of Chadli's rule, reformers decided that a state-controlled economy in a repressive one-party system was doomed. Yet they were not prepared to accept the political excesses associated with pluralism, liberalization, and democracy. Although the dialogues and debates were unleashed to a degree never imagined, the decision phase was never implemented, at least not as it affected economic restructuring. The lid was blown off the political pot, and the debris was scattered far and wide. The ensuing chaos, including strikes, demonstrations, and rallies, frightened many not accustomed to political dissent. Preexisting sociocultural fissures developed into threatening chasms. Berberist cultural and linguistic demands were being articulated in militant political terms as was Islamic fundamentalism, with religious zealots pushing their case with increasing virulence.

Islamic appeals in Algeria have responded to socioeconomic grievances and cultural demands for integrity, authenticity, and identity. In dualistic messages, FIS was formulating a legitimate political discourse consistent with Algerian culture, history, and experience. This effort to define what is a good polity and to achieve popular sovereignty on the basis of Islamic traditions[49] seems essential for institution building and democratic development. To be sure, "the redefinition of collective identity in a hitherto undemocratic society is a risky step toward democracy."[50] Yet no meaningful democracy can emerge that does not first have popular sovereignty founded on a collective national identity, shared historic vision, and common cultural values. "This paradox of democratization in Algeria and elsewhere [in the Arab-Islamic world] is difficult to resolve. But no theorist or advocate of democracy could argue against popular sovereignty without creating yet another paradox: violating the basic democratic principle of universal political participation."[51] It is important to note that nowhere in the Arab world has a multiparty election in a formerly one-party state directly replaced a party in power. Thus, the ultimate test of democracy's "true" effect will be when such turnover takes place. This will also reveal the "true" measure of civil society's autonomy.

For its part, the military has violently demonstrated that it will not allow Algerian state and society to collapse. It has left little doubt that it is willing to use whatever force is necessary to ensure the political and territorial integrity of Algeria, even if this includes sacrificing unarmed civilians, real economic change, and many of the democratic freedoms that had been allowed to take root since October 1988 in ground scorched by decades of authoritarianism and political oppression. In a country where chaos has always been seen as never far from the surface, the iron-fist approach has always had certain popularity. The country appears to be in the process of reinvoking its dreaded past.

Notes

Parts of this material first appeared in John P. Entelis, "Introduction," State and Society in Algeria, John P. Entelis and Phillip C. Naylor, eds. (Boulder, Colo.: Westview Press, 1992). The author thanks Westview for permission to use these materials.

1. See Belaid Abdesselam, *Le gaz algérien* (Algiers: Bouchène, 1989); Mahfoud Bennoune, "The Industrialization of Algeria," in *Contemporary North Africa: Issues of Development and Integration*, Halim Barakat, ed. (Washington, D.C.: Center for Contemporary Arab Studies, 1985), pp. 178–213 and idem., *The Making of Contemporary Algeria, 1830–1987: Colonial Upheavals and Post-Independence Development* (Cambridge, Mass.: Cambridge University Press, 1988); Mahfoud Bennoune and Ali El-Kenz, *Le hasard et l'histoire: Entretiens avec Belaid Abdesselam*, 2 vols. (Algiers: ENAG/Editions, 1990); Gérard Destanne de Bernis, "Les industries industrialisantes et les options algériennes," *Tiers Monde*, vol. 12 (1971): 545–63; and Marc Raffinot and Pierre Jacquemot, *Le capitalisme d'état algérien* (Paris: Maspero, 1977).

2. See de Bernis, op. cit.

3. Karen Pfeifer, "Economic Liberalism in the 1980s: Algeria in Comparative Perspective," in *State and Society in Algeria*, John P. Entelis and Phillip C. Naylor, eds. (Boulder, Colo.: Westview Press, 1992), pp. 97–116.

4. John P. Entelis, "Algeria Under Chadli: Liberalization Without Democratization or, Perestroika, Yes; Glasnost, No!," *Middle East Insight* vol. 6, no. 3 (1988): 47–64.

5. See Abed Charef, *Octobre* (Algiers: Laphomic, 1990).

6. Robert A. Mortimer, "Global Economy and African Foreign Policy: The Algerian Model," *African Studies Review* vol. 27, no. 1 (March 1984): 20.

7. See John P. Entelis, *Algeria: The Revolution Institutionalized* (Boulder, Colo.: Westview Press, 1986).

8. See Rachid Tlemcani, "Chadli's Perestroika," *Middle East Report* (March–April 1990): 14–17.

9. See Karen Pfeifer, op. cit.

10. Ibid.

11. See Lynette Rummel, "Privatization and Democratization in Algeria," in *State and Society in Algeria*, John P. Entelis and Phillip C. Naylor, eds. (Boulder, Colo.: Westview Press, 1992), pp. 53–71.

12. See Karen Pfeifer, op. cit.

13. See Bradford Dillman, "Transition to Democracy in Algeria," in *State and Society in Algeria*, John P. Entelis and Phillip C. Naylor, eds. (Boulder, Colo.: Westview Press, 1992), pp. 31–51.

14. Jacques Fontaine, "Les élections locales algériennes du 12 juin 1990: Approche statistique et géographique," *Maghreb-Machrek* vol. 129 (July–August–September 1990): 124–140.

15. Arun Kapil, "Algeria's Elections Show Islamist Strength," *Middle East Report* (September–October 1990): 31–36.

16. See Jacques Fontaine, "Les élections locales algériennes du 12 juin 1990: Approche statistique et geographique," op. cit.; Arun Kapil, "Algeria's Elections Show Islamist Strength," op. cit.; and Economist Intelligence Unit, "Algeria: Country Report" (henceforth referred to as *EIU-CR*), 1990 (nos. 1–4), 1991 (nos. 1–4).

17. *EIU-CR* 1990, no. 4.
18. See Abbassi Madani, *Al-Mushkilat al-tarbawiyya fil-bilad al-islamiyya* (Educational Problems in the Islamic World) (Batna, Algeria: Dar Ribab, 1986), and idem., *'Azmat al-fikr al-hadith wa mubarrirat al-hal al-islami* (The Crisis of Modern Thought and the Islamic Alternative) (Algiers: Maktabat Rihab, 1989), and idem., *Al-Naw'iyya al-tarbawiyya fil-marahil al-ta'limiya fil-bilad al-islamiyya* (Educational Quality in the Schooling System of the Muslim World) (Riyadh, Saudi Arabia: Maktabat Duwal al-Khalij, 1989).
19. See Bradford Dillman, "Transition to Democracy in Algeria," op. cit., and Arun Kapil, "L'Evolution du régime autoritaire en Algérie: Le 5 Octobre et les régimes politiques de 1988-1989," *Annuaire de l'Afrique du Nord 1990* (Paris: CNRS, 1992), pp. 499-532.
20. See Arun Kapil, "Algeria's Elections Show Islamist Strength," op. cit.
21. *EIU-CR* 1990.
22. See *EIU-CR* 1990; 1991, no. 4.
23. William Lewis, "Algeria and the Maghreb at the Turning Point," *Mediterranean Quarterly: A Journal of Global Issues* vol. 42, no. 1 (Summer 1990): 72-73.
24. Arun Kapil, "Algeria's Elections Show Islamist Strength," op. cit., 31-36.
25. *EIU-CR* 1990, no. 4.
26. William B. Quandt, *Revolution and Political Leadership: Algeria, 1954-1968* (Cambridge, Mass.: MIT Press, 1969).
27. Robert A. Mortimer, "The Politics of Reassurance in Algeria," *Current History* vol. 84, no. 502 (May 1985): 201-204, 228-229.
28. See Karen Pfeifer, op. cit.
29. See Lynette Rummel, "Privatization and Democratization in Algeria," op. cit.
30. See *EIU-CR* 1988, nos. 1-4.
31. See John P. Entelis, "Algeria Under Chadli: Liberalization Without Democratization or, Perestroika, Yes; Glasnost, No!," op. cit.
32. See *EIU-CR* 1989; 1990, nos. 1-2.
33. See Jacques Fontaine, "Les élections locales algériennes du 12 juin 1990: Approche statistique et geographique," op. cit.
34. See *EIU-CR* 1990.
35. *El Moudjahid*, September 13, 1990.
36. *Horizon*, April 4, 1990.
37. Arun Kapil, "Algeria's Elections Show Islamist Strength," op. cit., 32-33.
38. See Bradford Dillman, "Transition to Democracy in Algeria," op. cit.
39. See *EIU-CR* 1991, nos. 1-4.
40. *El Moudjahid*, August 13, 1991.
41. *EIU-CR* 1991; 1992.
42. See Hugh Roberts, "A Trial of Strength: Algerian Islamism," in *Islamic Fundamentalisms and the Gulf Crisis*, James Piscatori, ed. (Chicago, Ill.: The Fundamentalist Project-American Academy of Arts and Sciences, 1991), pp. 131-54.
43. Maurice Lemoine, "L'Algérie au risque des impatiences," *Le Monde Diplomatique* vol. 48, no. 1 (July 1991): 1.
44. See Zehra F. Arat, "Democracy and Economic Development: Modernization Theory Revisited," *Comparative Politics* vol. 21, no. 1 (October 1988): 21-36; Larry Diamond, Juan J. Linz, and Seymour Martin Lipset, "Introduction: Comparative Experiences with Democracy," in *Politics in Developing Countries: Comparing Experiences with Democracy*, Larry Diamond, Juan J. Linz, and Seymour Martin Lipset, eds. (Boulder, Colo.: Lynne Rienner, 1990), pp. 1-38; and Samuel P. Huntington, *The Third Wave: Democratization in the Late Twentieth Century* (Norman, Okla.: University of Oklahoma Press, 1991).

45. Daniel Brumberg, "An Arab Path to Democracy?" *Journal of Democracy* vol. 1, no. 4 (Fall 1990): 120.
46. Ibid., p. 121.
47. Ibid.
48. Robert Bianchi, *Unruly Corporatism: Associational Life in Twentieth-Century Egypt* (New York: Oxford University Press, 1989).
49. Abdeslam Maghraoui, "Problems of Transition to Democracy: Algeria's Short-Lived Experiment with Electoral Politics," *Middle East Insight* vol. 8, no. 6 (July–October 1992): 20–26 at 25.
50. Ibid., 25.
51. Ibid., 26.

Re-Imagining Religion and Politics: Moroccan Elections in the 1990s

Dale F. Eickelman

nthropologist Benedict Anderson argues that national and religious communities are *imagined*. They transcend the boundaries of face-to-face communities but are also less than universal, with "finite, if elastic, boundaries—sovereign, and with a deep, horizontal comradeship."[1] The affinities of religious and political identities are actively shaped and constrained by how both the elite and nonelite conceive them. Although not infinitely malleable, political and religious identities are not fixed and enduring, as some of their adherents claim.

A case in point is that of a ruling monarchy in the late twentieth century. Hassan II would agree with Anderson's observation that it has been centuries since "serious" monarchies appeared to most people "as the only imaginable 'political' system," with subjects rather than citizens.

There is no doubt that the ranks of ruling monarchs have thinned over the last two centuries. From the seventeenth century onward in Western Europe, Anderson argues that "the automatic legitimacy of sacral monarchy began its slow decline."[2] Ruling monarchs may appear an endangered species in the late twentieth century, but Hassan II—both as practicing monarch and as a political observer who sometimes explicitly sets aside his role as ruler to reflect publicly on other nations' politics—cannot be accused of a lack of political imagination in sustaining royal authority in the modern era.[3] The Moroccan monarch, far from drawing on a conventional repertoire of an unquestioned "tradition" that fits uncomfortably with "modern" life, invents and transforms it, even while drawing on supposedly immemorial tradition. Hassan's invocation of "tradition" as the basis for the continued legitimacy of dynastic rule should not deflect attention from a process of creation and manipulation that sustains the credibility of dynastic rule to both Moroccans and the international community. After the January 1984 riots in several Moroccan cities, Hassan said in a televised address that he was like a doctor with a stethoscope to the heart of his people: he could sense every palpitation.[4]

There have been many "palpitations" since the beginning of Hassan's rule. Rémy Leveau, perhaps the most astute long-term French observer of Moroccan politics, goes so far as to say that the Morocco of the 1990s is as different from the Morocco of 1960 as Spain in 1975 (the year of Francisco Franco's death) was from the Spain of 1939 or 1947.[5] Even allowing for the hyperbole of Hassan's 1984 medical metaphor, his actions since the 1960s indicate a sensitivity to the growing political awareness of a younger, emerging generation of Moroccans and to the changing nature of domestic political activity.

This essay focuses on the flurry of electoral activities that began in April 1992, when Hassan announced municipal and parliamentary elections. Municipal elections had last been held in 1983, parliamentary ones in 1984. A constitutional referendum took place on September 4, 1992; municipal elections were held October 16, 1992; and direct elections for 222 parliamentary seats took place on June 25, 1993. Elections for the remaining 111 indirectly elected parliamentary seats took place on September 17, 1993.[6] The dates for both the municipal and the direct parliamentary elections were shifted several times, primarily because of the complexity in overhauling the electoral system to guarantee a higher level of integrity than it has had in the past. Similarly the number of seats in parliament was raised twice, from 306 in February 1993 to 327, then from 327 to 333 in May 1993. Complementary to these electoral activities, large numbers of educated Moroccans have become increasingly vocal about whether the "rule of law" (*siyyadat al-qanun*) prevails, and this has been reflected in both the September 4, 1992, constitutional referendum and Hassan's numerous speeches and interviews, intended to persuade Moroccans and the foreign community that human rights abuses and disregard for legal conventions will not be tolerated. Morocco's national press has become increasingly specific in reporting abuses by police and public authorities.[7] These abuses have long been known to most Moroccans. Unlike the recent past, however, they are now a matter of discussion in the press and in public, and the effect has been to curb abuses. These activities, and the responses of the monarchy to the rising tide of Islamic activism, increasingly broaden the definition of what is political in Morocco, and they suggest the direction that Moroccan politics may take in the coming years. Even if the end result of the electoral process was no significant change on the national level—neither parties perceived as linked to the monarchy nor the opposition obtained a clear majority—there now is greater awareness of what politics can become independent of the monarchy.

"SERIOUS" MONARCHY IN THE LATE TWENTIETH CENTURY

The Moroccan experience of royal authority challenges Anderson's claim that "'serious' monarchy lies transverse to all modern conceptions of political life," in part because the legitimacy of monarchies derives from divinity and not from "populations, who, after all, are subjects, not citizens."[8] Hassan II, who takes monarchies seriously, might have had Anderson in mind when he said in a September 1992 interview concerning Morocco's new constitution that "our monarchy is not a divine monarchy, as some wish to imagine; it is by law popular and religious. The Constitution says that sovereignty belongs to the people who express themselves directly, by referendum or by intermediary of their parliamentary representatives." After invoking the notion of the *bay'a,* the covenant of allegiance of a people to a Muslim sovereign, he concluded, "I will accept the constitution because I am its author and editor."[9]

Moroccans harbor no doubts concerning the dominant role of the monarch in the conception and orchestration of politics in Morocco. In a June 1992 interview, one member of the officially recognized opposition said, "There is no such thing as government in Morocco, only the king, because all major decisions are made directly by him." He cited two proverbs: "Talk is like a pillar with a slave woman behind it," implying that everything said gets back to one source, and "Anywhere you strike a bald head, you see blood," implying that the king is behind all major movements.[10] Sociologically viewed, however, the monarch's political action remains finely tuned to Morocco's changing political constituency. Speaking in spring 1992, Hassan reminded his public that over half of today's eligible voters were children when the last parliamentary elections were held in 1984.

Morocco's major demographic changes are on everyone's mind. In 1984, there were 21.5 million Moroccans, 79 percent of them born after independence in 1956. For this majority, colonial rule and the independence movement were events learned in school, not events experienced in the streets. Today there are twenty-six million Moroccans, for whom the major formative events include rapidly rising educational levels, rapid population growth, narrowed opportunities for emigration, and growing domestic unemployment and underemployment. Although Morocco never guaranteed employment for school graduates in the way that Egypt did, Moroccan graduates through the 1970s usually found jobs in the public sector. Employment for graduates is now the exception rather than the rule. The formative events for today's young Moroccan differ significantly from those that influenced an earlier generation.

One constant in Morocco is the formal image of the monarchy. Even in the August 20, 1972, speech of the throne, given shortly after the second attempted coup d'état in just over a year, Hassan spoke of Morocco in the year 2000 and reflected on the failed plot to overthrow him: "This is the price for the monarchy in this country to remain faithful to Maliki doctrine, according to which one should not hesitate to sacrifice a third of [the country] in order to preserve the remainder. As we have emphasized many times, with the exception of the Throne, the pathways to authority are open to everyone, the chances being equal for all citizens."[11]

The 1972 vision of the Moroccan polity, elaborated at a moment of intense personal pressure, corresponds fully with the present one. What has changed is that the "pathways to authority" are now perceived as significantly more open than in the past. Morocco's new constitution, ratified in the September 4, 1992, referendum, reaffirms that expressing a critical opinion on the monarchy or Islam or failing to respect the king is off-limits.[12] In an interview granted to a French television station on the eve of the referendum, the king explained why he could not accede to a greater devolution of power: "I can delegate my powers, but I do not have the right to renounce my prerogatives on my own initiative, because they are also religious ones."[13]

When challenged by opposition political parties to conduct fair and "transparent" elections—a condition for their participation—Hassan responded with a speech that emphasized his role as arbiter (*hakam*), the ultimate guarantor of the integrity of the electoral process, and he invoked the Qur'an and Moroccan monarchic tradition to legitimize this role.[14] The monarch subsequently appointed an electoral commission to oversee implementation of the electoral process, technical rules for registration, delineation of electoral districts, and other matters.[15]

The current representation of the monarch as arbiter is in large part a "re-invented" tradition, akin to Hassan's claim that the 'Alawi dynasty, and Hassan in particular, "grew up imbued with the spirit of decentralization, having faith in it, persuaded that true democracy is local democracy." Similarly, Moroccans in their thirties and forties, most of whom know political activists who have served terms in prison, heard the monarch call on the youth to mobilize and join political parties to increase the numbers of "the Moroccan civil army, summoned to conquer the twenty-first century."[16] Of course, the call on youth to join political parties implicitly urged them to join *authorized* political movements rather than the various unrecognized Islamic groups whose strength is unknown but may include some 20 percent of Morocco's population.[17]

The cover of Rémy Leveau's *Le fellah marocain: Défenseur du trône* shows a brown woolen *jallaba*, the long, heavy garment worn by Moroccan tribespeople and peasants in the winter months, as if it were being worn, but empty of a human face or body.[18] It was intended to symbolize the book's main point—that the mainstay of the monarchy through the 1960s was Morocco's rural majority of tribespeople, peasants, and landowners, whose politics Leveau discerned through the analysis of election results and the profiles of candidates for parliamentary and local elections. For the government, the 1963 elections identified a significant cohort of rural notables, those who, in Gaetano Mosca's phrase, allow the rulers to rule.[19] They also identified the strengths and weaknesses of the national political parties.

The 1969 and 1976 municipal elections and the September 1984 parliamentary elections, which I witnessed, suggest the changing face of Moroccan electoral politics. Having analyzed them in detail elsewhere, I depict only their broad contours here.[20] In a town in western Morocco where I was conducting research in 1969, those people who noticed the elections at all viewed them with amusement. Few bothered to cast ballots, and those who tried to do so were told by the militia officer (*makhazni*) at the polling place, "Don't trouble yourself. It's already been done." Several years later I was shown the electoral registers—page after page of voters registered only as "Fatima," with no identifiers of age and residence (other than electoral district). At the time, however, municipalities had no budgets of their own, and in "peripheral" areas of the country—for practical purposes, everywhere except the major coastal cities—municipal councils and their counterpart rural communes were under the "tutelage" of the Ministry of the Interior. At least in the rural areas, the attitude toward government corruption was that it would cease if the king could be informed of specific abuses.

The 1976 municipal elections differed significantly in character. One reform that followed the attempted coups of 1971 and 1972, both involving elements of the military, was to open the country's political system to an emerging generation of local and regional leaders. Municipalities and rural communes were given some fiscal autonomy and the authority to hire workers and contract for services. There were signs of fraud, by candidates and by local officials interfering in favor of one party or another. For example, political parties and candidates were identified by color, an important consideration where many voters were illiterate, but on election day, the colors of ballots were switched. In rural areas, gendarmes set up roadblocks near some polling places to prevent election monitors from overseeing ballot counting. Some candidates, for their part, offered feasts for constituents, after which envelopes containing cash were distributed in a side room.[21] Yet in some regions, some political parties made an excellent showing by not engaging in such practices.

The June 1983 municipal elections and the September 1984 parliamentary ones showed a sophistication on the part of the Ministry of the Interior, political parties, and the electorate that would have made Chicago's late mayor, Richard J. Daley, proud. During the entire voter registration period, Ministry of the Interior officials were required to provide daily reports to their superiors on the likely party affiliations of voters. Thus if a number of younger voters—some of whom were known to be affiliated with one of the secular left parties—began to register, youth fitting that profile might later be denied registration on a technicality, while the registration of other voters with other profiles would be facilitated. In many districts, elections were conducted without incident, but in others, irregularities occurred—election supervisors were reportedly asked to leave the room while other officials added ballots to the urn after elections had closed, for example, or fraudulent counts took place. Although such incidents were common, tactics were more subtle than in the past. After all, gerrymandering and other sophisticated practices require considerable skill. By the 1980s, the Ministry of the Interior had enough educated cadres and sufficient communications capability to implement the complex system of daily reporting described here. Cruder instruments of state control would have backfired. Yet many candidates were equally adept at finding ways to manipulate the system to their advantage.[22]

Significantly, political activists were sufficiently convinced of the integrity of the electoral system to participate in it. Even more than in the past, elections were an effective means of discerning emerging political activists at local levels. Successful candidates obtained, so to speak, a stake in the existing political system and thus were co-opted. But it would be wrong to impute all election results to the manipulative skills of the palace. By the 1980s, most elections were seriously contested. If some constituents voted in lineage or residential blocs, they did so after determining which candidate would work most effectively for their interests.

Elections provide a major opportunity for political activism. In the 1992 municipal elections, 11,513,809 voters registered nationwide. Voter turnout was a plausible 75 percent of eligible voters, although there was considerable regional variation. Thus, only 51 percent of registered voters participated in the elections in the six provinces of northern Morocco, and some rural communes showed suspiciously high turnouts. In the end, 22,500 municipal councillors were elected, with the number of candidates five times that number.[23]

MASS HIGHER EDUCATION AND THE POLITICAL IMAGINATION

In any discussion of Moroccan politics, Islamic radicalism is just off-stage. Most of the Moroccan media treat the topic gingerly, reporting the monarch's comments and carrying lengthy accounts of activism in countries such as Algeria, Tunisia, and Egypt. Some stories reproduce detailed accounts from foreign media on the contents of videotaped and audiocassette Islamic sermons forbidden in Morocco.[24] An exclusive focus on religious activism deflects attention from the more profound changes taking place throughout the Muslim world, particularly in Morocco, which are correlated with mass higher education and mass communications, factors that have begun to profoundly affect how people think about authority and responsibility in the domains of religion and politics.

As throughout the Middle East and North Africa, mass higher education in Morocco has expanded significantly in the last two decades, as shown in figure 14.1.[25] Mass higher education in the Arab and

FIGURE 14.1
Secondary and Post-Secondary Enrollment
in Morocco, 1955–1992 (000s)

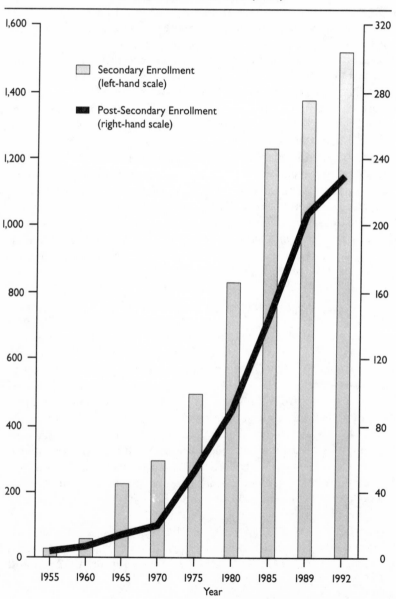

Muslim worlds is reshaping conceptions of self, religion, nation, and politics. It is as significant as the introduction of printed books was in sixteenth-century rural France.[26] Ironically, however, we know more about literacy in medieval and pre-modern Europe than in the contemporary Muslim and Arab worlds. Many scholars have noted linkages between advanced education and religious activism, but this focus on extremism deflects attention from both conceptual innovations and emerging networks for communication and action.

Religious activism in the political sphere, the claims of its adherents notwithstanding, is a distinctively modern phenomenon, and its supporters are principally the beneficiaries of mass higher education. Mass education may be important in itself, but also suggests basic transformations in ideas of what people accept as legitimate political authority.[27]

For the most part, mass higher education is a recent phenomenon in the Middle East and North Africa. It began in earnest only in the 1950s, with Egypt's commitment to universal schooling following the 1952 revolution. Fifteen to twenty years later—that is, by the 1970s—after large numbers of students began to complete the advanced educational cycles, its consequences can be more clearly discerned. The timing of educational expansion varies for other parts of the Middle East. Major educational expansion in Morocco began after independence in 1956, accelerated in the 1960s, and today almost matches the rate of population growth.[28] From 1957 to 1992, the university system expanded its enrollment from 1,819 to 230,000 students.[29]

A complementary measure of change is the circulation of books and magazines. As of 1982, the Arab world produced forty books per million inhabitants, far below the world average of 162 titles per million. Although more recent figures are unavailable, the gap appears to be closing rapidly.[30] Moroccan writer Mohammed Bennis recalls with excitement his student days in Fez in the 1970s, when the first "little" intellectual journals began to flourish in Arabic, rather than in French, which had been the dominant language of the educated elite. In lectures and public meetings, students began to interrupt colleagues who did not express themselves in Arabic. The shift from French to Arabic and the growing number of participants in higher education significantly increased participation in debates about politics, culture, and society.[31] The intellectual effervescence of the 1970s that Bennis describes saw the first cohort of Moroccans emerge who acquired their pervasive "habits of thought" in Arabic, the country's national language.[32] Pressure from this cohort created a demand for a "re-imagining" of Islam and national identity. In the last few years a significant readership for "quality" books in Arabic has developed in Morocco. For the increasingly influential cohort of university graduates, reading is a means of "appropriating," organizing, and making objective ideas of society, politics, and self.[33] Among the results of mass higher education are a changed sense of authoritative discourse, the emergence of a sense of religion as system and object, and altered conceptions of language and community.

Mass education fosters direct, albeit selective, access to the printed word and a break with earlier traditions of authority. Muslim activist discourse, such as that of Morocco's 'Abd al-Salam Yassin, assumes a familiarity with the language of Marxist and other "Western" discourses, against which it confidently reacts.[34] Belief and practice are now expressed in public and explicit forms and are more directly related to political action than previously. The rise of this new dominant discourse affects equally the expressive forms of the state and its religious and secular opposition. Secondly, mass education and mass communications encourage the conception of religion and politics as self-contained systems that can incorporate features from other systems. Thus when Islamic activists in Morocco declare that they are engaged in the "Islamization" of their society, they make explicit their sense of one system of ideas and practices—theirs—acting against the system of beliefs and practices held by other members of society. Finally, the standardized language of mass higher education encourages new senses of community and affinity. Benedict Anderson argues, for example, that the rise of written vernacular languages in Europe and the spread of print technology have created language communities wider than those of face-to-face interactions, yet narrower than the communities created by shared sacred languages.[35] With modifications, this premise can be transposed to the Moroccan context.

One indication of shifts in the religious and political imagination of a younger, educated generation in many parts of the Middle East is the effort of the state to co-opt fundamentalist discourse. In Morocco in the 1960s and early 1970s, both the monarchy and its political opposition employed a "developmentalist" idiom in which "religious" issues were separated from "political" ones. By the late 1970s, the public language of the monarchy's supporters was much more religiously oriented, and the monarch asserted that he was developing a cadre of Ministry of the Interior officials trained in administration and Islamic thought. He claimed that his political actions were modeled on those of the Prophet Muhammad: "In all modesty, Hassan's school is the school of Muhammad V and the school of Muhammad V is that of the Prophet. Most of us know the Prophet only as messenger of God. His political and diplomatic life remain unknown and we await the day when someone firmly attached to his religion and proud of its teachings will write on this subject."[36]

From North Africa to Jordan, Egypt, and Turkey, the impact of modern mass education is pervasive. In the context of a set national curriculum, in which Islamic studies is one subject among many, students are taught about the unity of Muslim thought and practice in a way guaranteed to see Islamic doctrine—at least as inculcated in formal education—as a doctrine conveyed by state authorities to secure their own ends.[37]

MOROCCO'S "NEW" ELECTORAL POLITICS

In mid-1992, a member of the Moroccan opposition noted: "Hassan II's major achievement in the 1960s was to eliminate the possibility of a leftist takeover of the government, as had happened in so many other newly independent countries." He went on to explain that in the 1950s, the left had emerged as a strong organizer of the independence movement. Even prior to accession to the throne, however, Hassan had created a nucleus of people around him prepared to remove that danger. The same observer continued: "Before his death, even Mehdi Ben Barka said that Morocco had in effect a right-wing coup which ejected the leftist forces from power. Leftist opposition was set aside until 1976–1977, when it began cautiously to emerge from eclipse."[38]

In the spring of 1992, Moroccans heard their monarch raise many themes related to local democracy and elections. The king also spoke of a new constitution, which would "take into account the conjuncture [of Morocco's current situation] and legitimate aspirations."[39] They had before them recent examples of the monarch's avoiding unnecessary confrontation, including the banning, ostensibly by local authorities, of the traditional May Day parade in Casablanca. Islamic activists had regularly closed off one of Casablanca's main streets for Friday prayers, and the parade, which fell on a Friday in 1992, would have required the police to clear the street. Citing technicalities, local authorities refused to issue a parade permit, although last-minute authorizations were granted in Rabat and elsewhere. The motive was evidently to prevent a confrontation between religious activists and the secular left.[40] The banning of a parade may not initially appear to indicate political flexibility, but this action, like the monarch's last-minute acquiescence in allowing a massive pro-Iraqi demonstration in Rabat on February 3, 1991, during the Iraqi occupation of Kuwait, indicated such flexibility to politically aware Moroccans.[41] Often the most effective use of authority is knowing when not to force an issue.

The major interest in the 1992–1993 elections was the growing transparency of the political process. "Opposition" political parties, defined as those whose leaders have not been selected for ministerial appointments, refused to participate in the election campaigns or to vote in the constitutional referendum unless the monarch guaranteed the government's "neutrality." They also won a concession in lowering the voting age: the monarch announced that Morocco's voting age would remain at twenty-one; the opposition, which formed a unified bloc (*kutla*) for the purposes of dialogue, argued for eighteen. In June 1992 it was lowered to twenty.

Notwithstanding events such as the sentencing in April 1992 to two years in prison of labor leader Noubir Amaoui for alleging the corruption of government ministers to a Spanish newspaper and for refusing to retract the allegations, Moroccan politics have become more open. Security for the Amaoui trial in Rabat was unusually tight, and some journalists and attorneys were injured by the police. The conduct of the trial appeared to many as atavistic. At the same time, however, the activities of human rights groups are regularly reported in the press. In an interview with a French newspaper, the monarch went so far as to say that Morocco had no political prisoners. When the interviewer pointed out that a private human rights group said there were, Hassan II replied that the Islamic activists detained were not political prisoners, but individuals who sought to derail religion. "[Islam] is my reserved domain, fortunately for Morocco, Africa, and the world. I hope that all advocates of liberty will encourage this responsibility, which is mine."[42] In the same interview, he announced the closing and destruction of the Tazmamart military prison because it had "no more reason to be." The Moroccan press has more latitude now to report on political and human rights events.

In his speech of the throne on August 20, 1992, Hassan also called for a major re-examination of the rights of women and a revision of the *mudawwana,* the legal code that governs family law administration in Morocco.[43] From mid-February until mid-March, Moroccans were treated to daily accounts of the trial of a senior Casablanca police official for sex crimes involving an estimated 1,500 videotaped victims. The trial was conducted with a speed almost unprecedented for the Moroccan judiciary and with procedures that led many to publicly call into question the independence of the courts. For the month of Ramadan, the circulation of Moroccan newspapers soared as journalists honed their investigative (and tabloid) skills and published more details of the case. The identities and actions of senior security officials were made public for the first time, and the king, in a speech commenting on the case, reaffirmed support for the security services, but he also promised major reforms, saying that no one was above the rule of law.[44]

Politically active Moroccans raise the question of why these apparently significant political changes are occurring now. One political leader offered the following assessment:

> Morocco is now undergoing fundamental political changes. After seventeen years, domestic politics have been de-linked from the Saharan conflict. The Sahara issue caused a closing of ranks and of minds for many years.
>
> We are seeing the first stage in the break-up of the system of power in Morocco. In the 1970s and 1980s we asked the question, "What is the role which political parties can play in the monarchy?" Now the question has changed to "What is the role of a monarchy in a modern society?" Technically this is a forbidden question, but Hassan knows that this is the issue on everyone's minds.
>
> For the first time, we are challenging decisions made by the king. Our talk about democracy is really double-talk. What is really at issue is the nature of the monarchy, which people are talking about out loud for the first time.[45]

The monarch is aware of a major generational change in Morocco. The economic situation is not promising, and, despite major efforts to reduce population growth, the population continues to grow faster than the country's economy. The dream of young Moroccans is to get a passport and work contract and leave Morocco to support their families. In the summer of 1992, Moroccans heard frequent reports of illegal immigrants drowning or being caught by Spanish authorities as they tried to cross the Straits of Gibraltar in small boats. The Mediterranean is no more effective a barrier to illegal immigration to Europe than the wire fence along the U.S.-Mexican border. Young Moroccans trade information on the easiest countries to enter, with Italy a favored destination through 1992 because unlike France and other European countries, it did not require entry visas for Moroccans. *Love in Casablanca*, a Moroccan film released in April 1992, nicely captured the desperate economic situation in a scene where two lovers, meeting in a park, see a man watching them. The man, a well-known Moroccan comedian, reassures them: "Don't mind me. I'm not a voyeur. I'm an unemployed graduate with no place to go." Morocco is also witnessing a new form of entrepreneur—those who have made fortunes in contraband *(trabando)* and narcotics. The banning of 400 candidates from the municipal elections for alleged ties to drug smuggling in September 1992, increased drug arrests in the beginning of 1993, and the announcement of a major program, with significant support from the European Community, to restructure the economy of the Rif to break narcotics cultivation suggest a major effort to link economic issues with Morocco's political future.[46]

"The monarchy is at an impasse," suggested a Moroccan political scientist.[47] The king realizes that too much tinkering with the system will reaffirm that the entire system can be changed. The decision to lower the voting age from twenty-one to twenty is an example. In 1980, Moroccans voted in a referendum to lower the age at which a regency was no longer needed to sixteen, and this was an argument reportedly made to the king to persuade him to lower the voting age to twenty after having publicly stated that he was not prepared to do so.

Has the outcome of the parliamentary election been perceived as fair? The 1992–93 cycle of referendums and elections initially augured little promise. In September 1992 *Le Monde* reported that 97.25 percent of Morocco's 11,804,038 registered voters went to the polls for the constitutional referendum, "evidently paying little attention to the calls for abstention," and 96.84 percent of the voters approved the initiative. After all, as some Moroccans said, the monarch personally urged an affirmative role, so that a vote against could be regarded as a direct challenge to his will. Reporting on *Le Monde*'s coverage—a standard practice for Moroccan editors wary of censorship—one Casablanca newspaper ran a story in the next column depicting similar results in a recent constitutional referendum in Djibouti.[48] In contrast, both turnout and results for the municipal elections were generally plausible, with political activists often complaining not of central government intervention but of its lack in the case of flagrant abuses such as the purchase of votes by some candidates.

A major concern is that the voices of Islamic activists are not heard. Hassan specifies that he uses the term "Muslim" and not "Islamic" to describe the nature of his rule, "although if we had used the term 'Islamic' we would not have shocked anyone."[49] Still, sympathetic merchants in Casablanca give money to activist causes for building mosques and prayer rooms in schools, offering subsidized housing for university students, piecework (below minimum wage) for women whose husbands do not wish them to leave the house, and social services where government services are inadequate. Islamic activists scrupulously avoid making explicit political statements, although the shell of one inactive but authorized political party is ostensibly used by an activist group.[50] Unlike neighboring countries, Morocco's government has plausible religious credentials. In the late 1970s, Hassan picked some of the best students of the *shari'a* (Islamic law) faculties in Morocco's universities and sent them the École des Cadres of Kénitra, the elite school for the training for Ministry of the Interior officials. Using a style reminiscent of the French Protectorate's Direction des Affaires Indigènes, these cadres were subsequently used to penetrate Islamic activist movements, to manipulate them, and to engage them in effective public dialogue. The result is to hold such movements more in check than is the case for most other Middle Eastern countries.[51]

How effective will Hassan be in adapting Morocco's existing political forms to challenges? As in all politics, much depends on the pace of change. To date, his ability to re-imagine tradition in a manner convincing to both Moroccans and the international community is beyond question. An older generation of Moroccans with access to the monarch aver that one reason he remains successful is that he listens to all opinions and reads his mail. As one official said, any letter couched in the traditional formulaic opening, "Yes, my Lord, may God strengthen you" (*na'am sidi a'zzak allah*) and closing with "To our victorious master, made triumphant by God, wide of vision (that is, any interpretation is possible)" (*li-sidina al-mansur b-illah, wasi' al-nazar*), can offer frank suggestions, advice, and criticism, since the author, in employing conventional etiquette, indicates acceptance of the monarch's authority. Of course, the main question is whether such conventions of compliance are known and accepted by Morocco's first generation to receive mass higher education. In 1992, 13.48 percent of candidates for municipal councils had university degrees. Only 6.2 percent did in 1983. Likewise in 1993, 60 percent of the candidates for parliament had a university education.[52] The number and profile of politically aware Moroccans is rapidly changing, and the apolitical "periphery" of Morocco in the 1960s has ceased to exist.

Islamic activism is an element of the "new" politics. Although the monarch raises the topic often in interviews with the foreign press, the general silence of the domestic press indicates the continuing sensitivity of the topic. An underlying assumption in much of the debate about Islam and democracy is that "Islam" determines Muslim conduct. An example from the U.S. "quality" press will suffice. The author of an article entitled "Another Moslem Invasion of Europe" argues that "European civilization" faces its third major invasion from the forces of Islam, who reside in a four thousand mile-wide belt of tension running from just east of the Canary Islands to Central Asia. In this "vast arc," "Western-style concepts" such as "democracy, personal freedoms, and the rule of law are denied." Note the use of the passive voice, which disguises the identity of the denier. This third "invasion," by demographic growth and labor migration, is said to equal the threat posed to Europe by the expansion of Islam in the eighth century and the expansion of the Ottoman Empire in the late sixteenth and early seventeenth centuries.[53]

Those who argue that "Islam" and democracy are compatible invoke objectifications of Islam or make it a concrete, timeless body of doctrine unconstrained by space and time. Morocco's electoral and political experience confirms neither extreme, but better fits Michael Hudson's notion of democratization: "By 'democratization' I am referring not to an ideal condition of democracy but rather a process through which the exercise of political power by regime and state becomes less arbitrary, exclusive, and authoritarian."[54]

The June 1993 parliamentary elections were characterized by last-minute maneuvers to limit the possibility of any single party emerging with a parliamentary majority. In late May, the requirement that all candidates had to affiliate with political parties was relaxed. This move allowed unaffiliated candidates, primarily those seen as affiliated with the government, including ministers, to enter the race for parliamentary seats. This move may also make it difficult to enforce party discipline in the future.

Nonetheless, the June 1993 election results give reason for cautious optimism. According to official statistics, 62.75 percent of Morocco's 11,398,987 registered voters participated in the parliamentary elections. The nongovernmental "opposition" parties gained a significant number of seats over those they held in the prior parliament, but they still fell short of a majority. The parties associated with the government correspondingly lost. Complaints about election irregularities were confined to specific localities and were not imputed to central government officials. As one report on the elections concluded, a level of "censorship, self-censorship, fear, intimidation, and official corruption remains,"[55] but there were significant improvements over prior elections.

The reasons for the large number of invalid votes, 13 percent of the 7,153,211 votes cast, appear to vary with region, but even the number of invalid votes can be read as a sign of greater democratization and the increasing sophistication of the electorate. As with the October 1992 municipal elections, some candidates reportedly sought to purchase votes. In some regions of Morocco, such as Casablanca and Khouribga, the "market value" for votes varied between 50 and 100 Moroccan dirhams, roughly the same as for the October 1992 municipal elections. Unfortunately, polling station reports (taqrir 'an 'amaliyat ihsa' al-aswat) do not distinguish between empty envelopes and votes invalidated for other causes. However, interviews that I conducted with polling station officials and party observers in one locality the day after the elections suggest that the majority of invalidated votes were due to blank envelopes, and a survey of election results in one area where detailed results were accessible suggested a correlation between a high incidence of "nul" votes and votes for a candidate—who nonetheless lost—reputed to have purchased votes. In some areas, such activities were limited because candidates engaged attorneys to monitor the practices of their rivals and efforts by some candidates to secure the support of local officials. Threats by rival parties to report illegal practices to local electoral commissions and to other authorities itself indicates a greater confidence in the "rule of law." There is no way of knowing the degree of abstention or of empty-envelope voting for religious reasons, although Islamists in some areas encouraged abstention.

There are flaws in Morocco's current electoral experience, but in contrast with the past these flaws cannot be imputed to a grand design from the center. Despite their claims to the contrary, Moroccan political parties unevenly cover the country. Unlike the situation that existed immediately after Morocco's independence in 1956, no party has deep roots in all the rural areas, where local candidates with no committed party affiliation other than cooperation with the government, usually in the form of local officials, still prevail. Often grudgingly, even the defeated parties acknowledge a "transparency" (shafafiyya) in the 1992-93 elections.

Morocco's current electoral experience is clearly incremental. The steps taken are cautious ones, and the time between the steps provides opportunities for future "corrective" action. The delay between the June 25 direct parliamentary elections and the September 17, 1993, indirect ones, provided yet another perceived opportunity for manipulation from the top. Nonetheless, most Moroccans are convinced that the conduct of the current elections breaks with past practices, allowing "democracy" to begin to acquire a specific substance and the "rule of law" to become more than a slogan.

Notes

1. Benedict Anderson, *Imagined Communities: Reflections on the Origin and Spread of Nationalism,* revised edition (New York: Verso, 1991 [orig. 1983]), pp. 6–7.
2. Anderson, op. cit., 19.
3. Consider, for example, a January 1992 interview with a Saudi newspaper in which he stated, "In my role as a political person and not as king of Morocco," he would like to have seen the "experiment" with "fundamentalist" (*usuli*) rule in Algeria allowed to proceed, so that the religious activists, with their "confused" ideas about religion and politics, could have been put to the test of practical political rule. Interview, *Al-Sharq al-Awsat,* January 13, 1993, p. 7. Official Algerian reaction to Hassan's comment presumed that he was speaking as head of state.
4. Hassan II, televised address to the nation, January 24, 1984.
5. Rémy Leveau, *Le sabre et le turban: L'Avenir du Maghreb* (Paris: François Bourin, 1993), p. 13. From 1958 until 1965, Leveau was a technical advisor to the Moroccan Ministry of the Interior. Among his responsibilities was laying the groundwork for the country's first municipal and parliamentary elections.
6. The 111 indirectly elected seats in parliament include sixty-nine provincial delegates, chosen from among the various elected municipal counsellors, seven from the Chamber of Artisans, ten from the Chambers of Commerce and Industry, ten from the Chamber of Salaried Workers, and fifteen from the Chamber of Commerce. *Al Bayane* (Casablanca), October 27, 1992, and February 20, 1993; personal interview of Ministry of the Interior official in Rabat, July 16, 1993. The king originally announced his intention to hold elections on the second Friday of October 1992.
7. See Ann Elizabeth Mayer, "Moroccans—Citizens or Subjects? A People at the Crossroads," *Journal of International Law and Politics* (forthcoming), for an analysis of the new constitution and work by official and private human rights groups in Morocco. Also see Susan Waltz, "Making Waves: The Political Impact of Human Rights Groups in North Africa," *Journal of Modern African Studies,* vol. 29, no. 3 (1991): 481–504.
8. Anderson, op. cit., 19.
9. Interview with the French television channel, Antenne 2 (France), reported in *Al Bayane,* September 5, 1992.
10. Personal interview in Rabat, June 11, 1992.
11. Cited in *Le Matin* (Casablanca), August 21, 1972, p. 1.

12. *Al Bayane* (Casablanca), August 22, 1992, pp. 2–3, reproduces the full text of the constitution. Moroccans were given two weeks to review the text of the constitution's 102 articles prior to the September 4 referendum.

13. Reprinted in *Al Bayane* (Casablanca), pp. 2, 9.

14. Reprinted in *Le Matin du Sahara* (Casablanca), p. 1.

15. "S.M. Le Roi communique aux partis politiques les résultats de l'arbitrage sur les questions electorales," *Al Bayane* (Casablanca), May 21, 1992, pp. 1, 3.

16. "Le discours de S.M. Le Roi à la séance d'overture du 5e colloque national des collectivités locales," *Al Bayane* (Casablanca), April 23, 1992, p. 3.

17. Personal interview of senior university official in Rabat, May 21, 1992.

18. Rémy Leveau, *Le fellah marocain: Défenseur du trône* (Paris: Presses de la Fondation Nationale des Sciences Politiques, 1976).

19. Gaetano Mosca, *The Ruling Class: Elementi di Scienza Politica,* Hannah D. Kahn, trans. (New York: McGraw Hill, 1939).

20. See Dale F. Eickelman, "Royal Authority and Religious Legitimacy: Morocco's Elections, 1960–1984," in *The Frailty of Authority,* Myron J. Aronoff, ed. (New Brunswick and Oxford: Transaction Books, 1986), pp. 181–205, and Dale F. Eickelman, "Religion in Polity and Society," in *The Political Economy of Morocco,* I. William Zartman, ed. (New York: Praeger Publishers, 1987), pp. 84–97.

21. In a practice that still apparently continues, people sell their votes for a specified price. The rate current in Casablanca in October 1992 was between fifty and one hundred Moroccan dirhams ($5.37 to $10.75 U.S.). On entering the polling station, voters are handed an envelope and a sheaf of multi-colored printed papers, one of which is placed in the envelope and deposited in the balloting box. The voter leaves the polling place with the unused ballots, which can be verified by a representative of the candidate. As a sign of greater voter sophistication, many voters in Casablanca deposited envelopes containing no ballot in the voting urn, concealing from the candidate's "inspector" the uncast ballot for his candidate. For descriptions of these and other current practices, see *Al Bayane* (Casablanca), September 25, 1992, and October 21, 1992, and François Soudan, "La victoire des nuls," *Jeune Afrique,* October 29–November 11, 1992, pp. 18–19.

22. Accounts of irregularities must necessarily be anecdotal, although the Moroccan press also carried numerous accounts of vote fraud. In one instance, a foreigner (personal communication, November 22, 1984), the friend of a provincial governor, listened to the governor discuss with his subordinates the details of who would win—and by how much—in the elections that occurred several days later.

23. Official figures are reported in *Al Bayane* (Casablanca), September 26, 1992, and October 24, 1992. For regional results of northern Morocco, see Mohamed Temsamani, "Elections communales du 16 octobre 1992: Des résultats pleins d'enseignements," *Les Nouvelles du Nord* (Tangier), May 14, 1993, pp. 22–23.

24. Following the assassination in 1992 of Faraj Fawda in Egypt, *Al-Ishtiraki* (Casablanca), June 21, 1992, carried a two-page story, "*Shara'it al-tatarruf 'ala l-rasif: Jins wa-fitna wa-tahrid*" (Extremist Cassettes on the Sidewalk: Sex, Rebellion, and Incitement). The story was based on an article that appeared in an Egyptian newspaper.

25. Data for Figure 14.1 are derived from Royaume du Maroc, Ministère du Plan, Direction de la Statistique, *Annuaire statistique du Maroc, 1991* (Rabat: Direction de la Statistique, 1992), and from *Al Bayane* (Casablanca), September 28, 1992.

26. See Natalie Zenon Davis, *Society and Culture in Early Modern France* (Stanford, Calif.: Stanford University Press, 1975), pp. 189–226.

27. For a fuller treatment of this notion, discussed in summary form below, see Dale F. Eickelman, "Mass Higher Education and the Religious Imagination in Contemporary Arab Societies," *American Ethnologist*, vol. 19, no. 4 (November 1992): 643–55.

28. At the opening of the 1992–1993 academic year, Morocco's Ministry of National Education reported that 3,940,300 students were enrolled in the country's primary and secondary schools, an increase of 9.2 percent over the prior year, *Al Bayane* (Casablanca), September 24, 1992.

29. Aziza Bennani, "L'Université Marocaine: Évolution et Adaptation," *Al Bayane* (Casablanca), September 28, 1992.

30. Khalil Sabat, "Le livre imprimé en Egypte," in *Le livre arabe et l'édition en Egypte*, Yves Gonzalez-Quijano, ed., special issue of the *Bulletin du CEDEJ* (Cairo), No. 25 (1989): 18.

31. Personal Interview of Mohammed Bennis in Mohammediya, July 16, 1992.

32. Pierre Bourdieu, *Homo Academicus* (London: Polity Press, 1988), and M'Hammed Sabour, *Homo Academicus Arabicus* (Joensuu, Finland: University of Joensuu Publications in Social Sciences, 1988).

33. Michael Albin, "Moroccan-American Bibliography," in *The Atlantic Connection: 200 Years of Moroccan-American Relations, 1786–1986*, J. Bookin-Weiner and M. El Mansour, eds. (Rabat: Edino Press, 1990), and Roger Chartier, *The Cultural Uses of Print in Early Modern France*, L. G. Cochrane, trans. (Princeton, N.J.: Princeton University Press, 1987): 6–11.

34. 'Abd al-Salam Yassin, *La révolution à l'heure de l'Islam* (Grignac-la-Nerthe, France: n.p. 1981). This French edition was translated by Yassin, formerly an inspector of French education in Morocco.

35. Anderson, op. cit.

36. Hassan II, *Discours et interviews* (Rabat: Ministry of Information, 1984), p. 162.

37. Mohamed El Ayadi, "Le modèle social marocain à la lumière du discours scolaire," Thèse de doctorat du troisième cycle en sciences sociales (Paris: Université de la Sorbonne Nouvelle, 1983).

38. Personal interview in Casablanca, June 14, 1992.

39. Speech reported in *Al Bayane* (Casablanca), April 23, 1992, p. 3.

40. A Moroccan official (personal communication, June 3, 1993) suggests an even greater complexity of motives that led to the parade not taking place: "In many reports I've seen, the May [Day] parade was forbidden by the authorities. This is not the truth. The leftist [parties] wanted the parade to take place on one of the largest streets of Casablanca. The authorities refused. They feared a spontaneous demonstration of 'Islamists' in the street. The leftists, scared to see Islamists infiltrating the parade and drawing the light from them, didn't insist. They invoked the refusal of the authorities to permit them to demonstrate on that particular street [Boulevard El Fida] to cancel the May Day parade for that year [and also] presented their refusal as solidarity with [Noubir] Amaoui [an imprisoned labor union leader]."

41. Authorities refused, however, permission for a subsequent demonstration in Casablanca, apparently at "the instigations of the American embassy, [which] was very angry" that the authorities "allowed the [Rabat] demonstration of February 3" (personal communication, Moroccan official, June 26, 1993).

42. Interview in *Libération* (Paris), reprinted in *Al Bayane* (Casablanca), July 8, 1992, pp. 1–2.

43. Published in *Al Bayane* (Casablanca), August 22, 1992. See also the king's remarks, "Recevant des deleguées d'associations feminines," *Al Bayane* (Casablanca), May 3, 1993, p. 9.

44. The police official, Hajj Muhammad Mustafa Tabit, was arrested on February 18 and condemned to death on March 15. Moroccan newspapers, but not the broadcast media, carried daily reports. For an English summary of the trial and its implications, see Fiammetta Rocco, "The Shame of Casablanca," *The Independent on Sunday* (London), May 9, 1993.

45. Personal interview, Casablanca, July 1992.

46. *Al Bayane* (Casablanca), February 12, 1993.

47. Personal interview in Rabat, June 23, 1992.

48. *Al Bayane* (Casablanca), September 6, 1992. Although Moroccan papers are cautious about initiating negative reporting, they are free to reprint reports from foreign journals. An exception was the exact wording used by Noubir Amaoui to "slander" senior government officials.

49. *Al Bayane* (Casablanca), September 5, 1992.

50. Personal interview of Moroccan government official, July 22, 1992.

51. Leveau, op. cit., 37.

52. *Al Bayane* (Casablanca), October 24, 1992; *Le Matin du Sahara* (Casablanca), June 27, 1993, p. 2.

53. Paul Johnson, "Another Moslem Invasion of Europe," *The Los Angeles Times*, December 20, 1991.

54. Michael C. Hudson, "Democratization and the Problem of Legitimacy in Middle East Politics," *Middle East Studies Association Bulletin*, vol. 22 (1988): 157.

55. International Foundation for Electoral Systems, "Morocco: Direct Legislative Elections, June 25, 1993" (Washington, D.C.: International Foundation for Electoral Systems, 1993), p. 3.

Islam and the State in Algeria and Morocco: A Dialectical Model

Mary-Jane Deeb

THE MODEL

Why are Islamic fundamentalist movements so powerful, and cohesive in their organization, their ideology, and their popular support in some parts of the Muslim world, while in others they are weaker, more fragmented, less able to mobilize support or provide a real challenge to the state? Using two countries in the Maghrib, namely Morocco and Algeria, this chapter attempts to find some answers and to make propositions that could apply not only to North Africa but also to the rest of the Arab world and perhaps beyond.

A comparison of Morocco and Algeria is methodologically significant. If two Muslim countries in different regions of the world, say Sudan and Pakistan, were compared instead, the historical, geographical, and cultural differences would blur the major patterns of interaction between Islamic movements and the state. By choosing two countries within the same region, with the same culture, and a similar history, certain variables remain constant, while it is possible to isolate others that have more significantly affected the strength, organization, and degree of radicalism of Islamic movements as forces of opposition to the state.

In 1972, Abdelbaki Hermassi, the Tunisian sociologist, wrote a seminal work, *Leadership and National Development in North Africa: A Comparative Study,* the thesis of which was that political systems and institutions at one stage of the political evolution of a nation, shape the next stage of the politics of that nation. He looked at three different approaches to colonialism (the segmental, the instrumental, and the total) by three French administrations in Morocco, Tunisia, and Algeria, and at the impact those approaches had on the ensuing leadership and state formations at independence.[1]

One can argue that this model is Hegelian. According to Hegel history evolves through a dialectical process of continual conflict between one system of thought and politics (the thesis), and another system (the antithesis), that emerges from its own internal contradictions. The outcome of this conflict is the synthesis, or a new political system or system of thought, that emerges and seems to resolve the original contradictions. In time, however, this synthesis itself becomes subject to internal contradictions that lead to the emergence of conflictual forces and eventually to a new synthesis. The Hegelian system is dynamic, continuously moving forward to ever higher levels. It is not the steady development of reason that moves history forward as Diderot, Durkheim, or Auguste Comte would have us believe, but rather the "cunning reason" or the passions that push men to war and revolution to achieve ever greater freedom. The ultimate point in this dialectical process, according to Hegel, is reached with the realization of complete freedom for all men.[2]

Using a dialectical approach and building upon Hermassi's earlier paradigm in which the leadership that molded the present states in North Africa was the synthesis of the conflict between colonial powers and nationalist movements, we can now view as the new thesis the independent states that have developed their own internal contradictions and fostered new forces of opposition, the strongest of which are the Islamic movements today. The outcome of that conflict or the new synthesis will certainly be transformed social, political, and economic systems that will respond more adequately to the demands of their citizens, a process that may be actually unfolding before our very eyes.

I am proposing to look at two different political systems in the Maghrib, the traditional monarchy in Morocco and the nationalist-socialist state in Algeria, to identify the internal contradictions from which a number of opposition forces have emerged. I have isolated Islamic movements from other forces of opposition because they represent a dominant system of thought and advocate a new political system, and because they will certainly have an important role in shaping the political systems that will develop in the region.

MAJOR PROPOSITIONS

The first proposition is that the more pluralistic the state is, the more numerous the loci of legitimate authority, the more likely the opposition is to be fragmented and multidimensional. The corollary to this proposition is that the more centralized and the more monolithic the state, the more likely the opposition is to be centrally organized and monolithic as well.

The second proposition is that the more closely the state is to being identified with traditional religious institutions, the less the popular support for oppositions that wish to overthrow that state on religious grounds. The corollary to this proposition is that the less close a state is to being identified with traditional religious institutions, the greater the support for opposition movements that want to overthrow it on religious grounds.

The last proposition states that when the state, while modernizing, tolerates the existence of traditional institutions and forms of social organization and allows them to change and evolve gradually, over time, religious opposition is less likely to be violent, and to insist on drastic reforms to "protect religious and cultural institutions" that are being undermined by the policies of the state. The corollary to this proposition is that the more rapid the process of modernization and the more force from the top is used to implement it and to undermine traditional institutions, the more likely the opposition is to be violent and to demand an immediate halt to the process.

MOROCCO: THE TRADITIONAL MONARCHY

From the sixteenth century until the 1960s there were three centers of religious legitimacy in Morocco, and despite competition among the three none was able to claim sole control over the religious sphere. There was the monarchy, whose members claimed to be Sharifians and descendants of the Prophet; there were also the urban-based clerics or *'ulama* whose training and education gave them the right to be major religious interpreters; and finally, there were the maraboutic brotherhoods, whose social base in rural areas assured them of large followings. Those brotherhoods in turn were numerous and varied, and did not see eye to eye either with each other or with the more orthodox adherents to Sunni Islam among the *'ulama*.[3]

From the sixteenth to the nineteenth centuries the main struggle was between the *makhzan* or central power of the monarchy, and the *zawiyas* of the brotherhoods whose power was not only religious but economic and political as well. The major role of the *zawiya* was one of arbitration and mediation between tribes that allowed their political influence to extend throughout *bilad al-siba* or areas beyond the central power's control. Consequently, whenever the powers of the *makhzan* increased and spread, their own diminished, and vice versa.

The '*ulama,* on the other hand, had less political power than either the central powers or the *zawiyas* until the end of the nineteenth century when they began to play a more active political role. Part of the explanation lies in the European penetration of Morocco at the time and the gradual undermining of the power of the *makhzan,* and its inability to defend the region against the encroachments of the "infidels."

Some of the '*ulama* took an anticolonial position that did much to enhance their power and legitimacy. The *makhzan* became gradually more dependent on the '*ulama* to bolster its waning powers. Other '*ulama* chose to collaborate with the French in return for guarantees of full religious freedom. By so doing they protected traditional religious institutions that might otherwise have been destroyed or undermined. Some of the *zawiyas,* such as the Wazaniyya and the Kataniyya, collaborated with the colonial powers and extended their power and influence under the French protectorate.

The conflict between the '*ulama* and the brotherhoods emerged only in the twentieth century with the reformist *salafiyya* movement, which was strongly influenced by the Islamic reformist movement in Egypt, and which became very critical of the *zawaya,* seeing them as the repository of backwardness, ignorance, and practices incompatible with the true teachings of Islam.

The struggle between the monarchy and the '*ulama* resumed after independence, with Muhammad V, and Hassan II after 1961, attempting to discredit both the '*ulama* and the *zawiyas.* The winner was the monarchy, which was able to consolidate religious power in its own hands, declaring the king Commander of the Faithful, and maintaining all the rituals of allegiance due to the monarchy.[4]

Despite a rather shaky start, the Moroccan state allowed the proliferation of political parties in the last two decades. The earlier dominance of the Istiqlal Party was undermined by the emergence of a number of parties representing various ideological tendencies in the Moroccan polity, and by the king's creation of artificial parties loyal to him to expand his control over parliament. Elections were often rigged, and the system is still not a free or democratic one, but it is undoubtedly a pluralist one.

Looking, therefore, at our dialectical model we see the Moroccan state having maintained a religiously and to some extent politically pluralist system over a long period of time. The second element in this model is that the political leadership not only is part of the religious equation, but the dominant part of that equation. Furthermore, the state has also maintained a "traditional" tolerance for ethnic pluralism in the society itself, allowing a great deal of autonomy and political freedom of expression to its very large Berber minorities in rural areas.

As in the rest of the region, nontraditional Islamic fundamentalists emerged in the 1970s and 1980s claiming an alternative source of religious legitimacy. They were at first encouraged by the state as a counterbalance to the leftist movements on school and university campuses. Today, in Rabat alone, there are twenty such groups that have their own organizations, leadership, and agendas.[5]

Henry Munson, in his excellent study of Islamic fundamentalists in Morocco, categorized them in three groups: the traditionalists, the mainstream, and the radical.[6] The traditionalists include ex-members of Sufi orders, such as the late Faqih al-Zamzami (who died in 1989), and his sons 'Abd al-Bari', Shu'ayb, and Ubayy, who though they left the order retained many of their Sufi beliefs and ideas. Their basic criticisms focused on the very unequal distribution of wealth and power in Morocco and what they saw as the oppression of the weak and the poor. They appealed therefore to the poor and the disenfranchised as well as to small shopkeepers, blue-collar workers, and laborers. Thus one of the major internal contradictions of the state in Morocco is that as the state, or the monarchy, strengthened its position vis-à-vis other groups in society, it engendered opposition to its economic and political monopoly of power.

Al-Zamzami was the descendant of the Bin al-Siddiq family of sheikhs of the Darqawi Sufi order of northern Morocco. He preached social and political reform in the name of Islam but never advocated the overthrow of the king. He is considered a "saint" by some and a hero by others in Tangier and other areas in northwestern Morocco.[7]

The mainstream group, according to Munson, includes the Muslim Brotherhood, which was primarily influenced by the Muslim Brotherhood of Egypt and the writings of Hasan al-Banna and Sayyid Qutb. 'Abd al-Salam Yassin, one of the major leaders in the category of Islamic groups, had a traditional Islamic education at al-Yusufiyya University in

Marrakesh, and taught Arabic, but also spoke French and sent his children to French schools. He then apparently had a mystical experience and joined the Sufi order of the Butshishiyya for six years. After breaking away from the order he founded his own movement known as Al-'Adl wal-Ihsan, which was very much influenced by Sufism.

Yassin and other mainstreamers do not just call for reforms of the existing system, they call for the establishment of an Islamic state to be governed by Islamic laws and institutions. Although Yassin believes in public action and even sent his program to King Hassan, hoping he would endorse it, he has taken a stance against political violence in some of his writings, such as *Al-Islam wal-tufan*.[8] The focus of his criticism, like Zamzami, has been on social inequality and the disparity in wealth between the king and his entourage, and a large sector of the Moroccan population. This is perceived as un-Islamic by the mainstreamers in the movement.

Despite his writings and the support he has among high school and university students and teachers alike, the movement itself is weak. The Moroccan state, however, has imprisoned Yassin more than once, and has made it difficult for him to propagate his ideas.

Al-Shabiba al-Islamiyya (the Islamic Youth Association) falls under Munson's radical category, because it advocates violence against "members of the community who have been led astray," as well as the overthrow of the monarchical regime. Early on, it antagonized the regime by refusing to support the king on the issue of the Western Sahara and the Green March. When 'Umar Ben Jallun, a leftist leader of the General Union of Moroccan Workers, was assassinated in December 1975, the Shabiba was accused of the crime, and its members arrested and jailed, two of them being sentenced to death. The movement itself was outlawed and its leader 'Abd al-Karim Muti' fled to Saudi Arabia. It then broke up into several splinter groups including the Revolutionary Commission, the Islamic Students Vanguard, and the Movement of the Mujahidin.[9]

The Morocco case illustrates some of the propositions made at the start of this chapter, namely, that the Islamic opposition is fragmented, does not have extensive popular support, holds many different views concerning the establishment of an Islamic state, and has not been very violent. The reasons may be that the state it is opposing is closely linked to traditional religious institutions, has permitted some pluralism in its political system for over two decades, and has allowed traditional institutions such as the Sufi *zawiyas* to continue to exist while at the same time pursuing a modernization program which is transforming the society gradually. Furthermore, Morocco was never under Ottoman rule and suffered only from a brief and rather benign type of French colonial experience that did not destroy its traditional culture or institutions. Consequently, its traditional pluralism continued to thrive well into the twentieth century. The internal contradictions, however, are the disparity in wealth and power between those in power and a large sector of the populace, which will continue to feed the rhetoric of the Islamic opposition to the state.

THE NATIONALIST MODEL IN ALGERIA

The case of Algeria is quite different. Until the advent of French colonialism in 1830, Algeria resembled Morocco in a number of respects. Like Morocco, its Sufi brotherhoods were powerful loci of power throughout the rural areas, each with its own rites and rituals, its own "way" or *tariqa,* its own saints. Institutions of higher learning were located in the many cities of Algeria: Hanafi or Maliki, Sunni or Ibadi could find his mosque and discuss his preferred school of thought in those cities. The *'ulama* in their educational institutions, and the *qadis* or Muslim jurists who presided over *shari'a* courts, were powerful people indeed.

But the comparison with Morocco ends there. There was no monarchy, but an Ottoman administration responsible to the Porte in Constantinople. The ruling elite was foreign, and although Muslim, had no religious legitimacy as such. More often than not it was at odds with the *zawiyas* and there were armed confrontations.

The French experience also was very different from that of Morocco as Hermassi so well documented in his study. Not only did it occur much earlier historically than it did in Morocco, but it also attacked directly the very heart of the Algerian political and cultural system, namely, Islam.

The French administration attacked and closed down *zawiyas* and mosques, as well as the schools attached to these mosques. They confiscated religious property, interfered with pilgrimage, took over and ran religious institutions, appointing and remunerating *'ulama.* In so doing they weakened and undermined the legitimacy of both traditional institutions, and forced upon Algerians a language, culture, and a set of institutions that were foreign to them in the name of "civilizing" them.[10]

By the beginning of the twentieth century another major blow was delivered to the traditional Sufi orders, in the form of a reformist or *salafiyya* movement that began after the visit of the famous Egyptian reformer, Muhammad 'Abduh, to Algeria in 1903. Algerian reformers and legal scholars, such as 'Abd al-Halim Ben Smaia and Kamal Muhammad Ben Mustafa, began criticizing the brotherhoods, and the marabouts, and called for Muslims to return to a stricter code of Islam and to forsake the traditional *tariqas* based on superstition and erroneous beliefs.[11]

The reformist movement culminated with the formation of the Association of Algerian Muslim 'Ulama in 1931, under the presidency of Abdelhamid Ben Badis. The attacks on the *tariqas* continued and became more organized as the reformers used the mosques to attack the orders as heterodox and obscurantist. The outcome was what John Ruedy calls a "war of religion" between the *'ulama* and the traditional orders. The reformers were undoubtedly successful in undermining the credibility and legitimacy of traditional maraboutic orders, whose power had been already tremendously diminished by French policy toward them.

During the war of independence the association became part of the Front for National Liberation, the FLN. Its members collected funds for the *mujahidin,* helped and supported their families, organized boycotts of French businesses and institutions, and used mosques to mobilize support for the war and pass information about the political situation to its members.[12]

Algeria at independence was a society that had been ravaged, and whose culture and traditions had been battered for more than a century. It was a society that had to be rebuilt from top to bottom, that needed to re-invent its identity. The nationalist project of the ruling FLN was based upon putting the pieces of that shattered country back together by emphasizing the unity of the nation, a unified view of itself, its people, its beliefs, and its position in the world. The state had a vision that would not tolerate dissent for fear of division, that would not accept a multiparty political system for fear its social basis would be fractured. The state also held a modernist view of its future. It would move forward and industrialize and create a modern infrastructure, using its wealth to build a system of social services that would provide education, health care, employment, and housing to all its citizens, fairly and equitably. It was a view that rejected traditional views and institutions, which perhaps were even blamed for 132 years of French domination.

The new state's attitude toward religion was much the same. At first it sought the support of the Association of Algerian Muslim 'Ulama. One of its most famous members, Tawfiq al-Madani, was even asked to make statements in support of socialism and he would declare in January 1963, "Islam is a socialist religion, it is a religion of equity."[13]

The honeymoon between the state and its independently-minded 'ulama would not last very long, however. Gradually, all dissenting voices were silenced and the state "nationalized" religion, in the words of Jean Claude Vatin.[14] It created a Ministry of Religious Affairs that administered religious property, provided religious education and training in state-controlled and administered schools and institutes, built mosques, and appointed imams who received salaries like government employees and issued the Friday *khutab*. The role of the 'ulama, according to the state, was to serve a unified view of the state and of Islam, and discourage opposition and heterodoxy.

The Algerian state was undoubtedly successful in building a well-defined Algerian identity and a unified nation. In the process it also managed to silence all opposition—leftist, democratic, religious, ethnic, and tribal—in the name of national unification.

The state asserted a view of the Algerian Islamic identity that it presumed was or ought to have been universally accepted. Since the state was Muslim, that view posited, then Algerians need no longer fear for their culture and beliefs. The new state had the power and the means to forge a new identity that would weld Islam and the modern industrial world.[15]

Opposition to this monolithic model of Islam emerged at the very start of independence. Al-Qiyam al-Islamiyya (Islamic Values), a militant Islamic group, was the first to argue against the monopoly of Islam by the state, but was suppressed in the sixties. A decade later, a group with strong links to Al-Qiyam emerged calling itself Ahl al-Da'wa (People of the Call). They were at first tolerated by the state as a counterbalance to leftist organizations on school and university campuses. After the Iranian Revolution, however, it became clear that they constituted more of a threat to the state than the leftists, and so their leaders and members were arrested and imprisoned. Many of those would eventually become the founding members of the Front Islamique du Salut or the FIS, its better known acronym.

The internal contradictions within the state had emerged. Whereas the monolithic nature of the state had fulfilled an important function at an earlier stage, namely nation-building through a process of national unification, that function was no longer significant a quarter of a century later. It could no longer continue to maintain its unified stand politically, socially, or even economically, in a society that was modernizing and diversifying.

Under a lot of pressure from various opposition groups including those among the most vociferous, the Islamic groups, the state began introducing major reforms in all sectors—political, economic, and social—from the mid-1980s. It changed direction economically from a socialist state-controlled economy to a more market-oriented type, encouraging private-sector investment. After the fall of oil prices in 1986, it became evident that the state alone could not continue providing all the social services needed and that private-sector cooperation would help in alleviating the very high unemployment and in dealing with critical shortages in housing and construction.

Politically, the Algerian state introduced major constitutional revisions in February 1989, that opened up the political arena and allowed for a multiparty system.[16] The outcome of this new liberalization was the emergence of more than fifty different political parties, among which was the newly formed FIS. Other Islamic groups included Hamas whose leader Mahfoud Nahnah was critical of the FIS' methods of operating and stood for the establishment of an Islamic state in stages, through legal and nonviolent means. The Party for Algerian Renewal (PRA) led by Noureddin Boukrouh, the Da'wa headed by Sheikh Ahmad Sahnoun, and Al-Nahda, were other moderate Islamic movements opposed to violence, but with a similar agenda. There were also ethnically based parties such as the Rally for Culture and Democracy, a precursor of which had made a brief appearance in 1980 as the Berber Cultural Movement, but had been strongly discouraged by the state. Another such group was the Socialist Forces Front headed by Hocine Ait Ahmed, calling for political and cultural pluralism.

In local elections in June 1990 the FIS won 54 percent of the vote to the FLN's 28 percent, giving the FIS control over half the municipalities of Algeria's major cities. The December 1991 national elections resulted in a landslide victory for the FIS and a dismal defeat for the ruling party. The state with the military intervened and denied the Front a victory that it claimed would have put an end to the democratic experiment. Since then the state and the army have faced the FIS in daily armed confrontations that have resulted in a large number of casualties, arrests, death sentences, acts of violence, terrorism against security forces, assassinations of major political leaders, and the undermining of the state from within.

CONCLUSION

The internal contradictions within each state have engendered different types of Islamic opposition in organization and cohesiveness, as well as in mobilizational capacity. Whereas the Moroccan Islamic opposition is fragmented, weak, and critical of other similar movements and their leaders, the FIS in Algeria, although not the only Islamic group, is highly organized and well financed, has demonstrated highly developed mobilizational skills in the elections of 1990 and 1991, and has leaders that have been able to direct the movement and represent it with much success. The more moderate Islamic groups did not seem to fare as well in the elections. That may have been due to their inability to organize and mobilize people around their leaders and the fact that their agendas were not radically different from that of the FIS. Therefore, unlike Morocco where no one Islamic group was able to monopolize the role of major opposition to the state, in Algeria the FIS has undoubtedly played that role.

But it is the nature of the state itself that has engendered the different types of Islamic opposition in Algeria and Morocco. The traditional Moroccan political institutions and political culture of Morocco were maintained throughout the French colonial period. The state's approach to modernization at independence therefore was one of cautious gradualism: introducing change without undermining the traditional structures upon which its survival depended. Compromise honed over the centuries was the preferred way of exercising authority, and although the monarchy became the dominant source of power with Hassan II, the king learned early on to avoid alienating all groups simultaneously, and to have many voices of dissent rather than one unified opposition.

The more revolutionary and confrontational Algerian state that had fought the French by unifying the Algerian opposition, sometimes by force, was a very different entity. It was uncompromising in its attempt to forge a unified and modern Algerian nation from the fragmented and dislocated society left behind by the French at independence. Its approach to change was described by Rémy Leveau as a "construction volontariste forçant le destin et imposant sa volonté."[17] Algeria was to catch up with lost time and change very rapidly. Modernization would come from the top and would include all sectors of society. In exchange Algerians would have to give up their differences and unite behind their government. The reaction to this forceful way of modernizing the society was equally forceful, especially when it became evident that the state was failing to live up to its promise to provide for all the needs of its citizens, in exchange for which it had taken away their right to different political, economic, and social agendas.

Finally, it was the relationship of the state to religion that shaped the opposition to the state. Whereas the Moroccan monarchy was identified for centuries with the family of the Prophet Muhammad, and the person of the king was holy for Moroccans, this was not the case of the Algerian leadership. The religious aura combined with traditional continuity gave the Moroccan monarch a legitimacy that was perpetuated and cultivated very carefully. The Algerian leadership's legitimacy was rooted in the war of independence, and although Islam was recognized as the religion of the state, Muslim traditional leaders were by and large kept out of the decision-making process and their authority and independence undermined. It was therefore, easier for the FIS to depict the ruling junta as anti-Islamic, than it was for any Moroccan leader of Islamic movements to question the religiosity of the king.

The significance of this comparison is its implications for the rest of the Muslim world. If the model is applicable elsewhere then it may become easier to predict where an Islamic opposition may challenge the state more successfully and where the state and the Islamic opposition may work together more harmoniously.

Notes

1. Abdelbaki Hermassi, *Leadership and National Development in North Africa: A Comparative Study* (Berkeley and Los Angeles: University of California Press, 1972).
2. Fukuyama maintains that "Whether or not we acknowledge our debt to him, we owe to Hegel the most fundamental aspects of our present-day consciousness"; Francis Fukuyama, *The End of History and the Last Man* (New York: The Free Press: 1992), p. 59.
3. Jamal Benomar, "The Monarchy, the Islamist Movement and Religious Discourse in Morocco," *Third World Quarterly*, vol. 10, no. 2 (April 1988): 544.
4. Mohammed Tozy, "Monopolisation de la production symbolique et hiérarchisation du champ politico-religieux au Maroc," *Annuaire de l'Afrique du Nord* (Paris: CNRS, 1979), pp. 219–23.
5. Emad Eldin Ali Shahin, "The Restitution of Islam: A Comparative Study of the Islamic Movements in Contemporary Tunisia and Morocco," Ph.D. diss., Johns Hopkins University, 1990, p. 186.
6. Henry Munson, Jr., "Morocco's Fundamentalists," *Government and Opposition: Studies on North Africa* (London), vol. 26 (Summer 1991): 331–44.
7. Munson, op. cit., 335.

8. Shahin, op. cit., 264, 266.
9. Ibid., op. cit., 213–14.
10. John Ruedy, *Modern Algeria: The Origins and Development of a Nation* (Bloomington, Ind.: Indiana University Press, 1992, pp. 100–01.
11. Ibid., 102.
12. Mary-Jane Deeb, "Islam and the State: The Continuity of the Political Discourse of Islamic Movements in Algeria from 1832 to 1992," paper delivered at a conference on "Islam and Nationhood," Yale University, New Haven, Conn., November 1992, p. 19.
13. Raymond Vallin, "Muslim Socialism in Algeria," in *Man, State and Society in the Contemporary Maghrib,* I. William Zartman, ed. (New York: Praeger Publishers, 1973), pp. 50–51.
14. Jean-Claude Vatin, "Popular Puritanism Versus State Reformism: Islam in Algeria," in *Islam in the Political Process,* James Piscatori, ed. (Cambridge: Cambridge University Press, 1983), p. 110.
15. Deeb, op. cit., 24.
16. See Robert Mortimer, "Islam and Multi-Party Politics in Algeria," *The Middle East Journal,* vol. 45, no. 4 (Autumn 1991): 578–79.
17. Rémy Leveau, *Le sabre et le turban: L'Avenir du Maghrib* (Paris: François Bourin, 1993), pp. 128–29.

Index

Pact of 1857, 24, 48; general strike of 1978, 153; *habous* reforms in, 92; intelligentsia of, 46; Italian occupation of, 30; liberalization in, 153-154, 156; mission to Turkey of, 42; modernization in, 24, 34; National Assembly of, 202, 208; National Security Council of, 156; and *nizami* army, 42; Ottomans in, 23-26; personal status laws of, 157; political participation in, 202, 206-208; rebellion of 1864, 24; and reform *fatwas*, 45-47; reform movements in, 149, 151; `ulama of, 28-34, 48

Tunisian Communist Party (PCT), 206, 213

Tunisian Human Rights League, 156

Turabi, Hassan, 139

Turkey, 34, 56, 59, 116, 263

U

`ulama, xvi-xviii, 38-39, 63, 68, 95, 134, 140; in Algeria, 77-80, 133-135; Arnold Green on, 28-29; of Fez, 39-40, 43, 56; and *ijtihad*, 47; in Morocco, 54-58, 60, 61, 64; on *nizam* armies, 42-43; Qadhafi on, 192; on taxes, 44-45; in Tunisia, 28-34, 48; `Abd al-Salam Yassin on, 182-183. *See also* Association of Algerian Muslim `Ulama

Umayyads, xiv

umma, 23, 25, 27, 30, 40, 59, 66, 67, 95, 111, 139, 172

Unionist Democratic Union (UDU), 212-213

United States, 202

V

Vanguard Socialist Party (PAGS), 210, 213, 229

Vatin, Jean-Claude, 89, 283

Voltaire, xiii, 75

W

Wahhabis, 62, 73, 106, 119, 188

al-Wazzani, Muhammad Ibn al-Hassan, 59, 63-69

Wazzaniyya, 278

Weber, Max, 50, 118

Westernization: in Algeria, 226; of elites, xvi, 34, 82, 169; of intellectuals, 64, 68, 115, 126-127; of the military, 113; `Abd al-Salam Yassin on, 171, 176, 182-183

Western Sahara, 205-206, 265, 280

women, 13, 44, 46, 78, 93, 226; in Algeria, 78, 230; emancipation of, 46, 92, 93; in Mizab, 13; in Morocco, 179-81, 264, 267; status of, 93; support for MTI of, 153; in Tunisia, 157; `Abd al-Salam Yassin on, 170, 180-181

World Bank, 228

World War I, 30, 32, 33, 75, 81

Y

Yahiaoui, Mohamed Salah, 239

Yassin, `Abd al-Salam, xix, 167-184, 262, 279-280; *Al-Islam wal-tufan*, 280

Yeltsin, Boris, 223

Young Moroccans, 58

Young Tunisian Movement, 29-33

Young Turks, 31, 55, 59

Z

zahir, 61, 63, 179

Zakariya, Fouad, 99

zakat, 43, 215

al-Zamzami, Faqih, 279, 280

zawaya, 60-61, 62, 79, 109, 110, 278, 280, 281

Zionism, 33, 97

Zitouna University, 29, 30, 31, 104, 109, 152; dismantling of, 92; name of, 153, 156

Znibar, Ali, 55